Right Out of California

Right Out of California

THE 1930S AND
THE BIG BUSINESS ROOTS OF
MODERN CONSERVATISM

Kathryn S. Olmsted

THE NEW PRESS

NEW YORK
LONDON

Requests for permission to reproduce selections from this book should be mailed to:
Permissions Department, The New Press, 120 Wall Street, 31st floor, New York, NY
10005.

Published in the United States by The New Press, New York, 2015
Distributed by Perseus Distribution

LIBRARY OF CONGRESS CATALOGING-IN-PUBLICATION DATA

Olmsted, Kathryn S.
  Right out of California : the 1930s and the big business roots of modern conservatism /
Kathryn S. Olmsted.
    pages cm
  Includes bibliographical references and index.
  ISBN 978-1-62097-096-6 (hardcover : alkaline paper) — ISBN 978-1-62097-139-0 (e-book)
    1. California—Politics and government—20th century.   2. California—Economic
conditions—20th century.   3. Conservatism—California—History—20th century.
4. Labor disputes—California—History—20th century.   5. Agricultural industries—
Political activity—California—History—20th century.   6. Businessmen—Political
activity—California—History—20th century.   7. Business and politics—California—
History—20th century.   8. Social change—California—History—20th century.
9. Depressions—1929—California.   10. New Deal, 1933–1939—California.   I. Title.
  F866.O483 2015
  320.5209794—dc23
                                                                                  2015013928

The New Press publishes books that promote and enrich public discussion and
understanding of the issues vital to our democracy and to a more equitable world.
These books are made possible by the enthusiasm of our readers; the support of a
committed group of donors, large and small; the collaboration of our many partners
in the independent media and the not-for-profit sector; booksellers, who often
hand-sell New Press books; librarians; and above all by our authors.

www.thenewpress.com

Composition by Westchester Books Group
This book was set in Goudy Standard

Printed in the United States of America

10 9 8 7 6 5 4 3 2 1

For Eric

CONTENTS

Right Out of California

INTRODUCTION

When Herbert Hoover went through his mail in the summer of 1933, he grew steadily more furious about the policies of the man who replaced him in the White House. Ensconced in his modernist mansion in the hills above Stanford University, where he had retreated after his recent defeat, Hoover wrote one bitter letter after another to his fellow Western businessmen about the shortcomings of Franklin Roosevelt's New Deal. Roosevelt trafficked in "constant misrepresentations and illusions," Hoover seethed; the president's New Deal policies would lead to the "destruction of the savings of the people" and the "impoverishment of the country." In fact, Roosevelt was just using the Depression as "an excuse for imposing socialism under new euphemistic phrases."[1]

Contemplating Roosevelt's policies, Hoover lamented the end of the gold standard, the beginning of unemployment insurance, and the ways the industrial recovery program "terrorized" Americans. Referring to Roosevelt's agricultural price supports, Hoover complained that the country was trading away its heritage of liberty "for a fictitious price of wheat."[2]

Yet Hoover benefited from government programs that set "fictitious prices." Among Hoover's many investments were four large California ranches, including one with 240 acres of cotton fields. And Hoover's son Allan, the ranch manager, was eligible to become one of hundreds of thousands of cotton growers who signed subsidy contracts with the federal government.[3]

1

Thus Herbert Hoover—the man soundly defeated by Roosevelt, the man who accused the New Deal of being fascist, communist, and socialist, the man who was organizing a nationwide revolt against Roosevelt's brand of social democracy—would himself profit from New Deal cotton policies. "My son, who runs the farm . . . will sell some cotton that he did not plant to the Secretary of Agriculture at a most profitable price," he wrote to his friend Frank Knox, publisher of the *Chicago Daily News*. Hoover sarcastically suggested that he would need to "seek emancipation from the Income Tax" because of the extra income he would receive from the subsidies.[4]

Many wealthy, conservative California growers joined Hoover in pocketing the Agricultural Adjustment Administration's checks. Unlike Hoover, some of them publicly admitted they were happy to do so. Philip Bancroft, a prosperous fruit grower and Republican Party activist, wrote admiringly to the secretary of agriculture of his "enthusiastic appreciation of the splendid work that you and the entire Administration have been doing on behalf of our industry."[5] J.G. Boswell, owner of one of the largest cotton ranches in the world, chortled that he was "letting out his belt / Anticipating all he'll get from Franklin Roosevelt."[6]

Western growers also welcomed other New Deal programs, including the loans of the Farm Credit Administration and infrastructure programs that promoted agriculture. The Public Works Administration, the Reconstruction Finance Corporation, and the Bureau of Reclamation built dams and irrigation systems for California growers, including massive new canals through the state's rich agricultural valleys. Agribusiness leaders had benefited from federal irrigation and transportation spending for decades, and they greeted the New Deal's expansion of these programs with enthusiasm. But the New Deal differed from those older government programs because, unlike the big-spending Republicans of the nineteenth century, the New Dealers put resources into helping farm owners *and* into defending organized labor.

For decades before 1933, the federal government had supported management against labor. At a minimum, American companies in the pitched labor battles of the 1870s through the early 1930s could count on the U.S. government to turn a blind eye to employer violence against striking workers. And at times, including the Great Railroad Strike of 1877, the Pullman strike of 1894, and the West Virginia miners' strikes of the early 1920s, they could call on federal troops to break strikes.[7] The judicial system also assisted big business. The U.S. Supreme Court sided with employers who fired their workers for joining or even sympathizing with unions, and the courts routinely issued injunctions to stop strikes.

Then, in the 1930s, during Roosevelt's New Deal, the federal government began to change the ways it intervened in the economy. It started serving labor as well as management. Congress and the Roosevelt administration empowered workers by going so far as guaranteeing their right to join unions. Section 7a of the 1933 National Industrial Recovery Act said that workers "shall have the right to organize and bargain collectively through representatives of their own choosing." By 1935, when the National Labor Relations Act superseded Section 7a, the Roosevelt administration was unequivocally protecting industrial workers' right to organize and to demand higher wages and better conditions from their employers. It was these New Deal labor policies—particularly when they helped people with dark skin or relatively radical beliefs—that prompted businessmen to launch a counterrevolution that would continue into the next century.

Ironically, Californians, like other Westerners, knew well what good the federal government could do. The vast expanse of the American West had served, as historian Richard White has written, as the "kindergarten of the American state."[8] The U.S. government first expanded its powers in the West, where it conquered Native peoples, explored prairies, dammed rivers, irrigated fields, and divided and administered the land. But the Great Depression and the New Deal made California conservatives much less enthusiastic about government power. Already, they worried that the worsening Depression might bring Bolshevism to America. Now that the government was intervening on behalf of workers in the shadow of the Bolshevik Revolution, many Western business leaders saw a strong government as a menace to liberty.[9]

The agribusiness barons of California did not just complain about the changes the New Deal brought. They organized. To attack labor, they formed and funded industry groups to lobby local governments to outlaw picketing and imprison union leaders. They hired publicists who branded strikers as Communists and tried to turn the public against them. To combat what they saw as the broader problem of New Deal labor laws, they hired political consultants who understood how to use concerns about cultural changes to turn middle-class Californians against government policies that benefited workers. These conservatives, a new breed of activist, discovered and funded media-savvy, right-wing office seekers who would spread their message.

The new conservatives often connected the economic changes they deplored with the cultural changes they feared. Californians on the political right expressed anxiety that the "color line" was becoming blurred in the 1930s, as Mexican Americans, Asian Americans, and African Americans moved into spaces and jobs that had previously been off-limits to them.[10] They worried that the traditional, patriarchal family was under siege as women began to take on more economic responsibilities and leadership opportunities. Traditionalists also disliked the emphasis on class struggle in the art and novels of the Depression decade—particularly in the work of Californians like photographer Dorothea Lange and, most famously, a young novelist named John Steinbeck, who described the desperation and celebrated the resiliency of farmworker families.

The Western growers helped to cultivate and nurture the antilabor, antistatist movement that dominates American politics today. By the end of the Depression decade, the philosophy, tactics, and leaders of modern conservatism had emerged in California. Soon Western capitalists would help spread their movement to the rest of the country. The modern Republican Party came right out of California.

National Leader

At first glance, it might seem odd that California in the 1930s would be at the vanguard of a new national political movement. The state was far from Washington, D.C., both in actual miles and in the daily concerns of national politicians, and it was lightly populated. The 1930 census counted 5,677,000 people in California, or about 4.6 percent of the national population of 122,775,000.[11] Moreover, if an enterprising political or business leader from the nation's capital or New York wanted to visit California and take stock of the local situation in 1930, he or she would have had to set aside two weeks just to get there and back by train.

But then the rise of the commercial aviation industry shrank the nation and expanded California's political power. Although air travel was still new and flights were slow and costly by modern standards, the diaries and letters of politicians and businessmen record their excitement at traveling coast to coast in less than twenty-four hours. "I am in sunny California," wrote Lawrence Richey, Hoover's secretary, to a friend in Los Angeles in 1933. "I left Washington Sunday afternoon at 3:30 and arrived in San Francisco at 11:45 Monday morning. It was surely a great trip and it is wonderful to think that we can reach California in such a short time."[12]

California was not just easier for national political leaders and businessmen to get to during the 1930s, it was also richer, more populous, and more politically significant than it had been just a few years before. The number of its electoral votes swelled from thirteen in the 1920s to twenty-two in 1932, and then to twenty-five after the reapportionment of 1940. In other words, the state's relative political importance almost doubled from 1930 to 1940.[13]

The state received more electoral votes because it had more people. Its population leaped 65 percent from 1920 to 1930, and then jumped another 21 percent during the Depression decade—14 percent higher than the national growth rate. During the 1920s alone, California added the equivalent of the entire population of Iowa or Virginia—and most of these new residents were American-born, not immigrants.[14]

California's move from the periphery to the center of national politics in the 1930s can be seen in a list of the names of the people who play roles in this story: U.S. presidents Herbert Hoover, Richard Nixon, and Ronald Reagan; celebrated authors Upton Sinclair, Lincoln Steffens, Carey McWilliams, and Langston Hughes; economist Paul Taylor; university leader Clark Kerr; World War I propagandist George Creel; and actor James Cagney. There are also people less known to the public, but not less significant: law enforcement and security figures like General Ralph Van Deman, called the "father of military intelligence," and General Pelham Glassford, the hero to many for his role in the Bonus Army March of 1932. Of these people, only Nixon and Steffens were native Californians. The rest came from somewhere else.

California's migrants were uncommonly willing to experiment with radical solutions to political problems. National policy makers in the 1930s regarded California as a little nuts—"one H—— of a state," as Franklin Roosevelt's chief political strategist, Louis Howe, said privately.[15] California's large and vibrant Communist Party had dynamic leaders who were especially effective at leading strikes. Some of the party's most successful labor organizers inspired tens of thousands of workers to walk off their jobs and demand better treatment.

The non-Communist left in California was also extensive and energetic. The 1930s was an era when Sinclair could credibly campaign for governor as a democratic socialist pledging to take over parts of the state's economy. As journalist Carey McWilliams wrote in his memoir, "California—particularly Southern California—was the place to be in the years from 1934 to 1939; in no other part of the country did so much happen so fast."[16]

Workers across the United States demanded higher pay during this era, but California was unique because some of its biggest strikes occurred on farms as well as in factories. In the first two years of the New Deal, there were huge, violent strikes in the state's Central Valley, in the irrigated Eden of its southeastern desert, and on the coastal wharves. In 1933 alone, fifty thousand farmworkers refused to harvest crops and walked out of the fields to protest wages as low as 10¢ an hour. The largest agricultural strike in U.S. history happened in the San Joaquin Valley in 1933 when close to twenty thousand cotton pickers went on strike. The nation witnessed the second general strike in its history when the entire city of San Francisco shut down to protest state repression of a longshoremen's strike in the summer of 1934.

Books and other artistic accounts of these labor battles helped shape public perception of the Depression. Many artists, writers, and Hollywood stars tried to assist the farmworkers and support their radical organizers. The poverty of the farm laborers contrasted so sharply with the artists' idealized vision of California—a land that should have been filled with sunshine and happiness—that they felt compelled to point out the contradiction.

John Steinbeck would play the most important role in publicizing the farmworkers' troubles to the rest of the nation. Steinbeck would also help embed some of the most pervasive myths about the time in the American consciousness. Readers of his novels learned that these strikes were led exclusively by white men; that women and people of color played only supporting roles; and that Communist labor organizers, as well as the growers, provoked violence. The truth was more complex—and, to those invested in maintaining the current social order, more threatening.

The massive California farm strikes incited political reaction as well as artistic inspiration. At first, the growers responded to the strikes with hired goons and official repression. Up and down the state, vigilantes beat pickets with axe handles and clubs, soaked them with fire hoses, and smothered them with tear gas. Local law enforcement officers arrested picketers on trumped-up charges of "vagrancy" and union organizers on felony charges of conspiracy. Very quickly, however, they realized that they needed to invent new kinds of political mobilization.

Novelist Wallace Stegner famously said that California is like America, only more so.[17] The battles in the California fields were similar to struggles that would take place elsewhere around the country, but they began earlier and were marked by more systematic and calculated violence than the national fights they prefigured. The state's multiracial, multiethnic workforce of migrants and immigrants, of women and men, foreshadowed the coming transformation of American labor. The battles over these changes would remake American politics and policy.

Most scholars have looked elsewhere—the South, Midwestern cities, or Wall Street—for the origins of modern conservatism. When historians bring the West into this story, they examine the housewives or defense workers in the suburbs of the Sun Belt. Alternatively, when they focus on class rather than region and analyze the role of business leaders in creating the New Right, they primarily discuss the members of the Liberty League and other Eastern industrialists. But these stories leave us with an incomplete and misleading understanding of the sources and motivations of conservative leadership.[18]

In this book, I argue that modern conservatism first emerged in its fullest form in the 1930s, in reaction to the New Deal. This movement began in California, and not in its suburbs but in its fields, where racial conflict shaped political attitudes. California agribusiness leaders consciously manipulated fears of cultural change—particularly disruptions to racial segregation and traditional gender roles—to mobilize grassroots opposition to Roosevelt's labor policies.

The engineers of this Western conservative movement realized that their argument had more power if it encompassed culture as well as money. Business leaders understood that they had to persuade people that Franklin Roosevelt's administration imperiled their religion, their liberty, and their family—their very way of life as they knew it. These Western corporate leaders developed ideas and strategies that would define the conservative movement for decades to come—and that would eventually have enormous consequences not just for the labor movement but for income inequality in America.

Compromised Reform

These conservatives saw the New Deal as an existential threat. "SINCE WE HAVE MOVED LEFT WE CAN SEE THE MONSTROUS RUSSIAN DOCTRINE BEING ACTUALLY APPLIED OF GRADING DOWN THE WHOLE POPULATION TO THE LEVEL OF THE LEAST PROSPEROUS," wrote newspaper publisher William Randolph Hearst in 1935, with a characteristic overuse of capitalization. "Is this the New Deal or the NEW DEATH?"[19]

But California agribusinessmen feared, or professed to fear, the New Deal all out of proportion to the actual threat it posed. Roosevelt's administration did much to help them and little to harm them. Indeed, the California growers despised and feared Roosevelt's labor policies even though those policies *did not apply to agricultural workers*.

The key piece of New Deal legislation that protected workers' right to organize, Section 7a of the National Industrial Recovery Act, did not cover farmworkers or domestic workers. The New Dealers deliberately left out these workers to secure the support of Southern lawmakers who represented plantation owners who did not want their sharecroppers or maids to join a union. Later, the Social Security Act and National Labor Relations Act would also exclude farmworkers. The Roosevelt administration was not interested in supporting farmworkers because they were overwhelmingly African Americans in the South (who could not vote), Mexican immigrants in the Southwest (who also could not vote), or white migrants in the West (who found it difficult to meet residency requirements to vote).[20] The fragile New Deal coalition needed the cooperation of conservative Democrats, who would have bolted if FDR had not placated them. The New Dealers tried mightily to appease owners of large plantations, farms, and ranches—who had been among the Democratic Party's most important supporters since before the Civil War.

Franklin Roosevelt, after all, was no radical. He never wanted the government to take over the nation's factories, farms, or banks—and it did not do so during his administration. He did support labor unions, but only because he and his allies hoped that workers could unite to raise their wages without direct government redistribution of wealth. For the most part, the New Deal tried to maintain a social order that largely benefited white men. Throughout the labor struggles in California, Roosevelt and his advisers dismissed and marginalized those who proposed more radical solutions.

Still, the New Dealers' attempts to distance themselves from more radical alternatives were not comfort enough to the California growers and their allies. During the labor struggles of the 1930s, these businessmen discovered how to bash the center for coddling the left—and, perversely, to do this at precisely those times when the center was *distancing itself* from or failing the left. Yet for their pains, the New Dealers were attacked for being too radical. As the center defined the left as the enemy, the right claimed that the center *was* the left. This dynamic was new to American political culture in the 1930s, but its creators would soon refine it and export it to the rest of the nation.

1

REVOLUTION AND REACTION

In the winter of 1933–34, John Steinbeck drove to a sleepy fishing village on California's central coast. He and Francis Whitaker, a friend from nearby Carmel, found the house they were looking for and climbed to the attic, where two frightened men were hiding from lynch mobs. Steinbeck's friends were helping these men, and they thought the young novelist might want to hear the fugitives' story—and then tell it to the world.

The storytellers, who refused to give Steinbeck their real names for fear of reprisals, had recently fled the violence and terror of the largest farmworker strike in U.S. history. Beginning in October 1933, eighteen thousand pickers had walked out of the fields of California's cotton empire, which stretched a hundred miles up the San Joaquin Valley. The workers, mostly Mexican Americans and Mexican immigrants, wanted a raise. Their pay was 15¢ an hour, at a time when the national minimum wage for many industries was 25¢. When the local and state police could not break the strike, the growers recruited vigilantes. The vigilantes brought clubs, tear gas, and guns.

In the attic that day, the men told Steinbeck what they had witnessed during the previous few months: the rousing speeches by strike leaders around the workers' campfires, the assaults on picketers, and the murder of strikers by vigilantes. They told him of the families who participated in the strike and the man and woman who led it: a charismatic, thirty-three-year-old Irish American named Pat Chambers; and a remarkable twenty-one-year-old from Georgia, Caroline Decker, whose fiery speeches and attractive features prompted the newspapers to label her the "blonde flame of the red revolt."[1] Without regular salaries and with bounties on their heads, these union organizers lived in tents, went to bed hungry, and risked prison, injury, and death to do their work.

The union leaders were eager to tell their story to their visitors. They knew that Whitaker, a blacksmith and metal sculptor, was helping raise money and awareness for the farmworkers by alerting his friends in the artists' colony in nearby Carmel-by-the-Sea, where poets, playwrights, authors, and painters gathered to learn about leftist causes.

Steinbeck, though, could potentially do even more for the cause. He had not published much of note by that point—a few historical romances and mythic tales—but some of the union's most prominent supporters saw talent in him. A native Californian, born and raised in Salinas, he could reach a wide audience if he could be persuaded to write about the West's real social dramas.

Steinbeck saw the dramatic potential in the strike: there were heroes and mobs, idealists and pragmatists, compromises and murders. Soon after the meeting in the attic, he wrote his literary agent that he wanted to write a first-person, nonfiction account of the cotton strike through the eyes of the men in the attic, whom he would pay for their story. The agent responded with enthusiasm, but suggested that he write fiction instead.[2]

And so Steinbeck began to write his first great novel, the book that would transform him from an obscure regional writer into the one of the most acclaimed American authors of the twentieth century. With *In Dubious Battle*, Steinbeck became the "most versatile master of narrative now writing in the United States," according to the *New York Times*.[3] *In Dubious Battle* would also lay the foundation for the monumental *Grapes of Wrath*, Steinbeck's novel about migrant farmworkers in California that would come to define the Great Depression for generations of Americans.

American readers loved Steinbeck's Depression novels, in part because they believed he was writing the history of their times—a view that Steinbeck encouraged. "In this book I was making nothing up," he wrote to his agent as he finished *In Dubious Battle*. "In any of the statements by one of the protagonists I have simply used statements I have heard used."[4] A few years later, after he wrote *The Grapes of Wrath*, he explained why he did so much research for his books: "I'm trying to write history while it is happening and I don't want to be wrong."[5]

Steinbeck wanted to be more right than the facts allowed. In his fictional account of the great cotton strike, the cotton turned into apples; the comely blonde firebrand became a ruggedly handsome (male) firebrand; Pat Chambers became "Mac," a rigid, insensitive ideologue; and the male and female Mexican workers changed into white men.[6] And thus the author transformed a tale of dark-skinned men and women striking under the leadership of pragmatic leftists into a story of a struggle among white men of various kinds—of brave white workers resisting rapacious growers and manipulative Communists.

In Dubious Battle marked not only Steinbeck's first major literary success, but also the beginning of Americans' embrace of convenient myths about the Great Depression and the New Deal. Steinbeck's version of the strike is the one that we know today. He wrote fiction, but it has become history. It is this difference—between stories and histories, between documented facts and comforting myths about the Great Depression and the New Deal—that this book seeks to explore.

The cotton strike of 1933 signaled the beginning of massive, Communist-led labor struggles and the subsequent conservative reaction in California. There would be abductions, near-lynchings, and murders; imprisonments and trials and appeals; electoral campaigns and dirty tricks; movie stars who almost lost their careers over the strikes, and a Nobel Prize–winning novelist who made his. As Communists pushed for worker organization and, ultimately, revolution, reformers in Washington discovered new ways of responding to the radical challenge. California would become the battlefield of a labor war as liberals, conservatives, and radicals clashed over the best response to one of the greatest crises in the history of capitalism.

Food Factories

Just a short time earlier, no one would have predicted that California could become the birthplace of an important national political movement. When Bert Hoover stepped off the train in Menlo Park, California, in the fall of 1891, he found a bucolic farm removed from the nation's political and economic controversies. Stanford University, where he intended to enroll that fall, had just opened its doors and was so desperate for students that it accepted the lightly educated farm boy from Iowa even after he failed the entrance examination. The San Francisco peninsula at that time was both relatively uninhabited and isolated: there were no bridges linking San Francisco to cities across the bay.

Yet by the end of Hoover's life, in 1964, Stanford—thanks in no small measure to Hoover's promotion of it—would become a leader in higher education on the West Coast, and there would be seven bridges, including one authorized during his presidential administration, linking the peninsula to the rest of the state. The changes to Stanford and its surrounding area mirrored the progress of California as a whole. In one lifetime, the far West moved from the political and economic margins of the country to its center.

California owed its transformation in no small measure to agribusiness. A state founded on gold had become a state dependent on farms. In the 1920s, it moved into the top three states in terms of value of agricultural output. California had the most diverse agriculture, the most productive and profitable farms, the longest irrigation canal, the biggest winery, and the largest agricultural cannery. And much of the rest of the state's economy relied on agribusiness: from the processors who put the fruit and vegetables into cans, to the railroads and shipping companies that transported them, to the marketing companies that created the sun-drenched images that sold California farm products and the California dream around the globe.[7]

On average, these farms—or "ranches," as Californians often called them—were much larger than those in other parts of the country. Only 2.2 percent of the nation's farms were in California, yet the state was home to more than 36 percent of America's large-scale farms, those with a gross income of more than $30,000 in 1929.[8] There were, to be sure, many small growers in the state, but in certain crops and environments—cotton in the Central Valley, vegetables in Imperial Valley—the large growers wielded disproportionate power.

Because California farms were so large on average, relatively small numbers of farmers worked their own land or harvested their own crops. In California, about one-third of agricultural laborers worked on their own properties, while two-thirds were hired hands; in the nation as a whole, the proportions were reversed, with more than 70 percent of farmers working their own lands and only about 30 percent working for someone else. California author Carey McWilliams coined a phrase to describe agriculture in his state: "factories in the field."[9] As the Federal Writers Project guide to California explained, "Farming here is not farming as Easterners know it; most of the ranches are food factories, with superintendents and foremen, administrative headquarters and machine sheds."[10]

Some of these growers were individual owners, like Joseph Di Giorgio, a Sicilian immigrant who owned a forty-thousand-acre ranch in Delano and the largest fruit packinghouse in the world, or J.G. Boswell, known as the King of Kings County, whose cotton empire stretched over tens of thousands of acres.[11]

Many of the largest ranches, however, were farmed not by individuals but by corporations, including the California Packing Corporation, which controlled twenty thousand acres of orchards and canneries in ten states, and mammoth conglomerates such as the Transamerica Company, the Kern County Land Company, and Miller & Lux, all of which owned at least one hundred thousand acres of prime California croplands.[12]

For decades, California growers relied on immigrants to pick their crops. Waves of Chinese, Japanese, Filipino, South Asian, and Mexican laborers surged and receded with the harvest seasons. In the 1920s and the early 1930s, Mexicans and Mexican Americans comprised the majority of workers for the largest growers, especially in the vegetable fields of Imperial County on the Mexican border and the cotton ranches in the vast Central Valley. When workers could not find jobs, they had no safety net: no unemployment insurance, pensions, or welfare.

Picking cotton and vegetables was grueling work, especially so in California. Pickers worked from dawn to dusk year-round. In the summers, the temperatures in the inland valleys routinely topped one hundred degrees; in the winters, thin clothing could not protect laborers from the chill of the thick ground fog that covered parts of the Central Valley. In flush times, they could earn enough to pay for gas to drive to the next job and for a dinner of canned salmon, corn bread, and onions. In difficult times, they were marooned in squatters' camps with no fuel to drive away. They gathered dandelion greens and ate them with boiled potatoes. Given the lack of nourishing food, children suffered disproportionate rates of illness and mortality. The specters of influenza, pneumonia, and nutritional deficiencies like pellagra stalked the workers' camps.[13]

Because the growers knew that many of their workers were foreign, and because they saw them as very different from themselves, they felt justified in paying them abysmal wages. "What a Mexican should be paid is just enough to live on, with maybe a dollar or two to spend. That's all he deserves," one Southwestern grower told economist Paul Taylor.[14] A cotton grower explained to Taylor that he preferred Mexicans to Anglos because "you can't tell the whites so well what to do."[15] Whites could vote and could not be deported, while Mexicans and even Mexican Americans lived in fear that they could be sent over the border if the growers decided they were agitators.

Farm organizations lobbied fiercely to maintain a lax immigration policy, arguing that they could not find Anglos to take the backbreaking, low-paying jobs they offered. "We, gentlemen, are just as anxious as you are not to build the civilization of California or any other western district upon a Mexican foundation," Parker Frisselle, the owner of a five-thousand-acre raisin farm in Fresno, testified to Congress in 1926, arguing against one of many ultimately unsuccessful bills to limit immigration from Mexico. "We take him because there is nothing else available."[16] Another grower contended that Anglo workers refused to perform painful, tedious work in the fields. "You can not get white labor to go in the beet fields and on their hands and knees, chop out the plants; you can not get them to dig in the mud for celery; it is not the kind of work that white people engage in."[17] And if they did, there was something wrong with them: the only whites who picked fruits and vegetables in California were "derelicts" who were "physically, mentally, and temperamentally unfit," one grower spokesman insisted.[18]

After the Great Depression began in 1929, however, there were many apparently fit white people willing to take these jobs—because they had no other choice. Throughout the Great Plains and the Southwest, plummeting crop prices and a series of environmental disasters brought misery to farmers. Hundreds of thousands of tenant farmers in Oklahoma, Arkansas, and Texas began to drift to California in hopes of finding work in the Western fields.[19] These desperate Americans competed for scarce work at low wages. In 1932, there were 142 would-be farmworkers in California for every 100 jobs.[20]

The growers took advantage of the labor surplus by cutting workers' pay. From 1930 to 1931, wages dropped from $3.45 per day on average to $2.78 (or even less if the workers needed "board," or a residence in a tent or shack provided by the grower). If the pickers worked all year long, they would earn about $868 annually, or a little less than the poverty line in California. But most farm laborers worked less than 60 percent of the time and earned only $300 to $400 a year. In 1932, the average wage plunged to $2.14 a day and reached its nadir in 1933 at $1.91 for a twelve-hour day.[21]

To feed their families, men and women worked in the fields alongside their children. In contrast to the gendered images of the American family farm, with the "farmer's wife" safely ensconced inside the home, California crops were picked by parents, grandparents, and children as young as six years old. The working families often lived in huts made of packing crates, scrap tin, and cardboard scrounged from a nearby dump.

The largest growers had an impersonal, industrial relationship with their workers. "The old fashioned hired man is a thing of the past. He has left the farm," said George Clements of the agricultural department of the Los Angeles Chamber of Commerce. Clements believed that growers who paid their workers more than the market would bear were wasting their money, and, by extension, in the case of corporate growers, stealing the shareholders' money. The farmer "who does not wake up to the realization that there is a caste in labor on the farm," he said, "is sharing too much of his dollar with labor."[22]

Western growers built powerful wage-fixing organizations to ensure that competition did not force them to share too much with their workers. During World War I, farm employers colluded to set maximum wage rates throughout the American West. The push to keep prices down was justified as an essential part of the war effort. After the war, many growers decided to keep these wage-fixing organizations or start new ones. Supported by farm bureaus, chambers of commerce, and growers' protective organizations, these labor bureaus recruited workers when they were needed, sent them away when they were not, and pressured farmers to pay them all the same wage. Because the finance companies supported the labor bureaus, growers could not get loans if they paid more than the wage set by the bureau. Through these agencies, farmers discovered the power of their own collective action while they denied it to their workers.[23]

As farmers continued to slash wages through the early years of the Depression, many workers grew increasingly restive, and some struggled to form unions. But the workers were rootless, impoverished, and divided, and thousands of strikebreakers stood ready to take the jobs of any who dared to walk out of the fields. The growers intimidated strikers and hired vigilantes to assault them. In this dangerous atmosphere, the American Federation of Labor (AFL) declined to organize California farmworkers. As one AFL organizer said, "only fanatics are willing to live in shacks or tents and get their heads broken in the interests of migratory laborers."[24]

The Radicals

Some "fanatics" were willing to live in shacks and brave assaults to help migrant laborers—first during the early years of the twentieth century, and again during the Depression. These radical men and women responded to the injustices of industrial capitalism by proposing to replace it with a new system of common ownership of the means of production.

Beginning in 1905, a radical labor union, the Industrial Workers of the World (IWW), popularly known as the Wobblies, organized farmworkers along with timber workers and miners of the West. As anarcho-syndicalists, the Wobblies sought to inspire workers in all industries, including agribusiness, to join one big union that would topple capitalism and the political system that supported it. Wobblies spouted militant rhetoric, led strikes, and committed acts of industrial sabotage. The union counted just one hundred thousand members at its height right before World War I, but it terrified corporate leaders.[25]

Even though they were the *Industrial* Workers of the World, the Wobblies saw the workers in the factories in the fields as the real American proletariat—the laborers most likely to respond to their language of class warfare. In California, the IWW set up union locals in Fresno, Redlands, and Imperial County and led free speech fights up and down the state to defend its right to teach about revolution. The Wobblies' most important unionization campaign took place in an overcrowded, pestilential farm labor camp outside of Wheatland, north of Sacramento, in 1913. When deputy sheriffs came to the camp to arrest the IWW organizers, workers fought back.

Four men died in the battle, including two workers, the district attorney, and a deputy sheriff.[26]

The state of California responded to the Wheatland riot in two ways: first by trying to improve living conditions for migrant pickers, and then by crushing the IWW. The progressive Republicans who held power in Sacramento created a new state agency, the Commission of Immigration and Housing, to inspect migrant farmworker camps and force growers to offer laborers basic necessities like toilets and clean drinking water. Progressives argued that the best way to destroy radicalism was to provide a decent standard of living for the working class.[27]

At the same time, state and local governments repressed the Wobblies by making it a crime to belong to a radical union. One scholar has called the campaign against the IWW "the most explicit, straightforward, and altogether remarkable effort in modern America to use the power of the state, backed by law, to stamp out a radical organization."[28] Local officials throughout the Midwest and the West, where the Wobblies were most active, charged tens of thousands of IWW members with violating vagrancy laws, or being on the streets without a "lawful purpose." More seriously, state legislatures passed laws against "criminal syndicalism," which meant belonging to an organization that advocated a change in industrial ownership.

Some anarchists did commit violent crimes in their efforts to overthrow capitalism. In 1910, an anarchist bomb killed twenty-one people at the headquarters of the *Los Angeles Times*, a notorious opponent of labor unions. Over the next few years, California suffered more anarchist attacks: in 1916, ten people died in San Francisco when a bomb exploded during a parade celebrating military preparedness; the next year, an explosion rocked the governor's mansion in Sacramento; two years later, a banker's wife was killed by a bomb hidden in her garden in Oakland. But the reaction to these isolated acts of terror was disproportionate. The state could and did send people to prison for murder, but state legislatures went further, making it a crime to belong to any organization that opposed capitalism. As a 1919 *Oakland Tribune* editorial argued in support of California's criminal syndicalism law, "There will have to be a summary policy adopted toward dynamiters, Bolshevists, I.W.W. and the whole brood of anarchists. It should be enough to know of their general tendency and sentiments without having to fasten spe-cific crimes upon them."[29]

The U.S. Supreme Court upheld California's criminal syndicalism law. Over the next few decades, the court sustained convictions for syndicalism or sedition even if the defendants or the groups to which they belonged never carried out or even planned violent acts. The laws aimed to prevent radical groups from spreading their message and gaining converts.

The Wobblies faced extralegal repression as well. Growers and business leaders recruited local vigilantes, including members of the Ku Klux Klan and the American Legion, to threaten, intimidate, assault, and sometimes lynch their organizers. While government officials prosecuted and impris-oned IWW leaders for organizing unions, they seldom charged the vigilan-tes who attacked and murdered them. Wobbly members saw the "rule of law" as just another way for people with wealth to maintain their power and privilege.

The anti-Wobbly campaign destroyed the IWW, which shrank to a tiny, insignificant organization by the mid-1920s. Prosecutions for criminal syndicalism virtually ceased until state officials found a new breed of "fa-natics" who worked to organize unions and overthrow capitalism: the lead-ers of the Communist Party.

American Communists first formed organized parties in 1919, two years after the Bolshevik Revolution in Russia.[30] Convinced that capitalism was near collapse, they joined the Communist International, an organization with its headquarters in Moscow, and supported its pledge to use "all avail-able means, including armed struggle, for the overthrow of the international bourgeoisie and for the creation of an international Soviet republic as a tran-sitional stage to the complete abolition of the State."[31]

The U.S. government tried to destroy the Communist Party before it could take root in American soil. Federal agents arrested suspected Com-munists and deported noncitizens during the Red Scare of 1919–20. In the Department of Justice's antiradical division, a young bureaucrat named J. Edgar Hoover began to compile thousands of files on radicals and to build the institutional capacity of the government to monitor and harass them. Although the federal government spied on radicals, it lacked the power to prosecute them. The United States had no national peacetime sedition act, and despite numerous attempts, Congress failed to pass one until 1940.[32]

State and local governments eagerly stepped into the breach. Like the Wobblies, Communists routinely received short jail terms for vagrancy, blocking the sidewalk, disturbing the peace, or picketing. Leaders were charged with violating state sedition statutes, criminal syndicalism laws, or "red flag" laws, which outlawed the use of revolutionary banners. By the mid-1930s, almost every state had passed some sort of law against the vaguely defined crimes of "sedition," "syndicalism," or "insurrection."[33]

Just as Communists endorsed any means necessary to destroy capitalism, anticommunists believed they needed to be ruthless in smashing the Red threat to the American government and way of life. Communists menaced every important conservative institution: as internationalists, they pledged to obliterate the nation-state; as Marxists, they promised to confiscate private property; and as atheists, they swore to destroy the church. Most important, conservatives believed that the Reds endangered the American family by making men dependent on the state and taking women outside of the home to work.

Middle-class Americans were especially receptive to arguments that communism threatened their families. In the 1920s, as American women cut their hair, hiked up their hemlines, and headed to the voting booths for the first time, some traditionalists fretted that the American family might collapse under the strain of modernization. To these social conservatives, Communists were frightening because they embraced changes in gender roles and advocated for even more.

The anticommunists were extremely successful during the 1920s. Government repression and internal dissension caused the Party to dwindle to just 9,300 members by 1929.[34] The antiradical campaign worked so well that most states stopped prosecuting Communists.[35] In a land of consumerist plenty, of automobiles and moving pictures and jazz clubs, a few thousand Communists no longer seemed as threatening.

Then came the Party's greatest recruiting opportunity in history.

The Crisis

Up until the Great Depression, Herbert Hoover had enjoyed a fantastically successful career as a businessman, cabinet officer, humanitarian, and, finally, president. After graduation from Stanford, he amassed a fortune of $4 million as a gold mining engineer and executive in Australia, Russia, and China. In 1914, when World War I broke out in Europe, he organized an unprecedented voluntary effort to distribute food to millions of civilians displaced by the fighting. When the United States joined the war in 1917, President Woodrow Wilson asked Hoover to head the Food Administration, where he oversaw a campaign to exhort Americans to produce more food and consume less. The success of "meatless Mondays" and "wheatless Wednesdays" helped the government avoid strict rationing plans.

After the war, Hoover built a house in Palo Alto and established the Hoover War Library, later renamed the Hoover Institution. But he lived in California infrequently over the next ten years as he embarked on his national political career, first as commerce secretary to Presidents Harding and Coolidge, and finally, as the crowning achievement in a life filled with impressive accomplishments, as the first president from west of the Mississippi.

Then, just one year after his election, Hoover confronted the worst economic crisis in the nation's history. The gross national product began to plummet: adjusted for inflation, it was down 10 percent in 1930, 16 percent in 1931, and 29 percent in 1932.[36] Some 30 million Americans—the jobless and their families—lost their sources of income as unemployment soared.[37] Many Americans looked to Washington, desperately hoping that their government could do something to bring back their jobs and restore prosperity.

As a man who had been born in a tiny cabin on the prairie, an orphan who had made himself into a millionaire through hard work and intelligence and good luck, President Hoover believed firmly that the federal government should not give direct relief to suffering Americans. Instead, he encouraged business leaders to work together to solve the crisis in the spirit of cooperation and community. He convened a conference of industrial leaders in Washington, D.C., and extracted a promise from them to maintain wage levels. He urged railroads and local governments to step up their construction programs. When gross domestic production continued to slide, Hoover agreed to the Democratic Congress's demand to create a new government agency, the Reconstruction Finance Corporation, to loan money to the largest banks and railroads. Finally, in July 1932, he signed a bill sending federal aid to the states for public works. But he steadfastly refused to give direct government relief to the unemployed, for fear of making them dependent on government and weakening their commitment to hard work and individualism.

His policies did not work. The depression worsened. By 1932, between a quarter and a third of Americans were out of work. One-fifth of all commercial banks failed, taking tens of thousands of families' life savings with them.[38] Local officials warned that they could see mass starvation in their cities if Washington did not send more aid.[39]

Outside of major cities, and throughout the rural United States—in Appalachia, and Mississippi, and the California valleys—families lived in squatters' camps on the banks of streams, cobbling together tin, packing crates, and sheets of canvas to make homes for their children. Mothers stretched their corn or beans to make two small meals a day. Babies starved to death; children fainted from hunger in schools, if they were lucky enough to be in school, or in the fields, if they had to work to help support their families. Waste and disease overwhelmed sanitation systems and immune systems; dysentery, diphtheria, typhoid, and even plague swept through the encampments of the homeless. The United States had known depressions before, but never one that devastated so many families for such a long time.

Many Americans began to blame Hoover for the economic policy failures that led to the Depression and for his apparently callous dismissal of its human costs. An exceedingly wealthy investor himself, Hoover seemed to have little empathy for the common man. An aloof, intensely private person, he often spoke in a monotone, eyes cast downward, hands in his pockets, jangling his keys. Cartoons depicted him as a remote, dour man oblivious to the human tragedy around him.

His presidency reached its lowest point in the summer of 1932 with the "Bonus Army" debacle, when thousands of World War I veterans camped near Washington, D.C., to demand the immediate payment of a service bonus due them in 1945. Most members of the Bonus Army left the capital when the Senate refused to pass a bill paying them their bonus, but a few thousand stayed on in an abandoned building downtown and in shanty-towns on Anacostia Flats. When the D.C. police tried to force the veterans from the downtown buildings, the men resisted. Two were killed by the police. Hoover then sent in the U.S. Army to evict the remainder. General Douglas MacArthur exceeded his orders by proceeding to Anacostia Flats, where his men, on horseback and in tanks, set upon the veterans' encampment and burned their tents to the ground. The spectacle of the U.S. Army attacking its own veterans helped doom Hoover's reelection chances.[40]

Communists had been predicting the imminent collapse of capitalism for decades, but the crisis of the 1930s provided them with compelling evidence for their argument. In response, the Party organized demonstrations, marches, and strikes—all in hopes of awakening workers to the need for revolution. Communists also began setting up their own separate unions, rather than continuing to work within the capitalist ones. However, the Communists realized that their potential recruits wanted immediate, concrete gains like 5¢ more an hour, not promises of a Leninist utopia. Party organizers adapted themselves to the workers' needs and emphasized the financial benefits of joining a Communist union.[41]

In particular, Party leaders targeted the people they viewed as the most "oppressed and inarticulate" of Americans: farmworkers.[42] If anyone in America wanted a revolution, the Party leaders reasoned, it would be the men and women who picked cotton twelve hours a day and then went home— or rather, went homeless, and slept in ditches.

In California, the state Communist Party leader, Samuel Adams Darcy, made it his priority to organize and politicize migrant pickers. Young, tall, and burly enough to intimidate smaller men, Darcy had displayed such leadership and management skills in New York that he alarmed the Party's national leaders, whose experience in internecine quarrels had honed their survival instincts as well as their paranoia. Seeing him as a potential rival, Party leaders exiled him to California, where they hoped he would fade into obscurity. Darcy responded by working hard to revitalize the California Party, which he transformed from an obscure sect with fewer than three hundred members into a disciplined, dynamic force in the region's labor politics. At their peak in the 1930s, Communist unions in the state claimed tens of thousands of members, and more than one hundred thousand Californians voted for Communist candidates for statewide offices.[43]

The Party created a farmworkers' union called the Cannery and Agricultural Workers Industrial Union, or CAWIU. The leaders of this new union knew that their jobs could be dangerous. Throughout the state, the organizers risked injury and death. In one of the worst cases of mob violence, during a tree pruners' strike in Vacaville, a group of forty masked men snatched six young CAWIU leaders from the city jail, drove them out to a deserted area, flogged them with straps, sheared off their hair, and slathered them in red enamel paint. The vigilantes left the organizers alive, but too wounded and terrified to continue leading the strike.[44]

But in March 1933, a new administration took over in Washington, and the labor situation in California changed overnight. The promise of Franklin Roosevelt's New Deal inspired tens of thousands of agricultural laborers to exercise what they believed was their new right to join a union. These workers would test the limits of the New Dealers' vision of recovery and reform.

The Reformers

At first glance, Franklin Roosevelt seemed an unlikely champion of the working class. Born into one of the nation's most patrician families, he enjoyed the untroubled life of the elite: ponies, governesses, hunt breakfasts, yachts, prep school, and trips to Europe. His school chums and neighbors included Vanderbilts and Astors; his extended family contained a president. He waltzed with debutantes and sailed with commodores.[45] He could walk four miles straight without stepping off his father's estate above the Hudson River. Because the American economic system had been very good to him, he might have become one of the most fervent defenders of the status quo.

Instead, Roosevelt was a dedicated advocate of progressivism, which was America's alternative to socialism. Rather than arguing for government ownership of factories and farms, as did European socialists (and the much smaller number of American socialists), American progressives wanted to reform the private enterprise system to save it from revolution. Like his cousin Theodore, who was one of the nation's leading progressives, Franklin Roosevelt believed in using the government to force employers to make their factories safer places for their workers. While serving in the New York legislature in the 1910s, Roosevelt helped to pass laws mandating workers' compensation, factory inspections, and limits on the hours that women and children could work each week.

As governor of New York beginning in 1929, Franklin Roosevelt remained committed to using government policy to help the neediest citizens. He called for old-age pensions, unemployment insurance, and restrictions on antiunion injunctions; he fought for public works projects and larger relief payments to the hungry. The governor believed that society had a moral obligation "to prevent the starvation or the dire want of any of its fellow men and women who try to maintain themselves but cannot." New Yorkers, he said, must use their government to extend aid to these unfortunate citizens "not as a matter of charity but as a matter of social duty."[46]

Progressives like Roosevelt did not want to confiscate or redistribute wealth, but they did believe that the government should prevent monopolies and ensure a decent standard of living for workers. One of Roosevelt's most influential advisers, as governor and later as president, was labor expert Frances Perkins. A one-time social worker, Perkins dedicated her life to advocating for government regulation of capitalism. As a New York state industrial relations official, she argued that the government should appoint fact-finding commissions and mediate strikes instead of reflexively sending in troops to back employers. She helped to shape Roosevelt's belief that government power should be used to level the economic playing field and give hope to the downtrodden.[47] During Roosevelt's term as governor, Perkins ran the New York Industrial Commission, which mediated strikes, mandated minimum standards for health and safety, and investigated complaints about working conditions. Perkins, Roosevelt, and other progressives believed that if the government did not enforce some rules in the marketplace, workers would starve.

Or they might revolt. Roosevelt argued that Americans could overthrow the government and the economic system if officials did not embrace policies that he (and his cousin Theodore) called "sane radicalism." As the Depression deepened in 1930, FDR proposed in a private letter to a friend that it was "time for the country to become fairly radical for at least one generation." The lessons of history, he said, proved that "where this occurs occasionally, nations are saved from revolutions."[48]

Roosevelt meant that government should be a neutral force in the marketplace rather than a tool of corporate capital. In 1930, as governor he helped to end a massive strike in the New York City textile industry by calling business and labor leaders to a conference and persuading them to accept arbitration. This was indeed fairly radical in a country in which state troopers and local police routinely suppressed strikes with brutal force. Throughout his governorship, Roosevelt refused to send in state troops to break strikes, opting instead to urge both sides to negotiate.

Governor Roosevelt was also quite progressive in his dealings with Communists. He preferred to parley with radicals rather than imprison them, arguing that harsh repression only helped the Reds to recruit new members. Once, in November 1932, shortly after his election to the presidency, when a group of Communists protested outside his Albany mansion, he surprised them with an invitation to come inside and discuss their demands directly with him. He urged them to put their faith in procedural liberalism and to wait for the new programs he would introduce as president.[49]

Conservatives believed that Roosevelt was coddling Communists. True leaders did not invite revolutionaries for tea; they ordered state troopers to crack their skulls. One anticommunist intellectual called progressives "misguided muddlers" who, although sometimes inspired by the "purest motives," allowed evil to take root in American soil.[50] Extremist anticommunists like Congressman Hamilton Fish, a Republican who represented Roosevelt's home district in the Hudson River Valley, denounced reformers as "pink intellectualists" who were more despicable than real revolutionaries.[51]

Roosevelt scoffed at the Red baiters, ridiculing the charge that modest regulations were the first step down the slippery slope toward communism. Indeed, he argued that regulation would rob radicalism of its appeal. The defenders of privilege, he noted, had charged him and his fellow progressives in the New York legislature with Communist sympathies back in 1911, before the Soviet Union even existed. "We were called Communists, we were called Radicals," he recalled. "We thought we were doing a heroic thing when we made it illegal for women and children in industry to work more than fifty-four hours a week. That's how radical we were."[52]

Governor Roosevelt's wife, Eleanor, agreed with her husband that conservatives manipulated fears of communism for their own political purposes. In 1927, Mrs. Roosevelt chastised a prominent business leader for his alarmist writings on communism, criticizing his group for "constantly sending out propaganda and letters of warning as to the Bolshevik who is to be found around the corner and under every bed." The country, she argued, was in more danger from the extremist anticommunists than from the Reds.[53]

In addition to pledging to help the working class, FDR made a point of seeking advice from people who had been marginalized in the past because of their religion or gender. In an era when most men of his class were overtly anti-Semitic, he socialized with many Jews and appointed them to top posts in his administration, including treasury secretary.[54] Roosevelt's willingness to listen to women was also unusual for his time. Eleanor was one of his most trusted advisers, and he would soon name Perkins as the first woman in history in the Cabinet. As he told Perkins after he appointed her New York's industrial commissioner, "I am willing to take more chances. I've got more nerve about women and their status in the world."[55]

Roosevelt popularized a new term for his political philosophy. The word "liberalism" was not common in American political debate before 1932. As a presidential candidate, Roosevelt sought a new word that would transcend partisan lines and signal a break with older (and outdated) political divisions. During his campaign, Roosevelt began calling himself a "liberal" rather than a "progressive."[56] He always distinguished his ideology from conservatism on one hand and socialism on the other. Later, when he ran for reelection as president in 1936, Roosevelt explained his political philosophy by quoting one of his favorite sayings: "'Reform if you would preserve.' I am that kind of conservative because I am that kind of liberal."[57]

Roosevelt emphasized that many American presidents in the past had supported an expansive role for government in the economy—that is, an expansive role for government policies that aided business. He would be different, he said, because he thought that government should help workers and farmers as well as business. "Each group has sought protection from the government for its own special interests," he said, "without realizing that the function of government must be to favor no small group at the expense of its duty to protect the rights of personal freedom and of private property of all its citizens."[58] This was a crucial point of Roosevelt's "new deal for the American people," which he promised upon accepting the Democratic Party's nomination: that the federal government would strive to protect the interests of those who had previously lacked power or representation in Washington.

Once elected, the new president proclaimed that his administration would no longer serve one interest group. The "rulers of the exchange of mankind's goods" had failed "through their own stubbornness and their own incompetence," he declared in his inaugural address. Now, the government would put people to work and build "greatly needed projects to stimulate and reorganize the use of our natural resources."[59]

A New Deal for Labor

Roosevelt's first policies to combat the crisis focused on economic recovery: saving the dollar (by going off the gold standard), saving the banks (with regulation and deposit insurance), organizing industry, and subsidizing farms. The two centerpieces of his early recovery effort were the Agricultural Adjustment Act (AAA) and the National Industrial Recovery Act (NIRA). With these laws, the federal government moved to revive industry and agriculture and to transform the American economy.

The AAA boosted farmers' income by giving them cash to reduce their acreage. In return for planting less cotton than they had the year before, for example, growers received $12 per acre from the Agriculture Department. Because the program reduced the supply, the price of cotton increased, and planters benefited from the higher prices as well as from the government checks. The federal government also set up numerous other agricultural programs to help farmers, including the Farm Credit Administration, which loaned money for farm mortgages, machinery, and supplies.[60] The federal government, in other words, loaned farmers money to grow crops—and also paid them not to grow a vast surplus. The AAA effectively accomplished its goal of raising farmers' income, which doubled in the course of the 1930s.

Under the NIRA, the government suspended antitrust laws and encouraged industries to form cartels with the goal of centralizing planning, raising wages, and inflating prices. Initially, the program was quite popular. But within a year, consumers began to resent its inflationary effects.[61] Although the law was supposed to reflect the wishes of consumers and workers as well as business, it disappointed just about everyone. If the Supreme Court had not ruled it unconstitutional in 1935, Congress probably would have killed it anyway.[62]

Still, judging from the election results of 1934 and 1936, most Americans supported Roosevelt's New Deal, and for clear reasons: because it delivered on its promises of relief, reform, and recovery. During Roosevelt's first term, real Gross National Product (GNP) grew by an average of 8 percent per year; after the recession of 1937–38, GNP increased by more than 10 percent per year until the United States entered World War II. Economic historian Christina Romer describes these rates of growth as "spectacular." Roosevelt's first term saw the greatest peacetime economic growth in U.S.

history. The United States did not return to full employment until World
War II, but that was only because joblessness had skyrocketed so dramatically
under President Hoover. President Roosevelt was reelected overwhelmingly
in 1936 because voters could see signs of recovery all around them.[63]

Like other Americans, Californians of many different political persua-
sions embraced the new administration's policies. *Touring Topics*, the magazine of the Southern California Auto Club (hardly a hotbed of radicalism),
enthused in early 1934 about the new spirit in the West after the change
in administration. "After four years of tragic adversity there is hope once
again . . . and faith in the ultimate destiny of a people," the editors wrote.[64]
Sacramentans applauded the National Recovery Administration (NRA)
with a "Sacramento Valley Prosperity Week" in October 1933, complete
with a civic parade with twenty-five floats, fifty marching bands, and ten
thousand cheering spectators, all to celebrate the nation's renewed confidence. The *Sacramento Bee*, a progressive Republican newspaper, rhapso-
dized: "There was hope. There was the rollicking spirit that everything is
going to be all right now. The New Deal." NRA, proclaimed the *Bee*'s reporter, stood for Now Rises America.[65]

Besides letting businessmen collude to raise prices, the NIRA also gave
something to workers: government protection for forming unions. Section 7a
of the act guaranteed that employees "shall have the right to organize and
bargain collectively through representatives of their own choosing."

Although workers had the right to join unions before the New Deal—
in the sense that members could not be put in jail simply for belonging—
federal law did not require employers to respect that right. A business owner
could fire any employee who joined a union; send spies into meetings to identify union members and report on their plans; refuse to hire someone unless
that person promised never to join a union; and require all employees to join
a company union. If an independent union did manage to surmount all these
obstacles and offer a collective bargaining proposal, a business owner could
refuse to deal with that union. As one scholar of labor relations wrote in
1938, "Under such circumstances, to speak of labor's right to organize was
clearly a misuse of terms. All that the employees had was a right to try to organize if they could get away with it; and whether they could or not depended
on the relative economic strength of the employers' and the employees'
organizations."[66]

The federal government occasionally intervened in disputes between workers and employers. Once, during the massive anthracite strike of 1902, President Theodore Roosevelt forced coal miners and operators to negotiate; more often, presidents sent in federal troops to break strikes. On the whole, the nation's laws and judges were so hostile to union organizing that employers could usually defeat strikes without any federal help.

As Samuel Gompers, head of the American Federation of Labor, wrote in 1919, "the whole machinery of government has frequently been placed at the disposal of the employers for the oppression of the workers."[67] Gompers and other labor leaders demanded that government restore balance in the marketplace by outlawing these antiunion practices.

Labor leaders won some important victories prior to the New Deal, most notably in 1932, one year before Franklin Roosevelt became president. The Norris–La Guardia Act, sponsored by two progressive Republicans, George Norris of Nebraska and Fiorello La Guardia of New York, outlawed the nation's most potent union-busting techniques. The law prohibited federal judges from issuing injunctions against nonviolent strikes and banned the infamous "yellow dog" contracts, which made refusal to join a union a condition of employment.

Then, in 1933, came the New Deal and the potentially revolutionary provisions of Section 7a. New York senator Robert Wagner, a champion of organized labor and an architect of the recovery bill, insisted that the NIRA had to guarantee workers' rights: "No 7a," he said at one point, "no bill."[68] Wagner believed it would be unconscionable for the government to allow businesses to raise prices without simultaneously encouraging workers to join unions, thus giving them a chance to raise their wages.

Although the text of Section 7a did not explicitly say whether its protections applied to agricultural laborers, congressional leaders and the Roosevelt administration quickly clarified that they did not. The New Dealers agreed to omit farm laborers from the NIRA for the same reason that they later excluded them from the Social Security Act and the National Labor Relations Act: powerful Southern Democrats wanted to maintain control over their tenant farmers and sharecroppers.[69] Moreover, the Roosevelt administration believed that the Agricultural Adjustment Act would protect farmworkers' interests because landowners, the theory went, would share their increased income and their subsidy payments with their workers. Therefore the government did not need to protect farm-workers' unions.[70]

The New Dealers saw practical advantages in industrial unionization: more money in workers' paychecks would boost consumers' spending power, which would in turn lead to national economic recovery. In addition, government protection for unions would help convince workers to support the existing economic system and ignore calls for radical change. Roosevelt's advisers had no idea that their labor policies would revolutionize the relationship between workers and their employers and bring about a fundamental shift of power in the American economy.

The Conservatives

In contrast to the energized radicals and resurgent liberals of 1933, conservatives were directionless, disorganized, and angry. They did not yet have a cohesive movement. But many business leaders—some embittered, some ambitious, and others just determined to hold on to their traditions and their wealth—began to agitate against the New Deal from its inception. And many of them came from California.

After he lost the White House in 1932, Herbert Hoover retreated to Palo Alto and his stunning home, an expansive, multilevel edifice with sweeping views of the rolling brown foothills of the coastal mountains and the red-tiled roofs of the university. There, he took long walks with his German shepherd and his Belgian sheepdog, read the thirty newspapers shipped by air to his home every day, answered his own mail, and wrote about the dangers of collectivism for popular magazines. He appeared to be relaxed and thriving in retirement, or at least so it seemed to a *Los Angeles Times* reporter who wrote of the former president's new zest for life and his pleasure in "doing what he pleases when he pleases."[71] But beneath the jocular exterior he showed to reporters, Hoover nursed powerful grudges. It was not just that he had lost the election in 1932; in Hoover's view, the nation had lost its soul. And because he was one of the few who recognized the peril, it was his duty to sound the alarm. Although some historians today see him as a "forgotten progressive," Hoover himself believed that there was a real and significant difference between his policies and those of the man who replaced him in the White House.[72]

Hoover blamed many events and people for the Great Depression, but he particularly favored explanations that were far away and back in time. While president, he maintained that European events, particularly the Treaty of Versailles, were at fault; the American president had little control. Once he was no longer in the White House, he discovered the singular importance of the presidency, and placed the blame for the continuation of the Depression squarely on the shoulders of his successor.

He laced his private letters with bitter invective against the New Dealers' monetary policies (they aim for the "destruction of the savings of the people in pursuit of demagogic pandering to those who have never saved anything"), their assaults on the Constitution (the spirit of the Bill of Rights was "being violated in every town and village every hour of the day"), and their crusade to undermine traditional values ("They would destroy our civilization just as most of the same people would destroy our religious faiths. Instead of a nation of self-reliant people they would produce a nation of sycophants eating at the public trough.").[73] In Hoover's view, Roosevelt wanted to incite class warfare, eliminate profit, undermine individualism, redistribute wealth, and, ultimately, replace private industry with government ownership. Those alive in 1933 were witnessing "the major battle of the Republic—Collectivism versus Individualism."[74] Some of the new president's advisers only feigned interest in reform, Hoover told his friends; deep down, they wanted revolution.[75] As for Roosevelt, he had "no social or economic or governmental philosophy or pattern"; he went where the mob directed. And at the moment, the mob marched toward Moscow.[76]

To avert this national catastrophe, Hoover believed, the American people needed to reinstall a Republican in the White House—preferably, one named Hoover. He believed that the GOP guarded the most sacred principles of the nation, including decentralized government, the gold standard, nationalism, thrift, prudence, and sobriety. He left deliberately vague the specific policies he would advocate: he would return to the gold standard, end "regimentation" and social experiments, and restore morality and individualism. But the general direction was clear—backward. Whatever his politics before 1933, the postpresidential Hoover was a reactionary. And he aimed to unite the Republican Party behind him.

Throughout the next few years, the former president tried to mastermind a comeback from Palo Alto—a comeback for the conservative movement and, he hoped, for himself. His friends told him not to speak out publicly at this point. He was so thoroughly discredited, they believed, that he could only hurt the cause. So, in those first lonely months, he reached out privately to like-minded Republicans across the country, venting his bitterness in the dozens of self-pitying letters he wrote from California. On good days, he was convinced that the nation was facing imminent economic ruin (good because that meant Roosevelt and the Democrats would soon face their day of reckoning); on bad days, he had to acknowledge Roosevelt's popularity but took solace in his religious belief that the liars and demagogues who had turned him out of office would be "boiled in oil" in another life.[77] And ultimately, when Roosevelt's policies led to national disaster, history would vindicate him. "When the American people realize some ten years hence that it was on November 8, 1932, that they surrendered the freedom of mind and spirit for which their ancestors had fought and agonized for over 300 years," he wrote to a friend, "they will, I hope, recollect that I at least tried to save them."[78]

Some wealthy California business leaders shared Hoover's consuming hatred of the New Deal and his fear of the coming socialist apocalypse. William Mullendore, an influential executive for Southern California Edison, stoked his outrage with frequent letters to Hoover, who had been his supervisor at the Food Administration during the war. Mullendore began writing an annual state of the nation letter to his fellow business leaders, hoping to awaken them to Roosevelt's "destruction of American institutions."[79] One of Mullendore's most enthusiastic supporters was Charles Collins Teague of Ventura County, the head of Sunkist citrus cooperative and the leader of several state farm and business groups. In Teague's view, the New Deal's alleged hostility to capitalism required business leaders to organize "some concentrated effort to prevent the destruction of those principles and policies that have largely been responsible for the greatness of the nation."[80]

Mullendore and Hoover found a particularly receptive audience for their anti–New Deal views in the Los Angeles area. Southern California employers prided themselves on their record of hostility to labor organization. Led by *Los Angeles Times* publisher General Harrison Gray Otis, the L.A. Merchants and Manufacturers Association was dedicated to destroying unions in the name of "industrial freedom" and economic growth. The deadly 1910 bombings at the *Times* had only confirmed Otis's archconservative views.

By the 1920s, when the U.S. Chamber of Commerce was publishing maps showing the most business-friendly areas as "white spots" amid a sea of black union-friendly cities, the *Los Angeles Times* publishers and other business leaders proclaimed their city "the world's white spot."[81] In the editors' view, the city's dedication to "free labor" had provided the raw capitalist energy to make it the first West Coast metropolis to reach the top-ten list of America's most populous urban areas in 1920. Yet this freedom was in danger, according to the *Times*. Union labor threatened to "besmirch" this white spot and "strangle its freedom."[82]

To maintain their control, antiunion employers relied on the Los Angeles Police Department's Red Squad, which gassed, beat, chased, and arrested left-wing protesters and picketers. The civilian leaders of Los Angeles gave unstinting support to the Red Squad in the 1920s and early 1930s. "The more the police beat them up and wreck their headquarters, the better," said one police commissioner in 1932. "Communists have no constitutional rights and I won't listen to anyone who defends them."[83] Up north, Chester Rowell, the Republican editor of the *San Francisco Chronicle*—a journal not known for its support of unionized labor—summarized the Southern California attitude to unions this way: "They know what to do with the radicals. They fight them, and if necessary shoot them."[84]

More than any one person, it was Harry Chandler, Otis's son-in-law and the man who inherited the *Times* when the general died in 1917, who helped shape Southern Californians' hatred of unions and radicals. Thanks to his vast farms, ranches, and tracts of urban and suburban housing—one of the greatest real estate empires in the West—Chandler was possibly the richest man in California. In addition to expansive holdings in Los Angeles and the San Fernando Valley, Chandler's many farming interests included a half-million-acre ranch in New Mexico, almost a million acres of land in Baja California, and a 280,000-acre cattle ranch straddling Los Angeles and Kern Counties. A friend and fishing buddy of Hoover's, Chandler used his paper to support the extreme right of the Republican Party and to destroy progressives—especially Democrats.[85]

The other leading Western opponents of the New Deal were men who, like Chandler, controlled huge swaths of California real estate as well as the flow of information to people who lived in the region. Joseph Knowland, publisher of the *Oakland Tribune*, used his newspaper to promote the

Republican Party and the interests of large landholders like himself. Know-land had served in the state legislature and in Congress from 1899 to 1915; his son, William Knowland, would enjoy an even longer career as state legislator and U.S. senator.

The man who sold the most newspapers in California also became a ve-hement enemy of the New Deal by 1934. William Randolph Hearst owned four of the five top-selling newspapers in the state, such as the *Los Angeles Examiner*, the *San Francisco Call-Bulletin*, and the *San Francisco Examiner*, and his real estate investments were almost as large as Chandler's—including, most famously, his 240,000-acre ranch surrounding his castle at San Simeon.[86] Earlier, at the start of his career in publishing, Hearst had been a champion of the working class. By 1933, though, he was beginning to drift to the right. In 1935, while still nominally a Democrat, Hearst ordered his employees to replace the words "New Deal" with "Raw Deal" in their news stories.[87] Regarded as a loose cannon and a demagogue by both Republicans and Democrats, Hearst still had the power to motivate and enrage the millions of people who read his papers.[88]

Nevertheless, it is important to remember that some Western business leaders supported the New Deal—at least when it directly helped their bot-tom line. A.P. Giannini, president of the Bank of America and one of the most influential bankers in the West, backed Roosevelt because his policies gave more power to regional bankers (as opposed to those on Wall Street) and more flexibility for those who, like Giannini, wanted to expand their branch banking system.[89]

California agribusiness leaders were extremely grateful for the generous subsidies of the Agricultural Adjustment Act. When J.G. Boswell, the Cen-tral Valley's cotton king, began raking in thousands of dollars from the Agricultural Adjustment Administration for plowing under some of his cotton, he reflected genially that Franklin Roosevelt was an "honest, intel-ligent and capable directing physician for this sick country of ours."[90]

The state's growers even successfully lobbied Washington to extend gov-ernmentally enforced marketing agreements to crops that were not initially covered by AAA reduction programs, such as fruits, vegetables, and nuts.[91] Charles Collins Teague, the citrus and walnut grower who agreed with Wil-liam Mullendore that Roosevelt threatened "fundamental American insti-tutions," nevertheless worked to persuade the Agriculture Department in

1933 to expand the AAA's scope to regulate and subsidize some of the crops that he raised. Through the AAA, he explained to his fellow growers, the U.S. government was providing "the opportunity for agricultural industries to avoid the demoralizing effect of disastrously low prices caused by over-production and uncontrolled surpluses."[92]

Western growers also cheered the New Deal's infrastructure programs, particularly the mammoth dams and irrigation canals in the Central Valley and Imperial Valley. Philip Bancroft, a grower, state Republican leader, and ardent opponent of the New Deal, did not hesitate to lobby for federal funds to build a tunnel under the Oakland Hills, near his home.[93]

In the earliest months of the New Deal, even the new government guarantee of the right to unionize did not worry the state's agribusiness leaders because they knew it did not apply to their laborers. After all, during the congressional debate over the National Industrial Recovery Act, Senator Wagner had stated unequivocally, "agriculture is specifically excluded."[94]

But many of the workers in California's factory farms did not understand that they had been left out, and they decided to fight for what they assumed were their rights. In the process, they would trigger a massive confrontation between big business and labor—and eventually between big business and the federal government.

2

THE GREAT STRIKE

Six days a week, Roy Dominguez rose before dawn to make his way to the cotton fields. With his mother, father, and seven siblings, he trudged barefoot along the furrows while the sun climbed into the San Joaquin Valley sky. He stooped and pulled fluffy cotton from the plant, wincing as thorns cut into his palms. Then he stuffed his harvest into a long sack and moved to the next plant. As the temperature reached one hundred degrees, he fought dehydration, fatigue, back pain, and brain-killing tedium. He would quit only when it was too dark to see, after he had harvested about sixty-five pounds of cotton and earned 45¢. In 1933, Roy was seven years old.[1]

Roy's mother, Pauline, a Mexican American woman born in the United States, could fill her sixty-pound sack twice during the day, earning between $5 and $6 a week, when she worked. The state of California mandated a minimum wage for women of $13.50 a week, but state law also required that women workers should carry only fifty pounds on their backs and that children should attend school, so she knew there was no use appealing to the law. Pauline wanted her children to learn to read, but she also wanted them to eat. The children had to work. "If they did not, they would starve," she explained.[2]

Workers like the Dominguezes had demanded higher wages in the past, but they never achieved any lasting success. Now, though, they hoped that President Franklin Roosevelt's New Deal would give them a better chance at winning some dignity and power.

Union Mad

California's Central Valley is framed by four mountain ranges: the Sierra Nevada to the east; the Tehachapi to the south; the Coastal range to the west; and the Siskiyou to the north. The Valley stretches some four hundred fifty miles north to south, and averages between forty and sixty miles in width. Its two great rivers—the Sacramento in the north and the San Joaquin in the south—meet in the river delta south of the state capital of Sacramento. Because of runoff from melting snow from the Sierras, much of the Valley had been marshland before investors and farmers reclaimed it during the nineteenth century.

The weather is hot, with an average high temperature of ninety-five in August, and relentlessly dry, for it seldom rains in California from May to October. Despite this aridity, the Valley showed "almost unbelievable fertility under irrigation," in the words of the Federal Writers Project of the 1930s.[3] After months of no rain, the dust chokes the air and hides the view of the mountains on either side. The acres of corn, peaches, nut trees, and cotton bake in the hot sun, along with the workers who harvest them.

In 1933, the Valley boasted a few large towns: from north to south, there was Sacramento, population 94,000; Stockton, 48,000; Fresno, 52,000; and Bakersfield, 26,000.[4] Mostly, though, the area was blanketed with white-tufted cotton fields, orchards hanging with red and yellow fruit, and the dusty streets and weathered storefronts of tiny market towns. The Valley would become the setting for the largest farmworkers' strike in U.S. history.

At the start of the New Deal, farmworkers joined other laborers in celebrating what they assumed was their new right to join a union. As soon as it passed in June 1933, the National Industrial Recovery Act (NIRA)'s guarantee of government protection for collective bargaining emboldened workers around the country. Labor leaders told workers that the president wanted them to organize: "Under the Industrial Recovery Act, the workers of the Steel Mills are CHALLENGED BY THE PRESIDENT OF THE UNITED STATES TO BECOME MEMBERS OF A LABOR ORGANIZATION," read one union flyer. "WILL YOU BE A SLACKER, or are you going to help him bring back the economic security of the steel workers?"[5]

Inspired by the NIRA, more than eight hundred thousand Americans joined unions in 1933 alone. Coal miners, autoworkers, oil drillers, fishermen, garment workers, newspaper reporters, and even motion picture actors tried to assert their power against their bosses by uniting. When employers balked at recognizing the unions, the workers walked off their jobs. The number of workers on strike jumped from 324,000 in 1932 to 1,170,000 in 1933; in Los Angeles, the citadel of the open shop, the number of strikers leaped from 20 to 13,000.[6]

But did the new labor protections apply to farmworkers' unions? Most New Deal officials from the start did not believe that farmworkers were covered by any federal labor policies. Secretary of Labor Frances Perkins later remembered that she did not think that the problems of agricultural workers should be part of her brief. "You read the act creating the Department of Labor and you thought of minerals, mines, factories, warehouses, ships, truck drivers," she said, "but you didn't think of farmers."[7] However, because the NIRA's language initially seemed broad enough to include all workers, on farms and in factories, alarmed farmers convinced New Deal administrators to issue a ruling that explicitly excluded agricultural workers from the law's protections.[8]

In summer and early fall of 1933, though, workers on the West Coast did not know that Washington officials had decided to deny the benefits of the New Deal's policies to agricultural laborers. Many California workers *believed* that the National Industrial Recovery Act protected them and that President Roosevelt wanted them to join a union.[9]

Federal officials in California grew nervous when they discovered that many farmworkers thought the National Recovery Administration would safeguard their rights. In July 1933, as a berry strike in El Monte threatened to spread to neighboring areas, one Department of Labor official wrote to another in alarm that the strikers were confident that the New Deal was on their side. "THEY ARE UNION MAD," he wrote, in strident capitals, "AND HAVE BEEN LED TO BELIEVE THAT THE GOVERNMENT UPHOLDS THEM IN THEIR STAND."[10] The New Deal turned discontent into hope. Workers who had despaired were now ready to organize.

The strikes of 1933 began spontaneously and spread across the state as crops ripened in the fields. Berry pickers in Los Angeles County demanded higher wages, joined later by pea pickers in the Santa Clara Valley. Throughout the summer and fall, the strikes followed the crops. Harvesters of sugar beets, apricots, pears, peaches, cherries, grapes, and lettuce refused to work as the crops spoiled. In all, thirty-seven strikes involving almost fifty thousand workers delayed or destroyed the harvests of about two-thirds of the state's fruits, vegetables, and cotton.

Organizers from the Cannery and Agricultural Workers Industrial Union rushed to these strikes to try to help the workers organize. The CAWIU helped workers win higher wages in the Alameda County pea fields in April and the Santa Clara County cherry orchards in June. Then the union's first big test came with the peach harvest in August.

The peach orchards of California stretched from Tulare County in the south to Butte County in the north, an area hundreds of miles long. Peaches are even more time-sensitive than other fruits: as trees hung heavy with ripening fruit, the late summer harvest was a time of maximum anxiety for growers and opportunity for would-be strikers. Workers in Fresno County seized the moment and demanded 5¢ more per hour to reach the minimum wage of 27¢ set by the National Industrial Recovery Act. When the ranch owners refused, the strike spread, and by the middle of August, four thousand workers had walked out of the orchards, shutting down the harvest of one of the state's most valuable crops.

Some individual growers decided to raise wages to avoid losing their fruit. Joseph Di Giorgio, who owned the world's largest fruit packinghouse, offered to pay 25¢ an hour to his pickers to avert a strike. At the urging of state mediators, the California Packing Corporation also agreed to a compromise wage of 25¢ an hour. But one large grower, H.C. Merritt, the manager of the four-thousand-acre Tagus Ranch, one of the most industrialized farms in the state, led a group of ranchers who resolved to hold the line at 17½¢ per hour.

To force workers to accept his offer, Merritt used all of the legal means at his disposal—and, for good measure, some extralegal means as well. He convinced a local judge to order an injunction against picketing, and California highway patrolmen enforced the ruling by chasing picketers from the roads. He persuaded the local sheriff to arrest strikers for vagrancy, trespassing, and disturbing the peace. He petitioned the governor for National Guard troops. He scoured local welfare offices for potential strikebreakers. He persuaded federal officials to stop giving relief to welfare recipients who refused to help him break the strike. He intimidated Mexican strikers by bringing federal officials to his labor camps to search for illegal immigrants. He evicted strikers from his land and dumped their belongings at the side of the highway. And finally, to make sure that his workers did not meet with outside agitators, he surrounded his ranch with private security guards, armed with rifles and machine guns.[11]

In such circumstances, to many of Merritt's workers, the Communist union organizers seemed a better ally than their capitalist employer. Especially when the local Communist on the scene was Pat Chambers.

Agitators

In 1933, Chambers's background was already shrouded in myth. Born in Ohio, he had spent five years at sea, it was said, and knocked around the West as a rigger in the oil fields. People murmured that he had endured beatings and jail time while trying to organize farmworkers' unions for the Wobblies. His real name was John Williams, but, like most Communists, he took an alias.[12]

Pat Chambers, left, standing with his fellow organizers during the cotton strike of 1933. Bancroft Library, University of California, Berkeley.

Chambers was short and slight, and his diction betrayed a lack of formal education, but his steady gaze and quiet self-confidence prompted larger and more privileged men to pay him respect. Chambers slept, ate, and took beatings along with the strikers. At the time of the peach strike, he wore a bandage over his jawbone, which a grower's thug had broken during an earlier labor action. He came to Communism through activism, not ideology. Chambers later claimed he had been unsure whether to sign on as a CAWIU organizer. "I was somewhat dubious about the Communists," he said, "about whether they knew what they were doing."[13] But it was clear they were doing *something*, while the IWW was essentially defunct and the American Federation of Labor was unable or unwilling to help. So he signed on with the Party and hopped a freight train, making his way to the San Joaquin Valley.

To evade the armed guards surrounding the Tagus Ranch, Chambers crawled through drainage ditches and under barbed wire in the moonlight.[14] Once in the camps, he was horrified both by the poverty and by the workers' grim acceptance of their fate. "I seen babies die of starvation," he said later. "And all they did was dig a grave, and that's it."[15]

Chambers was not known for his stirring speeches, and he never lectured the workers about the class struggle. He sat in the strikers' camps, resting on his heels, listening to them talk. Then he quietly offered terse suggestions. His own poverty helped convince the workers of his honest intentions. "These people seen that we didn't have anything, we didn't have any ulterior motives," he explained. "We had less than they had. If they went hungry, we went hungry."[16]

Chambers did not care much about Leninist dogma, or even fully understand it, as he freely admitted. His concern, first and foremost, was to help workers improve their living and working conditions. "The essence of leadership," Chambers recalled to an interviewer in 1976, "is not to portray yourself as some sort of know-it-all, but your ability to develop the people you are working with so they themselves can take the initiative and do the organizational drive."[17] Socialist leader Norman Thomas, who despised most Communists, nevertheless admitted that Chambers and other CAWIU organizers in the San Joaquin Valley were "level-headed and courageous" leaders who focused on the immediate concerns of the strikers.[18]

Chambers succeeded in persuading the workers to continue the strike long enough to threaten the harvest. Frantic about their potential losses, the peach growers began capitulating. Merritt held out the longest. But he, too, ultimately had to concede. He agreed to a compromise settlement of 25¢ an hour. The growers established 25¢ as the standard wage for peach picking throughout the Valley. In its most successful strike to date, the CAWIU had helped pickers to raise their wages by almost 50 percent.

The victory emboldened other farm laborers throughout the state. Workers fought for wage increases, while growers pushed back with violence. In Oxnard, police patrolled the sugar beet fields with shotguns and tear gas bombs. A farmer drove his truck into a crowd of strikers in Butte County, killing one man. In the bloodiest strike, in the vineyards near Lodi, local vigilantes carried guns and assaulted strikers with fists, clubs, tear gas, and fire hoses.[19]

In late September, the state's massive cotton harvest provided a perfect opportunity for workers to demonstrate their new powers of collective action. Chambers moved to the cotton fields and asked state Communist Party leader Sam Darcy to send his best organizer to help him.

The Blonde Kid Holding the Money

Chambers's partner in leading the cotton strike, Caroline Decker, did not fit the stereotype of a union organizer. At most two inches over five feet, and just one hundred pounds, Decker was barely past her twenty-first birthday. More Lana Turner than Mother Jones, she took pride in wearing the latest fashions, her high-heeled T-strap pumps kicking up dust as she walked the picket lines. But the bosses underestimated her at their peril: wherever the Communist Party sent her, from the mountains of Kentucky to California's cotton country, she inspired workers to join her union and go out on strike, even though she was threatened with beatings and death. The newspapers described her as intense, charismatic, and beautiful—the "blonde firebrand." Because of her precise diction, they called her a college girl.

But "Caroline Decker" was something of an invention—indeed, as much of an invention as "Pat Chambers." She was really Caroline Dwofsky, a child of immigrant Jews, a voracious reader who had never gone to university. She would become a central player in the California labor wars of the 1930s. She would also become a symbol of the promises and the dangers of the transformation of women's roles during the Great Depression.

Decker's parents, Bernard Dwofsky and Anna Raksin, had fled the pogroms in Ukraine as young adults and settled in Macon, Georgia, with many of her mother's relatives. The American South was dotted with colonies of Jewish immigrants in the early 1900s. Macon, the third largest city in the state, with a population of just over forty thousand, supported a Reform temple where Caroline went to Sunday School. Caroline's father owned an automobile accessory business that did well enough to pay for a modest home, the relative luxuries of electricity and a telephone, and music lessons for his three children. Caroline, the youngest, was born in 1912.[20]

Caroline grew up in a household full of the joys and tensions of immigrant families. Her grandfather, an old country gentleman with a Prince Albert coat and polished cane, spoke no English and heard little of what was said in any language. He loved to corner his grandchildren and bait them with his conservative political opinions, and then demand loudly that they argue with him in Yiddish. He also tried to encourage his secular children and grandchildren to cook kosher meals and celebrate religious holidays, but the next generation largely regarded the high holy days as excuses for parties. After her grandfather passed away, when Caroline was thirteen, the old traditions died with him.[21]

Little about Caroline's conservative father or grandfather suggested that she and her siblings would become radical activists. Their mother, however, tried to open their minds to new possibilities. Back in Ukraine, Caroline's mother's father, a middle-income merchant, had bribed the board of the local school to persuade them to admit his oldest child, in spite of her religion and gender. The intellectual life there exposed Anna to the revolutionary and artistic ferment of the era: she later told her children how she would gather in secret with other students to read banned literature. In between meetings, they would hide the books under the floorboards in outhouses.

When she moved to the relatively provincial environment of a medium-sized city in the American South, Anna continued reading and indulging her taste for European high culture. She walked miles to hear opera or see ballet. Despite their relatively modest means, she owned an extensive record collection for her fancy Victrola, with its capacious cabinet and mahogany horn.[22] She gave her children a glimpse of the possibilities beyond the narrow boundaries of her own life. She also gave her daughters a strong sense of security and independence.

When Caroline was in fourth grade, her family moved to Syracuse, New York, where her father opened a tire factory. Her brother began studying economics at Columbia University and learning about Marxism. Caroline first encountered radical ideas at her family's dinner table when her brother brought political activists home for hot meals and arguments. Rose Pastor Stokes, a feminist birth control advocate and founding member of the American Communist Party, came to dinner, as did Jay Lovestone and William Z. Foster, Communist leaders on opposite sides of a struggle over whether Stalin or Trotsky should rule the Soviet Union. Her brother introduced his family to African Americans who were challenging the color line at Syracuse University. As a teenager, Caroline learned about black civil rights, women's rights, and the class struggle. She listened as her father, a conservative small businessman, argued fiercely with his guests, and she watched her mother feed them and wash their clothes and worry about their safety. Fascinated by the discussions, Caroline and her sister, Esther, soon decided to join their brother in radical activism.[23]

Like Pat Chambers, Caroline did not know much about Marxist theory. She joined the Communist Party because it seemed to offer concrete ways for ordinary people to challenge the injustices of industrial capitalism. The Party organized marches on Washington, D.C., and state capitols throughout the nation; it launched unionization campaigns for the poorest workers in the country; and it demanded food for the hungry and housing for the homeless. "We were all young and intellectually active," Caroline remembered later, "and we were all . . . going to be saviours of the world!"[24]

Caroline became a speaker for the Young Communist League of Syracuse at the age of sixteen.[25] She discovered that the YCL provided an ambitious, rebellious girl with unusual opportunities for responsibility and influence. In theory, the Communists championed gender equity along with racial equality, atheism, and sexual freedom. In practice, the male Communist leaders were not keen on disrupting the gender norms that gave the men in the Party power and privileges.[26] Still, compared to other political movements at the time, the Party encouraged and employed many female speakers and organizers. The Communists' rhetorical commitment to gender equity helped to explain their appeal to some women—as well as the intense opposition they aroused in others.

The Party worked hard to recruit articulate young women like Decker. As an eloquent speaker—and, notably, as an attractive, native-born, female speaker with a Southern accent and a winning smile—Decker was an effective advertisement for a group hoping to reach beyond its base of recent immigrants.

The Communist Party also tried to broaden its appeal by stressing "questions of the most immediate interest to the workers," as leader William Z. Foster explained in 1930.[27] Party organizers helped workers to demand attainable, concrete goals: unemployment insurance, relief payments, old-age pensions, shorter workdays, higher wages, and an end to evictions. Decker participated in many of these demonstrations, marching with other Communists on the state capitol in Albany to demand more relief for the unemployed, starting Communist groups in the cigar factories in Binghamton, and helping to lead a massive demonstration of the unemployed in Pittsburgh.

The Pittsburgh march introduced her to the dangers of Communist organizing. As the marchers gathered, private security guards employed by local coal and iron companies began attacking them with batons and axe handles. Decker escaped unharmed, even though she was carrying the funds for the demonstration. Party leaders had given her the job of holding the money precisely because she did not look like a typical Communist. When the guards moved in with truncheons, the small, fair girl was on the sidelines, clutching a purse with the Party funds. "Who was going to assume that somebody like me," she recalled later, "this blond-headed kid, who looked like your neighbor's daughter or your own, had anything to do with this bunch of dirty, unemployed stragglers[?]"[28]

Soon Caroline moved from the hunger marches and police riots of Northern cities to an even more dangerous environment: the coalfields of Appalachia. When the Communists decided to organize the coal miners of Harlan County, in southeastern Kentucky, Caroline and her sister rushed to the scene.

The Harlan County miners' lives had long been desperate, but they became unbearable during the Depression. In 1931, workers saw their wages plummet from $3.90 to $1.65 a day.[29] When representatives from the noncommunist United Mine Workers tried to help miners, the coal operators tossed the organizers in jail, blacklisted union members from further employment, and evicted their families from their homes. The sheriff of Harlan County deputized hundreds of private security guards—"gun thugs," as the workers called them—in his campaign to destroy the union. The deputies beat, whipped, stabbed, imprisoned, and tortured union members as an American class war unfolded in Appalachia.[30]

As the United Mine Workers pulled out of Harlan County, the Communists moved in, and Decker begged Party leaders to let her go with them. Party officials decided to send Caroline and her sister to Harlan in part because they were women, and thus safer from violent assaults, and because they were native daughters of the South. Their Southern drawls might make their Party seem less foreign and threatening; at the same time, probably for the same reason, she adopted an Anglo-Saxon surname.[31]

In Harlan, Decker met activists who encouraged her to rebel and admonished her to conform—both of which were perfectly consistent with Communist Party doctrine on gender at the time. She learned rebellion from women like Dr. Elsie Reed, a physician who had backpacked across Soviet Siberia in her fifties.[32] Now nearing retirement age, Reed had driven down to Kentucky to attend to injured strikers. She provided a compelling role model for a teenage girl from Syracuse. Fearless, independent, and committed to social justice, Reed believed that women needed to make their own paths in life. "If a woman wishes to do anything unusual," she and a friend wrote in a memoir, "she must do it on her own initiative and responsibility."[33]

At the same time, Decker learned about proper gender presentation from the Party's chief propagandist, Al Wagenknecht. A co-founder of the Communist paper the *Daily Worker* and the producer of the Party's feature-length movie documentaries, Wagenknecht understood the importance of projecting the right image. And in Appalachia in 1932, a society with rigid gender roles, he believed that his girls should appear modest and decorous.

Wagenknecht took it upon himself to police the behavior and appearance of the Dwofsky sisters and the other young women who had come south to help the Party. He was horrified when Caroline's sister, in sympathy with the workers, dressed in donated, secondhand clothing and slept on a table in the Party headquarters. Wagenknecht ordered her to rent a room and clean up.[34] Caroline took the message to heart: she would always dress to project a genteel yet serious image.

Decker's decision to conform to strict gender roles helped the Party win converts *and* helped her to survive. While vigilantes assaulted male Communists, blew up their homes, and sometimes killed them, they generally left women alone. But women still lived with the fear that they might be attacked at any time. One night, as Caroline instructed five local Communists on how to organize a hunger march, a man rushed in to report that terrorists from the Ku Klux Klan had surrounded the house. Caroline helped to sneak the men out the back door, and then nervously made her way home to her rented room. She could see the Klan members in sheets following her, darting behind trees. "It was probably the scariest thing in my whole life," she remembered later. But they did not attack her. "This was one instance when being a woman—there were any number of instances in my life of that kind—when being a woman is what saved my life."[35] The Klan, which was devoted to Southern ideals of protecting white womanhood, let her escape. A male Communist might have been lynched.

Although the Communists succeeded in presenting themselves as upholders of strict gender roles in Kentucky, they did not try to conceal their egalitarian views on race. Their commitment to civil rights cost them supporters. White workers often told Caroline that they liked the Party's ideas about class, but not race. One night, a miner and his family shared their meager dinner with her, and then explained why they were not Communists. "You people, you're such wonderful people," they told her, "if you only weren't nigger lovers."[36]

Years later, Caroline was amazed at her foolishness. She had been very young—"young enough not to be afraid."[37] She celebrated her twentieth birthday at the center of America's bloodiest labor battle.

After surviving Harlan, Decker, now a seasoned organizer, traveled extensively in the East and Midwest, leading hunger marches, teaching classes on Communist doctrine, and organizing textile workers, shoemakers, and steel workers. She learned how to duck into doorways to avoid police assaults and how to ignore hunger pangs when the Party could not afford to pay her.

In May 1932, at a Party demonstration in Chicago, she met Communists from California and decided to accompany them back home. Among them was a strikingly attractive graduate student in history at UC Berkeley named Jack Warnick. Quite possibly, it was Warnick's presence in the delegation that prompted Decker to move out West.

Warnick was clearly no workingman. His hands were soft, his face clean-shaven, and his shirtsleeves neatly rolled above his elbows. He had intelligent green eyes and an earnest, scholarly air.[38] His fellow radicals noted his stunning good looks and precise diction. Caroline adored listening to him hold forth on the class struggle. Soon after they arrived in San Francisco, they were married in a simple ceremony in Grace Cathedral.

State Communist Party leader Sam Darcy quickly gave the young couple an assignment: they were to lead the new farmworkers' union, the CAWIU, and head down to its headquarters in San Jose. Although they did not speak Spanish and had never worked in the fields, Darcy ordered them to organize the state's mostly Spanish-speaking farmworkers. He gave them little direction and less money. They showed up in San Jose to discover that their office consisted of one room in a workers' hall and their staff included themselves and one other organizer.[39] Darcy told them to raise their own funds by giving speeches on street corners and pleading for donations. "We didn't even have two cents for a stamp . . . let alone anything for organizers," Decker remembered. "But . . . we were accustomed to not eating. If there was a buck and we had to put out leaflets, and we were hungry, we'd put out leaflets."

The union rarely played a direct role in initiating strikes: with only a handful of organizers, the CAWIU did not have the personnel to do that. "Nine times out of ten," Decker said later, "we would learn about these strikes from reading about them in the paper." Then they would hop on freight cars or borrow an old jalopy to drive to the strikes.[40]

Warnick specialized in raising funds from liberal sympathizers, while his passionate wife worked on the front lines. At bonfires in migrant camps up and down the state, she urged workers to unite and strike. She also helped to set up camp committees that could provide local leadership after she moved on to another strike. While she tried to educate the workers, she reached out to local businessmen and small farmers. Decker rejected the Communist Party's leaflets and wrote her own, emphasizing the common interests of workers and independent businessmen. Every night she would write and design a new leaflet, churn out copies on the mimeograph machine, and distribute them in the market towns and squatter camps of the agricultural valleys.

Then, in September 1933, she received orders from Darcy to go down to Tulare. Pat Chambers needed help with the cotton strike.

"Brawny Fists . . . All Along the Color Scale"

The biggest agricultural strike in U.S. history seemed to hinge on a relatively small difference in pay: the workers wanted $1 for every one hundred pounds of cotton they picked, while the growers offered 60¢. But both employers and employees understood that there was far more to the dispute than wages. The outcome of the strike would determine whether growers maintained control over the workplace and the workers, or whether the pickers could collectively demand a role in determining how they worked and lived. It was not only money but also power at stake.

To win the strike, Chambers and Decker needed to organize almost twenty thousand migrant pickers across an area one hundred miles long and forty miles wide. They would face attacks from private security guards, police officers, sheriff's deputies, and highway patrolmen. They would also grapple with the same kind of racial prejudice and gender anxiety that Decker had encountered in Kentucky.

Chambers and Decker faced challenges as old as American labor: how to get workers from different ethnic and racial groups to unite for a common cause. During the nineteenth century, union organizers had struggled to persuade native-born workers and immigrants to work together. During the San Joaquin strike, the CAWIU leaders confronted racial intolerance of a similar kind.

The cotton fields were overwhelmingly worked by Mexican immigrants, who made up an estimated 75 to 95 percent of the pickers. But working alongside them were white Southern migrants (called Okies, even if they were not from Oklahoma), black Southerners, and Filipino immigrants.

Many of the Okies had always thought they were superior to people with darker skins. In their view, the Mexicans were "just spics and they should be sent back to Mexico," one migrant woman remembered later.[41] The white Southerners usually lived in racially segregated camps; when they moved into strike camps with people of other races, they preferred to eat at whites-only tables. The Communists did not want to antagonize the Southerners by forcing them to integrate. But at the same time, the strike would not succeed unless the Okies moderated their white supremacist ideas. Moreover, racial equality was central to the Communists' worldview.

Chambers came up with a solution that respected the Okies' racial views while encouraging the white workers to transcend their prejudices. He and Decker provided the top leadership of the strike; he appointed Okie "lieutenants" as middle managers; and he chose heads for each of the four different ethnic groups. Chambers, Decker, and the ethnic leaders all ate together at one integrated table, setting an example for the rest of the workers.[42] The CAWIU leaders believed that the shared experience of struggle helped undermine the Okies' racial prejudices, although union organizers would continue to confront the challenge of white workers' racism throughout the 1930s.[43]

Many growers also viewed the darker-skinned workers, particularly the Mexicans, with disdain. Some of the wealthiest farm owners in the San Joaquin Valley had been born in the states of the former Confederacy, and they believed firmly in white supremacy. Wofford B. Camp, a cotton grower and Department of Agriculture official, cited the Ku Klux Klan as a good model for white men who needed to protect their "womenfolk" from dangerous agitators.[44] Some native-born Californians expressed amazement at the extent of the Southern migrants' racism. "Southerners," said grower J.W. Guiberson, "didn't think a Mexican or Nigger [was] anything but a slave."[45]

Because many growers viewed their workers with contempt, they could not believe that the pickers' grievances were legitimate. Some employers argued that their dark-skinned workers were led astray by outside agitators from New York (generally code for "Jews"). The Valley newspapers, which, except for the small *Merced Sun-Star*, were sympathetic to the large growers, frequently editorialized against the outsiders who tried to stir up the previously satisfied workers. "Our people are getting exceedingly weary of the activities of the professional Communist leaders, mostly from New York," explained the *Fresno Bee*, "who are motivated by no honest desire to improve working conditions, but rather propose to feather their own nests while promoting the cause of social anarchy and red revolution." These agitators would "loaf" between harvests, the *Bee* continued, and "descend on the scene like vultures who have smelled carrion from afar."[46] The *Tulare Advance-Register* insisted that the unions sowed "the red seeds of radicalism among an otherwise happy and contented people."[47]

The journalists who covered the strike for urban newspapers viewed it through a different racial lens. The reporters were accustomed to seeing

African Americans or Mexicans living in squalor, but the increasing numbers of white farmworkers astonished them. The stories in San Francisco newspapers focused on the Okies, even though they made up a minority of the strikers. Perhaps in a bid for sympathy from their white readers, the urban reporters wrote of the "tall fair men from the mountains of the South and their wives" who led "little towheaded children" around the filthy camps, as the *San Francisco Chronicle* described.[48]

Later, Americans would learn about the strike through the stories of two of these Okie men. Cecil McKiddy, the secretary of the strike committee, was a young migrant picker who was radicalized by the strike and would later die fighting against fascism in the Spanish Civil War. McKiddy's cousin "Big Bill" Hammett was a former itinerant preacher and small farmer who commanded respect from workers and growers alike.[49]

McKiddy would tell John Steinbeck about the dispute and provide inspiration for the character of Tom Joad in *The Grapes of Wrath*. Hammett, a rugged Texan with a flair for public speaking, would be immortalized by Steinbeck as London in *In Dubious Battle* and as Preacher Casy in *The Grapes of Wrath*.[50]

Steinbeck focused on these white men to the exclusion of the men of other races; indeed, he would write a novel about the cotton strike without a single nonwhite character. The Mexicans, in other words, were indispensable to the success of the strike, yet invisible to those recording its history. Not until the 1960s and Cesar Chavez's labor and civil rights movement would Mexican workers move to the center of the story of California labor struggles.

As they wrestled with challenges to their racial views during the cotton strike, some Californians also began to rethink their ideas about proper gender roles. Women provided critical support for the strike, both by refusing to work and by "manning" the picket lines. These female strikers could be just as assertive as the men (some were "*really* very militant women," Decker remembered later). They entered the farms to confront strikebreakers, begging and threatening the scabs to quit working, and sometimes assaulting those who refused.[51] "Don't forget," Decker told an interviewer years later, "the women and girls were out in the fields with [the men] and in the canneries with them and living in the Hoovervilles and the riverbeds." It never occurred to women in these circumstances that they belonged in the home—

wherever home was in a migrant camp—or that the strike should involve only men.[52]

But even as women played active roles in the strike, many men wanted them to return to idealized, clearly defined gender roles. Sometimes this male insistence on traditional gender norms could benefit the female strikers. As Decker had learned in Kentucky, men hesitated to beat up women picketers, while they had no such qualms about male strikers.

Moreover, women strikers could win sympathy from powerful men. At the peak of the dispute, Governor James Rolph was visibly moved by the struggles of a "widow lady" from Oklahoma who met with him as part of a delegation of strikers. A middle-aged woman with a thick Southern accent and gnarled hands, Percilla Carlo told the governor that she did not want a government handout. "There is nothing I hate worse than charity," she said. "We want food for our babies and a chance to make a living picking cotton." In this way, strikers suggested that their cause had nothing to do with revolution; it was about hardworking Americans who deserved a living wage. "I'm not a radical," she protested. "I'm a Seventh Day Adventist."

Rolph reacted emotionally to her presentation. "Of all the people here," he told Carlo, "you have impressed me with your sincerity."[53] He announced with great fanfare that the state would send food to the strike camps for the hungry workers and their families. "We're not going to force these strikers into arbitration by starving them out," he declared. "Not in my state!"[54] Much like the migrant mother in Dorothea Lange's famous photograph, who would stir compassion for Dust Bowl refugees later in the 1930s, Carlo put a maternal face on the problem of poverty among white Americans.

But while the figure of the suffering mother won sympathy, the agitating female organizer inspired fear. As an outspoken leader of a vast movement, Decker became a target for those who disapproved of women strike leaders and women Communists.

The newspapers described Decker as smart and impressive—her "keenness of mind and brilliance of expression is undeniable," according to a Visalia newspaper—but also as delicate and endangered. Stories emphasized how "slender," "diminutive," "attractive," blonde, and young she was.[55] She was always a "girl," while the female cotton pickers were "women."

The *San Francisco News* implied that Communist leaders had placed this girl in sexual peril by sending her to organize dark-skinned workers. "She

Caroline Decker and striking workers at union headquarters in Tulare during the cotton strike. Bancroft Library, University of California, Berkeley.

clenches her tiny fist and raises it in salute," the correspondent wrote. "It's answered by 50 brawny fists running the color scale from sun scorched white, glistening brown, to coal black. An occasional tattooed arm suggests that cotton pickers sometimes wander far afield." In the reporter's view, Decker herself was wandering far afield: a blonde woman, photographed in high heels and a polka-dot frock, making the dangerous choice to fraternize with dark-skinned men.[56] Moreover, the Party leaders, by putting her in that position, showed their contempt for gender norms and for their duty to protect a white woman's purity.

As a young, female radical, Decker struggled to be taken seriously by journalists and government officials. Although she was the union's best speaker, few of her words were preserved for us to read today. Whenever she spoke at a public event with a designated reporter, such as a government hearing or a court case, the employee charged with recording her words often declined to do so. "Caroline Decker . . . thereupon made a lengthy speech reviewing incidents occurring during the trial, and alleged unfair acts on the part of the court and the opposing counsel, and so forth," the court reporter later wrote of her response to sentencing in her own conspiracy trial.[57] Decker was one of the most interesting figures in these great strikes, yet we must search hard to find her voice in the historical record.

Like their husbands, the female farm owners also worried that Communist organizers like Decker imperiled their families and values. Conservative women began to organize against the strike and give interviews to the newspapers.[58] These women did not get much attention from the press or business leaders in the cotton strike. But in the coming year, as the growers intensified their campaign against the union, the conservative women would play an increasingly important role as publicists discovered how useful they could be—especially once they came to see the Communists, and those who supported them, as attacking the American home.

"Let's Clean Them Out Now"

To stop the harvest, the strike leaders needed to persuade pickers at hundreds of cotton ranches throughout the Valley to refuse to work until the growers met their demands. In the union's Tulare headquarters, a dark, fly-infested room furnished only with a bench, a rickety typewriter, and a soiled message board, Chambers and Decker planned their strategy.

They decided to supplement large picket lines at the biggest ranches with organized campaigns of "guerrilla picketing." Small caravans of men and women tried to intercept strikebreakers on their way to work or convince them to leave the fields once they arrived. They did this by blowing bugles, yelling exhortations and threats, and, at times, by entering the fields and chasing the "scabs."

In response, the growers forced the workers from their homes. On the first day, the owners of the largest ranches evicted the strikers from their company housing and dumped their belongings on the highways. But this strategy backfired when workers built their own camps on land owned by sympathetic small farmers. These tent cities of strikers dotted the Valley, with the largest encampment serving five thousand people outside the town of Corcoran. Within Camp Corcoran, each family set up its own "home"—usually burlap bags stretched between a car and a couple of poles. The stench of outhouses, trash, oil stoves, greasy cooking, and rotten food overwhelmed visitors from the cities.[59]

Despite the misery in the strike camps, the families kept up their spirits and their camaraderie. At Camp Corcoran, the workers laid out streets, set pipes for water systems, built temporary schools for children, and ringed the camp with makeshift barbed wire fences and armed guards. Behind the fences, the strikers sang and played guitars at night to boost their morale.[60] When the growers set up a loudspeaker outside the camp and demanded to speak with the leaders, the workers refused to identify them. Instead, they shouted in unison that the growers would have to talk to them collectively: "We are all leaders!"[61]

Like the grower who provided the land for Camp Corcoran, many small businessmen and farmers supported the workers. Some shopkeepers and farmers donated supplies like food, clothing, and fields for camping, even though they knew the large growers and bankers might respond by hurting their businesses, or even sending vigilantes to attack them.[62] The Tulare Farmers Protective Association threatened in a newspaper advertisement that the large growers would punish the local people if they continued to support the strike: "We the farmers of your Community, whom you depend on for support, feel that you have nursed too long the Viper that is at our door. These Communist Agitators MUST be driven from town by you, and your harboring them further will prove to us your non-cooperation with us, and make it necessary for us to give our support and trade to another town that will support and cooperate with us."[63]

When the evictions failed to stop the strike, the large growers created a new, company union to replace the CAWIU. Here they received help from

Enrique Bravo, the Mexican consul in Monterey, a vehement anticommunist. Bravo believed that his job was to assist the growers in ensuring that the harvest proceeded smoothly. He urged his compatriots to join a grower-endorsed, Mexican-only company union that he claimed would more faithfully represent Mexican workers' interests than the white-led Communist one. Most workers, however, distrusted the new union and refused to leave the CAWIU.[64]

Growers also tried to stop the strike by keeping workers from picketing their ranches. Early in the disputes, the California attorney general ruled that growers could use the highway patrol to clear the roads of picketers.[65] While the state troopers kept the strikers off the highways, the local law officers put them in jail. Police and sheriff's deputies arrested more than a hundred strikers on charges of vagrancy, trespassing, or disturbing the peace.

If there were not enough professionals to handle the strike, the sheriff deputized the growers or their employees and empowered them to carry tear gas and guns and to arrest the "agitators." After Herbert Hoover's farm superintendent was sworn in as a deputy, he promptly returned to the ranch and arrested eleven striking workers for "vagrancy." This happened routinely during the strike: sheriffs deputized growers, then the growers arrested their strikers, and, as if by magic, the strike was over at their ranch.[66]

The local judges and prosecutors helped to keep the strikers in jail. During a grape strike in Lodi the previous month, one judge had called strikers "nothing but a bunch of rats, Russian anarchists, cutthroats, and sweepings of creation." Lodi might "see a few hangings," the judge predicted, if the labor disputes were not resolved soon.[67] By contrast, during the cotton strike, the Madera County assistant district attorney showed unusual restraint when he urged growers to "give agitators a dose of castor oil rather than shoot them."[68]

It was obvious to everyone in the Valley that the growers might start shooting people, and soon. Some farm owners formed "protective associations," which organized mass meetings and increasingly brutal attacks on the strikers. In the town of Woodville on October 7, a group of about sixty mostly drunk vigilantes invaded a meeting of eight hundred workers and small farmers sympathetic to the strike. The strikers fought back using broken table legs and their fists and drove the growers from the hall.

Strikers demand the disarming of growers or arming of workers during the cotton strike of 1933. Bancroft Library, University of California, Berkeley.

As the strike entered its second week, the Valley became an armed camp. Growers trained guns on pickets and threatened strikebreakers with death if they stopped work; they zigzagged their cars along the highways, plunging from shoulder to shoulder, to terrify the pickets and force them onto the farmers' private property, where they believed they would be legally justified in shooting them. "The growers," said the Kern County undersheriff, "were just hoping one would put his foot across the line and he would have been plugged full of holes."[69] The state's labor commissioner, Frank MacDonald, told the press that violence could erupt in the Valley at any moment. "There is always an honorable and a fair way to deal with a difficult situation," he said, "and unless this course is pursued I greatly fear we will have something for which we will be apologizing for years to come."[70]

His fear was well founded. As MacDonald warned the press and the governor of the violence to come, "Cotton king" J.G. Boswell was privately advising the growers' protective association to find men with "guts enough" to go into the strike camps and "clean them out." "The cotton industry in San Joaquin will never be worth anything unless you do," he insisted.[71] L.D. Ellett, the head of the group, took the advice and convened a growers' meeting in Bakersfield. The men emerged to announce that they were organizing a "concerted drive on agitators" to chase them from the cotton belt.[72]

The growers claimed that they needed to use force because the union incited violence. But in fact the supposedly bloodthirsty Communist leaders counseled the workers *against* violence. Sam Darcy was horrified one morning when he discovered that workers had interpreted his call for a "business-like demonstration" at the Hoover ranch as code for a shoot-out. Hundreds of men showed up at the farm armed with shotguns. Darcy, who worried that a worker-led attack would prompt ruthless repression from the government, spent more than an hour convincing the men to disarm.[73]

Desperate for outside help, the strikers reached out to President Roosevelt himself. The day of the growers' conclave in Bakersfield, October 9, the union cabled the president with an urgent message: "We are threatened to be mobbed and our camps raided by gunmen and our women and children murdered." According to the workers, the "forces of law" were planning to allow a mob attack on strikers the next morning. Secretary Perkins forwarded the warning to Governor Rolph. "Feel every confidence that you will take any steps necessary to prevent violence," the secretary said, with optimism that quickly proved unfounded.[74]

That night, October 9, 1933, more than a thousand men converged on the small town of Corcoran north of Bakersfield for a growers' rally. The crowd filled the seats in the American Legion hall and spilled out into the streets. Surprised and thrilled by the number of people, Ellett and the other organizers moved the meeting across the street to the local ballpark, where farmers and businessmen from Kern, Tulare, and Kings Counties filled the bleachers.[75]

Facing the loss of their crops, the growers at the Corcoran ballpark were desperate and angry. Speaker after speaker exhorted the men to protect their crops and drive out the Communists who led the strike. The men passed a petition from hand to hand around the ballpark calling for the "legal elimination" of the union leaders. Ellett told the crowd that it was time for the employers to "take the law into their own hands." The men erupted in cheers.

Not everyone in the bleachers supported violence. One small farmer, M.B. Kearney, leapt to his feet to protest Ellett's speech. "I am strictly an American," he yelled, "and I do not believe in mob law." The other growers shouted him down. They wanted action. A few men stood up and cried: "Let's go across the track and clean them out now!"[76] That night, the growers organized a group of about four hundred men and armed them with baseball bats, pistols, rifles, and shotguns.

State officials, local law enforcement officers, and reporters spent an anxious night, awaiting bloodshed in the morning. Many observers searched for the best metaphor to capture the tension—a stick of dynamite, in the view of the state's labor commissioner, or a smoldering volcano, according to the *San Francisco Examiner*. Other papers called it a powder keg, waiting for a spark to burst into flame.[77]

The next morning, October 10, the growers lit the match. As about 350 workers gathered in the tiny Valley town of Pixley to listen to Pat Chambers, the growers and their allies decided to act. Chambers stood on a truck bed, urging the workers to remain nonviolent, but to protect themselves if they were attacked. As he spoke, a caravan of cars and trucks filled with forty growers roared into town and pulled up behind the workers. The men jumped out of the cars, brandishing pistols, rifles, and shotguns. Chambers told the crowd to move across the street into the union headquarters, a two-story redbrick building decorated with two large American flags.

As workers and their families rushed to the safety of the building, the growers pursued them and fired into the air. Delfino D'Avila, the local representative of the Mexican consul, angrily approached one grower and shoved his rifle barrel to the ground. Another grower bashed D'Avila's skull with the butt of his pistol and shot him dead. The vigilantes emptied their weapons into the fleeing crowd, killing another man and wounding eight people. Terrified women clutched their babies as the strikers attended to the wounded and the dead. The ambush had been entirely one-sided. "Not so much as a water pistol appeared in the hands of the besieged strikers," explained one horrified reporter. The flags adorning the front of the building were riddled with bullet holes.[78]

At the same moment, about seventy miles to the south, some of the most prominent growers of Kern County confronted pickets near the town of Arvin. After shouting insults at each other, the growers and workers began pushing, shoving, and throwing punches. Then the growers began shooting. One Mexican striker was killed, and several pickets and growers were injured. No one was ever convicted of that day's murders.[79]

The killings in Pixley and Arvin brought national and international attention to the state, with a *New York Times* reporter proclaiming that there was "civil war" in the cotton fields and the Mexican consul denouncing the murders of his delegate and the two strikers, all Mexican citizens.[80] Consul Bravo sent a telegram to the governor noting that the workers were "unarmed and in perfect spirit to abide by the laws," yet the farmers showed "radical tendencies, using force and being armed." He urged the governor to order the local authorities to disarm the growers.[81]

The county grand jury responded quickly but reluctantly to the cries for justice. The jury indicted eight ranchers for murder, but at the same time charged Pat Chambers with two counts of criminal syndicalism—for allegedly inciting the workers to violence in his writings and in his speech at Pixley. The court set his bail at $10,000 to make sure that the union could not afford get him out of jail.[82]

Newspaper editorial boards, citizens' groups, and religious leaders cried for government officials to stop the violence. "This is an emergency," the usually antilabor *San Francisco Chronicle* scolded in a front-page editorial. "These crops need to be picked, and picked now. The peace of California needs to be preserved—now."[83] The Episcopal diocese of San Francisco demanded that the state "take immediately all steps necessary to maintain peace and order in all strike areas." In Tulare County, many citizens were appalled by the growers' brutality. The ministerial association of Visalia, an organization of Christian pastors, called the killing of the strikers "an inexcusable act of violence" and urged the government to hold the guilty parties accountable.[84]

Historically, the state government maintained the right and the power to intervene in labor disputes. Some governors—Franklin Roosevelt, for example, during his stint as governor of New York—might have tried to mediate the dispute themselves. But at this moment of economic crisis, California suffered from a crisis of leadership in Sacramento.

Governor James Rolph, a self-made multimillionaire shipping tycoon and former mayor of San Francisco, was a beaming, glad-handing politician known more for his charisma than his convictions. The rotund, florid Rolph arrived in sober, dry Sacramento in 1930, his sixty-two-year-old body some-what worse for wear after all the decadent years in Baghdad by the Bay. "Thank goodness," commented Will Rogers, "we won't be reformed during this administration at least."[85]

Sunny Jim, as his friends called him, had distinguished himself in San Francisco in part by his cheerful insistence on avoiding conflict—the *San Francisco Chronicle* endorsed his bid for a second term as mayor on the basis of "his good-humored unwillingness to offend anybody."[86] But it was Rolph's tragic fate to arrive at the capitol as class conflict tore the state apart, and even Sunny Jim found it difficult to avoid taking sides.

This conflict evader with friends in organized labor and industrial agri-culture, this San Francisco–bred, old-style city boss, now had to confront the biggest, bloodiest agricultural labor strike in the nation's history. Worse still, he faced it in frail health, as he recovered from a life-threatening ill-ness that had sent him to the hospital just one week before the strike. In the midst of the conflict, the *Sacramento Union* noted that he looked "far from well" and had "aged and failed physically since his last illness."[87] In-deed, the strike—and other stresses to come—would soon prove too much for the governor.

Rolph read the newspaper accounts with increasing alarm but seemed paralyzed by indecision. He refused to help the growers by sending the Na-tional Guard to break the strike, but neither did he chastise the sheriffs for abetting the violence. The governor's passivity helped the planters, who had money, guns, and law officers on their side.

Believing in the promise of the New Deal, the cotton strikers and their supporters decided to appeal to a higher authority than Governor Rolph. In San Francisco, Roosevelt's man in California packed his bags for a flight to Visalia.

The New Dealers' involvement in the strike would mark a new era in agricultural labor relations. Up to this point, because the growers could con-trol strikers with assaults and threats, they had not developed more sophis-ticated tools. But soon, as the nation's politics began to change and the national press shone a spotlight on their operations, the farm owners would realize that they needed to move beyond physical intimidation to political organization.

3

A NEW DEAL

On October 18, 1933, George Creel alighted from his airplane and stepped onto the tarmac. He had come to California's San Joaquin Valley on a mission from the president. Creel's arrival signaled that the cotton strike had taken on national significance. It was the largest labor strike in U.S. agricultural history; it threatened one of the country's most valuable crops; and it had resulted in the deaths of three men. As the chief New Deal administrator for California, Creel was determined to force the employers to the bargaining table and mediate the dispute before the Valley's cotton crop went to seed, taking with it the New Deal's hopes for national recovery.

Creel's first task was to persuade all the relevant actors—the state government, the growers, and the strikers—that they should listen to him at all. His authority to intervene was dubious at best. Although President Roosevelt wanted the strike to end, the federal government lacked statutory authority to do anything about it. Creel took comfort in his certainty that everyone involved would be better off if they put their faith in him and in the process of neutral, expert fact finding. He was from the government, and he was there to help.

Shades of Gray

Most Americans old enough to remember the Great War knew George Creel's name. Once a zealous journalist who hounded evil monopolists and corrupt politicians, he had put down his muckrake and joined the government's propaganda team in 1917 to help promote the war effort and suppress dissent. As the head of Woodrow Wilson's Committee on Public Information, he made sure that every American understood his or her duty to Halt the Hun and Enlist Now! and Wake Up! because civilization was calling. Now after fifteen years in private life as a writer for glossy magazines, he was working for the government again, this time as the West Coast head of Franklin Roosevelt's National Recovery Administration (NRA).

Famously short of temper as well as stature—he was only an inch or two taller than Caroline Decker—Creel had made many enemies over his long career. They described him as thin-skinned, petulant, and self-absorbed—"a little shrimp of a man with burning dark eyes set in an ugly face under a shock of curly black hair," in the words of writer John Dos Passos.[1] They also viewed him as inflexible and arrogant. Journalist Mark Sullivan contended that Creel's universe had "no shadings and no qualifications. His spectrum contains no mauve, nothing but plain black and plain white."[2] Although this self-confidence served him well as a journalist and propagandist, it would not be an asset when he mediated the cotton strike.

Creel's first challenge as western regional chief of the NRA was to figure out exactly what the western regional chief of the NRA was supposed to do. The New Deal was trying to set up multiple national bureaucracies in a matter of weeks, and there was a great deal of confusion about duties and jurisdictions. Creel found himself in precisely the kind of situation he hated: one with many shades of gray, or mauve, and little direction on how to draw clear lines. In this ambiguous situation, he decided to write his own rules. Imposing authority and clarity where there were none, Creel chose an office in the customhouse in San Francisco "and calmly announced that I was the head of NRA for the Coast, and the sole source of authority."[3] Then he swung into action before anyone could ask awkward questions.

Next, Creel had to determine whether his authority extended to strike mediation. Soon after Creel's appointment, the president created another agency, the National Labor Board, to resolve the wave of strikes that followed the start of the New Deal. Senator Robert Wagner chaired this board, which in its first six months handled strikes involving more than a million workers. If the National Labor Board was in charge of resolving strikes, then Creel, as head of a different agency, had no power to intervene in them.

But Creel, who understood better than anyone how to spin a story, orchestrated a campaign to win more authority. In September, he noisily resigned his post, complaining in national newspapers that the president, in creating the National Labor Board, had made it impossible for him to do his job for the NRA. He then waited while business and civic leaders throughout the state protested his resignation, making him "the most discussed public man in California" as well as a leading contender for the governorship the next year, according to the *New York Times*.[4] California business leaders argued that Creel understood their interests and the Pacific Coast's needs.[5] In response, Roosevelt not only refused to accept Creel's resignation from the NRA but appointed him the western regional head of the National Labor Board as well. The president later assured him that "nobody else could handle it one-tenth as well as you do."[6]

Soon, Creel established himself as the czar for resolving labor disputes up and down the Pacific Coast. This was not an easy task, as California was "convulsed by strikes of every kind," as Creel said in a private letter.[7] In the first week of October alone, Creel dealt with strikes involving 2,300 lettuce pickers in Salinas, 2,000 garment workers in Los Angeles, 2,500 fishermen in Monterey, and 500 longshoremen in San Francisco.[8] But he seemed good at his job. Despite his reputation for abrasiveness, many California business owners commended Creel's energetic and decisive approach to settling industrial strikes.[9]

Then the cotton strike posed a new kind of challenge for Creel. The congressional debate over the NIRA, along with bureaucratic rulings afterward, made clear that the federal government's labor protections did not extend to agricultural workers. But strikers and civic leaders were clamoring for federal intervention. Three men had died and the crop was rotting in the fields, yet the governor had been unable to restore peace and order.

So Creel found a justification for intervening. He confidently told growers' representatives that he did, in fact, have the statutory authority to resolve California farm strikes because the state's fields were effectively industrialized. Since California farms were just like factories, Creel contended, their laborers should be treated like industrial workers. "Although agricultural labor comes under the Agricultural Adjustment Act," he explained to the state Chamber of Commerce, "the *industrial disputes in agriculture are under the jurisdiction of the National Labor Board*."[10]

In other words, six years before Carey McWilliams published *Factories in the Field*, Roosevelt's chief administrator on the West Coast was arguing that California farms were fundamentally different from farms in the rest of the country. And in this fluid period of the early New Deal, when regional administrators frequently made their own policy, Creel declared that this difference gave him the right to intervene in agricultural strikes. He issued an ultimatum to the governor: he would arbitrate the strike if Rolph did not. He repeated that threat several times over the next two weeks. "If they cannot settle it," he said, "the Federal Government can."[11]

Now that he had his rationale for mediating the strike, Creel needed a strategy to force the growers to agree to accept his intervention. After all, he could scarcely put the growers in jail if they refused to listen to him. But he did have influence over something very important to California agribusinessmen: their government loans and subsidy checks.

Threats and Promises

Creel planned to end the strike by pressuring the state government to set up an independent fact-finding investigation—and then to compel the growers to cooperate by threatening to withhold what the growers liked best about the New Deal. If their federal subsidies were at risk, they would be much more amenable to persuasion. Creel's message to the growers was simple: they needed to tell their thugs to stop shooting strikers, or else they would lose the checks they received from Uncle Sam.

One of Creel's assistants in the San Francisco NRA office, Irving Reichert, explained this plan in supposedly private communications leaked to the press. In a letter to the governor, Reichert excoriated the state government for allowing a "reign of terror" in the Valley and for failing to control local officials who "aided and abetted" the vigilantes. "Gangsterism has been substituted for law and order in the cotton areas," he wrote, and the governor had shirked his duty to protect *all* Californians, workers and employers alike. In a nation where state, federal, and local troops routinely put down strikes, Reichert advanced an almost revolutionary argument. "The protection of the state and its civil authorities," he insisted, "should be extended *not only to propertied interests but to working men as well*."[12]

In another letter, Reichert spelled out the consequences for the planters who refused to cooperate with government mediators. The federal government had given the growers "a very substantial amount of money" that was "inferentially conditioned" upon a "fair deal" for their workers, he explained. "It would be most unfortunate," Reichert warned, "if the government found it necessary to deny participation in this relief to certain growers because of their unfairness toward labor."[13] To underline this threat, Reichert's boss publicly invited the federal Farm Credit Administration to participate in any official mediation. "The government . . . has $1,000,000 invested in that cotton crop," Creel told the press. To protect its investment, the federal government had to intervene.[14]

While he threatened to cut off federal aid to the growers, Creel also offered government help to the strikers. He ordered the state government to send food relief—relief paid for by the federal government—to the strike camps. By sending in food, Creel made sure that the strikers would not be starved into submission. With this directive, Creel was following the new Roosevelt administration policy of sending relief to strikers unless the National Labor Board determined that the strike was "unreasonable and unjustified"—and Creel decided that the cotton strike was reasonable and justified.[15]

The New Deal's extension of relief to strikers was a shocking break from past practice. Now, for the first time in history, the federal government would feed people who refused to work.[16] As ordered, the government distributed more than $10,000 in free food to the strike area, at a rate of $5 a week for most families.[17]

The growers were incredulous that their government—the government they supported with their taxes—was dispensing "bountiful" federal checks to reward "able-bodied idlers" for refusing to work.[18] In their view, their tax dollars paid for the "pernicious" practice of "promiscuous free feeding."[19] In effect, the federal government was underwriting the strike.

As Creel pressured the growers, the tensions in the Valley continued to escalate. Rumors flew that strikers in Arvin had obtained a machine gun, terrorists were plotting to dynamite a cotton gin, and snipers were shooting people on the highways. According to a *San Francisco Chronicle* reporter, people in the Valley predicted that "blood will run in free flowing streams before this labor trouble in the cotton fields is ended."[20]

In tiny Pixley, four hundred deputy sheriffs patrolled the streets. Tulare and Kern Counties issued hundreds of permits for carrying concealed weapons.[21] Thousands of workers attended a funeral for the men shot in Pixley and Arvin.[22] Heavily armed lawmen stood uneasily on the streets as workers walked by with banners proclaiming "Bullets cannot stop our strike."[23]

After declaring that the governor had "failed dismally" to find a way to prevent further bloodshed, Creel called Rolph and urged him to set up a state-sponsored fact-finding commission. This commission would hear testimony from workers and growers and then suggest a compromise settlement. To maintain at least some state control and avoid the creation of a federal panel, Rolph quickly agreed. Then Creel faced the much more difficult task of getting both the Communist union and the farm employers to agree to cooperate. To this end, Creel flew down to Visalia and plunged into the crisis.

During his whirlwind visit to the Valley, Creel announced his intention to listen to all sides of the dispute and persuade them of the benefits of cooperating with a fact-finding panel. He met briefly with a group of growers and assured them that the state and federal governments would protect their interests if they participated.

Next, to the employers' fury, he talked with Pat Chambers in the Visalia jail, where the strike leader promised to cooperate with the state investigation. Creel emerged from the jail cell to tell the newspapers that he found Chambers "a reasonable person of excellent understanding and without ridiculous prejudice" who seemed "only too willing to cooperate with us and to settle the strike." He pressured the district attorney to allow Chambers to attend the fact-finding commission's hearings under armed guard.[24] The union probably demanded this concession as its price for participating in the hearings. But the growers were livid that the government had agreed to give a public platform to the most notorious Red in the state.

Creel concluded his visit with a trip to see Caroline Decker at the main strike camp at Corcoran. There, he found that he would have some difficulty winning the trust of the growers and their supporters.

The dusty Corcoran strike camp was crowded with tents and jalopies and hungry Okie migrants and Mexican immigrants. Evicted at gunpoint from their shabby company-provided huts, almost five thousand strikers now pitched their tents on this site, with their children and chickens and makeshift privies and kitchens. Decker had talked many times to the residents of this camp over the previous week, but this time she just asked them to listen to Creel.

Creel gave a rousing speech to the strikers, promising them that the New Dealers would work out an equitable settlement—if the workers would stop their strike and cooperate with the state commission. He also pledged the federal government's help in defending their First Amendment rights. "I tell you the constitutional rights of every man in that strike have got to be protected," Creel insisted, "and the Federal Government is ready to do it."[25]

Throughout the speech, Sheriff Van Buckner of Kings County stood uneasily on the edge of the crowd. A seventy-four-year-old, barrel-chested native of Kansas sporting a cowboy hat and a handlebar mustache, Buckner resented the meddling of imperious federal officials in what he saw as a local dispute with agitators and aliens. "Talk only in American!" he growled at the Mexican strikers.[26] The cotton growers were the upstanding men of his county. In his view, they worked hard, paid their taxes, and compensated their workers as well as they could in the frightening marketplace for agricultural commodities—one in which the price of cotton had fallen to one-third its 1929 price in four years.[27] Now it seemed the federal government was taking the side of the Mexicans—and the Okies and the Reds—and Buckner was fuming.

As Creel prepared to leave, Buckner and his deputies spotted a striker wanted for "inciting a riot" the week before—the riot being the strike meeting at Pixley that had allegedly provoked the growers into a murderous rage. The officers tried to arrest the man. Instantly, hundreds of strikers surrounded them, nonviolent but menacing, effectively daring the officials to take the man away. Boldly, Creel moved to the center of the crowd and demanded to know if the sheriff had a warrant. When Buckner produced one, Creel walked away. But the sheriff felt intimidated by the hostile crowd—and angry that, in his view, Creel had encouraged the riff-raff.[28]

From Buckner's perspective, Creel, an arrogant federal official, did not understand the local customs or economy. Creel had sided with foreigners and radicals, betraying his loyalties, and he had treated Buckner—the chief law enforcement man of the area—as if he were the hick sheriff of a "cow county."[29] The lawmen slunk from the camp without their prisoner, but with new grudges against the meddlers from Washington.

The Communists felt dissatisfied, too. Creel had told the workers to trust him and return to work, but the union realized that the workers' power flowed from their refusal to pick cotton. The Communists regarded all the New Dealers as captives of the capitalist exploiters. Sam Darcy, the California Communist Party chieftain, exclaimed with disgust that Creel seemed "to have no authority except to urge mediation and a return to work pending the outcome. That was all F.D.R.'s representative had to offer!"[30] Communist filmmakers would produce a documentary about the cotton strike that equated Roosevelt's NRA with Italian fascism.[31]

But in spite of the simmering anger of union leaders and farm owners alike, Creel achieved his goal. The union and the growers agreed to cooperate with the commission—although not necessarily to accept its recommendations. They merely conceded that they would help allegedly neutral experts find the facts, and then they would decide whether they agreed with those facts. The governor's commissioners rushed to Visalia in hopes of finding a peaceful solution to the crisis.

Facts and Polemics

Visalia in 1933 was a relative metropolis for the southern San Joaquin Valley. Its 7,200 residents shopped in the neat, tree-lined streets of the eight-block-long downtown, which featured restaurants, bars, shops, and filling stations. The cotton strike hearings would be held at the ornate, 250-seat civic auditorium, built in 1916 in California mission style and featuring a stage, balcony, and main hall.[32]

As the three members of the governor's fact-finding commission arrived in town, local newspapers wrote approvingly of two of the governor's picks for the commission. Archbishop Edward Hanna of San Francisco and Methodist theologian Tully Knoles of Stockton were among the most respected religious leaders in California, and widely regarded as safe, conservative choices.

But the third member worried the growers. Ira B. Cross, a labor specialist in the economics department at Berkeley, was a distinguished historian who had written about San Francisco trade unions. At the time of the cotton strike, he was working on his magnum opus, a history of the labor movement in California, which he would publish in 1935. In the growers' view, Cross had shown alarming sympathy for labor organizers in his earlier scholarship, and they wondered which facts this particular fact finder might choose to emphasize.

On the first day of the hearings, workers, growers, local business owners, and important visitors from the coastal cities filed into the auditorium. An "invisible line" separated the grim-faced strikers from the farmers in the audience, while the three commission members sat in the front, facing the crowd.[33] In the audience, famous and soon-to-be-famous observers quietly took notes. Socialist leader Norman Thomas came to learn about the challenges American farmworkers faced. He would use the information from the hearings to organize a tenant farmers' union in the South the following year.[34] Young Carmel, California, writer Ella Winter sat nearby, hoping to support the strikers and to write articles on the hearings for a national audience.

Two young economists who would play key roles in later political battles in California also listened attentively. Paul Taylor, a tall, handsome assistant professor who was an expert on Mexican labor in the West, came to advise Professor Cross, his senior colleague in the economics department at the University of California, Berkeley. Taylor would later marry the most celebrated photographer of the Depression, Dorothea Lange, and together they would produce one of the great documents of the Okie migration to California, their book *American Exodus*, which included Lange's iconic photos of Dust Bowl migrants accompanied by Taylor's commentary. Taylor would also serve as a consultant to the state and federal governments and conduct a lifelong crusade to protect the rights of small farmers and farm laborers.

Taylor brought along a promising graduate student, a twenty-two-year-old labor economist named Clark Kerr, who would soon become one of the most important leaders of American public higher education. A Quaker from a small town back east, Kerr was shocked by what he saw in the cotton strike. The Central Valley was "a long way from the peaceful Oley Valley in eastern Pennsylvania where I had been raised on a family farm," he later wrote. Labor disputes, politics, poverty: everything was so much more extreme in California. "Here was life in the raw as I had never seen it," he wrote. "There was hunger. . . . There was violence. . . . There was hatred."[35]

To document and understand the strike, Kerr stayed in Visalia for two additional months after the hearings finished. He drove his Model A Ford up and down the Valley, interviewing strikers, growers, and lawmen. In the end, he and Paul Taylor wrote a report on the strike, but did not publish it until decades later. Their summary, along with Taylor and Kerr's notes on the hearings, became key sources for scholars looking to tell the story of the conflict.

Kerr learned lessons from the strike that would shape his politics—and, because of the important role he would play in state affairs, the politics of California Democrats for years to come. He concluded that the Communist union organizers were impractical and untrustworthy, but too unpopular to pose any real threat to the state's government or economy. The greater danger, he believed, came from the right—from the growers who invoked the Red bogeyman to get more support for their real goal of keeping wages low.

Another man in the audience learned the opposite lesson. Richard E. Combs, a tall, red-haired Central Valley lawyer, had recently returned to his hometown of Visalia after finishing his law degree at Hastings College. Like Kerr, Combs said his life was changed by the cotton strike. But unlike Kerr, Combs saw the Reds, not the growers, as the true villains in the strike. He vowed to devote his life to exposing and punishing Communists in California—as well as the liberals, like Taylor and Kerr, who seemed oblivious to the dangers posed by the Reds.[36]

The seed of this conflict between these two men would bear poisoned fruit over the next three decades. Kerr would one day be the University of California president who opposed blacklisting radicals, and Combs the blacklister who would help end Kerr's career.

But all of that came later. In 1933, the lines dividing these two future adversaries had not become visible, and liberals like Kerr did not yet comprehend the extent of the farm owners' anger. The two men sat silently in the auditorium as the best speakers for the growers and the union presented their cases to the state's commissioners. The peace of the Valley, the economic recovery of California, and hundreds of thousands of dollars in wages rested on their decision.

The growers began the hearings on the offensive, attacking the commission members and their mission. Edson Abel, their attorney, said outright that the growers did not believe that the commissioners would treat them fairly. Abel then called a dozen witnesses, all of them large growers or owners or managers of the cotton gin and finance companies, who testified that they paid their workers as much as they could given the low price of cotton on the world market.[37] The growers had to deal with real-world prices and costs, Abel insisted: "The farmers are faced with a set of facts in this matter, not with theory."[38]

Two union leaders and one outside attorney cross-examined the growers. Big Bill Hammett, the tall preacher and cotton picker who was the union lieutenant in charge of the Okies, and Caroline Decker, full of passion and outrage, joined Abraham Lincoln Wirin, a Los Angeles lawyer who worked with the American Civil Liberties Union. They refused to continue unless the government brought Pat Chambers to the proceedings. Suddenly, just as Decker launched into a speech about the injustice of keeping Chambers away, two armed guards brought him into the auditorium and escorted him to a seat in the front row. The strikers in the audience responded with wild applause.[39]

Even after Chambers joined them, Decker took the lead in presenting facts and interrogating witnesses. The jailing of Chambers had allowed her to take charge of the strike, and she rose to the challenge. At the hearing, she presented the workers' case so effectively that the *Los Angeles Times* labeled her "the real brain" of the strike.[40] J.W. Guiberson, an intensely antiunion grower, grudgingly admitted she was a "real rip snorter" who was "too much for the growers' lawyer and a match for any lawyer." She could make a "darn good speech," he said.[41]

Yet the stenographer at the hearing considered her words so unimportant that he usually declined to write them down. ("Caroline Decker . . . rendered a brief summary of the strike for the benefit of the committee and before calling upon witnesses.")[42] Decker had succeeded in seizing an opportunity usually denied women in the 1930s: in effect, presenting a case before a government body. But even though she commanded center stage in the hearing, the state did not feel obliged to let future generations see the performance.

The stenographer did record the questions that Decker posed to other people, so we can see how she constructed her case by letting the workers tell their own stories about hours and wages. The workers testified to the misery of the rural company towns: the absence of running water; the single pit toilet serving hundreds of people; the sewage, disease, squalor, and malnutrition. Pauline Dominguez spoke of following the harvests, from beets to oranges, to lemons, to tomatoes, to beans, with her barefoot, hungry children working alongside her. Her little son Roy told the commissioners of his days in the fields, from sunrise to sunset, with no opportunity to attend school.[43] Lilly Dunn, who had cowered from the bullets at Pixley with a baby at her breast, testified that her children had no money for clothes, shoes, lights, running water, toilets, doctors, or even, in the worst times, nourishment. "One child died two years ago because of insufficient food," she said.[44]

The growers protested that the workers' witnesses had been coached. In response, Decker dramatically turned to the audience and dared the commission to choose any random worker to put under oath. The commission members declined and assured her that they were confident the witnesses had not been influenced or manipulated.[45]

The union also called to the stand a small farmer, M.B. Kearney, who electrified the audience with his tale of the meeting at the Corcoran ballpark on the night before the Pixley massacre. According to Kearney, L.D. Ellett, the growers' leader, had urged his followers to take the law into their own hands. The next day, these men had killed people at Pixley and Arvin. Pat Chambers asked indignantly if Ellett had been charged with criminal syndicalism for his inflammatory speech. "I am arrested under criminal syndicalism law because of an alleged statement, yet Ellett is free," Chambers pointed out.[46]

The growers were furious that the state government let Chambers serve as an official worker representative. When he attempted to cross-examine H.C. Merritt, the owner of the peach ranch where Chambers had led a strike in the summer, the rancher could not contain himself. "I didn't come here to be insulted by being asked questions by a dirty scum of a Communist," Merritt retorted. Professor Cross calmly told him that the commission would not accept any of his testimony if he did not respond to the union's queries. Merritt then agreed to let Chambers question him.[47]

Throughout the hearings, the union appealed to the federal government to assert its power in the Valley. Sounding more like a New Dealer than a Stalinist, Decker professed her faith in the government's ability to reveal— and destroy—the exploitative practices of capitalist agriculture. "We are sure that at this time when America's hope lies in the National Recovery Act," she said, "that the American people will expect your honorable commission to tear the lid off and expose the viciousness that lies back of this condition."[48]

Decker concluded by summarizing the poverty and oppression of the farmworkers and arguing for government recognition and protection of the workers' organizations. We do not know her precise words because the official state scribe summarized her oration with one dismissive sentence: "In her closing statement [Decker] presented to the Committee a list of the strikers' demands."[49]

The commissioners deliberated two days before announcing a surprising verdict: the growers should pay the strikers more and stop abusing their civil rights. "Without question," the fact-finding commission reported, "the civil rights of strikers have been violated." From now on, the commissioners insisted, government authorities should do more to protect these rights.[50]

The commissioners recommended a wage that was closer to the growers' offer than to the workers' demand. The growers proposed 60¢ per hundred pounds, the workers wanted $1, and the commission recommended 75¢.[51] The raise amounted to 60¢ a day for a man, or about 6¢ an hour. It was less for women and children. Still, the growers were angry that these officials would pressure them to pay more than they said they could afford—and then, adding insult to injury, to lecture them about violations of constitutional rights.

The growers fumed that they were the true victims of the strike, the real Americans whose rights had been trampled by outside agitators. "By all that is fair and just, have the American farmers no rights over Communists and aliens?" asked one Valley newspaper. The growers resented the "commission of highbrows" who presumed to lecture them on strikers' civil rights, while the "complacent" federal government fed the farmers' enemies.[52] In the planters' view, a group of cultural elites—a minister, a bishop, and a professor—conspired with government bureaucrats to punish rich and poor farmers alike. The planters would return to these cultural resentments again and again.

The conservatives' anger at the commission in general and Professor Cross in particular helped to trigger the first of many Red Scares at the University of California. Cross's tough questioning of the growers led some of them to conclude that he was, in the words of Sheriff Buckner, a "Communist pure and simple."[53] The mild-mannered economist received so much hate mail after the Visalia hearings that he ruefully suggested that he should deposit the collection of letters "in the archives of some hospital for the mentally unbalanced where it may be helpful in the study of various kinds of psychoses."[54]

Growers and local officials also noted the presence of seven University of California students among the strikers (out of twelve thousand at the university) and recommended an investigation of the UC to determine if its professors taught "the students to be socialists, to wave the red flag and to destroy America."[55]

There was nothing inherently liberal about public higher education in California. Growers and industrialists dominated the UC governing board, and many had received degrees from one of the two then-existing general UC campuses, in Berkeley and Los Angeles. Agribusiness barons in particular loved the UC for its extensive agricultural research programs based in Davis.

But during the cotton strike, growers and their supporters began to worry that radical elements were infiltrating their university. As with other state institutions, their support began to fade when they came to believe that a publicly funded entity was turning against their particular interests. The growers started to work with local law enforcement and private groups to monitor subversion in California colleges. Soon they would create a blacklist of professors with questionable views.

As the growers and the union considered the commission's proposals, people in the Valley feared that the violence might flare up again. Growers said strikers were invading ranches and slashing bags full of cotton; in response, local officials turned the Tulare County fairgrounds into a stockade where they imprisoned the strikers without charge and held them incommunicado. Sheriff Buckner said the situation was out of control and asked the governor to send in the National Guard. Governor Rolph refused, but did agree to dispatch one hundred more highway patrolmen.[56]

After meeting in Sacramento, state and federal officials agreed to endorse the commission's recommendation of 75¢ per hundred pounds and threatened to take away government benefits if the bosses did not comply. Creel told the growers that they would lose their loans if they refused, while the strikers would lose their food relief and their federal protection from local official and vigilante violence. In addition, the Department of Labor would begin importing strikebreakers to the Valley. Both sides protested briefly, with the growers threatening a "tax strike" and the CAWIU vowing to continue the work stoppage unless the union was recognized. But within two days, the growers, and then the union—convinced by Caroline Decker— accepted the compromise.

Necktie Parties

The three weeks of class warfare in California were over. The growers suffered a delay in the cotton harvest as well as dozens of injuries and nine arrests. Thanks to the strike, they paid an estimated $450,000 in additional wages.[57] In the end, though, the planters still prospered. The 1933 California cotton harvest brought in $12.4 million, an increase of about 150 percent over the previous year's $5 million.[58] In addition, the growers received millions in subsidies from the government in return for reducing their acreage. The New Deal had been good for the growers' bottom line.

For the workers, the strike helped them win a 25 percent raise—from 60¢ to 75¢ per hundred pounds—for the remainder of the short harvest season. Yet it cost the lives of two workers and one consular representative. Nine children starved to death in the camps, and one woman, allegedly denied hospitalization because she was the wife of a striker, died of pneumonia. The injuries to strikers were so numerous that no one bothered to count them. Federal officials deported an unknown number of Mexicans, and about one hundred workers went to jail on minor charges.[59]

The strike was lethal for Governor Rolph and his distinctive brand of moderately progressive Republicanism. The stress contributed to his ill health, and he suffered another stroke. He would endure several more health crises until the following June, when the tensions of his office killed him. His lieutenant governor, Frank Merriam, an archconservative antilabor man associated with what progressives called the reactionary wing of the Republican Party, became at once governor and the leading Republican candidate in the coming gubernatorial election.

Creel's efforts marked the high point of the New Deal's interest in helping farmworkers.[60] He asserted authority he did not really have and demanded that the growers share their federal largesse with their workers or risk losing their government checks. The Roosevelt administration quickly backed away from this position.

Creel did not try to institutionalize the gains of the strike. After all, the raise applied only to the current harvest season, which lasted about three weeks. The agreement did not extend to other crops or to the next year's cotton harvest. The federal government did not force the growers to recognize the union. Indeed, Creel did not want the growers to recognize the union. He even advised them privately to use the criminal syndicalism law to imprison the union's leaders.[61] He had found Chambers reasonable and pragmatic when he needed his help to end the strike. Now that it was over, he agreed that the Communist leaders should be locked up and prevented from causing any more trouble.

Nevertheless, despite the fact that the New Deal's efforts were timid, limited, and quickly disavowed, the growers felt victimized by them. The planters seethed that their federal government "petted and pampered and fed the reds and their charges, while harvest moon and torrid sun glowed over cotton fields' thwarted harvest," as one Valley newspaper fulminated.[62] The San Joaquin landowners were astounded that their own government, as one district attorney said, "came down here and definitely took the side of the strikers." Creel, according to Sheriff Robert Hill of Tulare County, "only made matters worse."[63] After the strike's end, many growers forgave Rolph for appointing the commission, but continued to loathe Creel.[64] One grower suggested that the NRA official could pay the ultimate penalty. "He won't be safe in the San Joaquin Valley," he told Clark Kerr. "I know at least a dozen men looking for him."[65]

In the growers' view, the Roosevelt administration was helping un-American immigrants and agitators instead of true patriots like the California farmers, the real "forgotten man" in New Deal America, as one newspaper said.[66] At the height of the strike, the president of the American Farm Bureau Federation insisted that he would be pleased to work for a couple of dollars a day. "With conditions as they are to-day," he said, with considerable but unconscious hyperbole, "I would rather pick cotton than own the land."[67] In his view, the organizers and New Dealers convinced the workers they were mistreated; they would happily pick cotton if not for the Reds and the feds.

Immediately after the end of the strike, the owners of California's factories in the field realized that they needed to work together if they wanted to maintain their control over labor. In November 1933, representatives from Pacific Gas and Electric Company, the Southern Pacific Railroad, Calpak, Bank of America, and about a dozen other large corporate growers and shippers met in San Francisco to devise a unified strategy to manage the agricultural strikes. The group directed two men, attorney Edson Abel of the Farm Bureau and raisin grower Parker Frisselle of the State Chamber of Commerce, to organize secret meetings of growers and their supporters throughout the state. Over the next few months, Abel and Frisselle visited more than twenty counties where they met with utilities executives, banks, canners, shippers, growers, and local law enforcement officers.[68] They began to plan their strategy for smashing the CAWIU and discrediting the federal officials who they believed protected and encouraged the union.

Even as a certain kind of order settled over California labor relations, union organizers anxiously noted an undercurrent of potential violence. As he stood trial for criminal syndicalism in Visalia, Chambers heard of a frightening event in San Jose, just down the street from the CAWIU headquarters. On the night of November 26, 1933, a crowd of thousands of people, incensed over the kidnapping and murder of a young local department store heir, gathered outside the city jail. Duck hunters had earlier that day found the victim's decomposing body floating in the San Francisco Bay, and two local men had confessed to the murder.[69] As the news of the confessions spread through the city, the mob began to gather. The leaders grabbed a thirty-five-foot pipe from a construction site and used it as a battering ram to rip the jail's iron doors from their hinges. They stormed up the stairway to the second floor landing, where they pounded a brick into the jailer's head before snatching their targets from their cells. The crowd watched as the leaders carried and dragged the prisoners across the street to St. James Park, where they stripped and beat the men and then hanged them until they were dead.[70]

Governor Rolph cheered the news of the lynchings. "I stand for law and order, of course," he said, before explaining that he really did not. "But," he continued, "as regrettable as was this lynching, I believe it was a fine lesson to the whole nation." If local law enforcement officers arrested any of the vigilantes, he added, "I'll pardon them all."[71]

Although the San Jose lynchings were not connected with union organizing, they terrified CAWIU leaders. If thousands of people in a large city could invade the jail for what the vigilantes called a "necktie party," with major newspapers there to pop their flashbulbs and illuminate the scene, then labor organizers were not safe in the relative remoteness of the lockups of the state's distant valleys.

In Visalia, Chambers's lawyer received $10,000 from a wealthy Los Angeles woman within hours of the lynching to pay his bail.[72] He hid in sympathizers' homes as his criminal syndicalism trial continued.

In the courtroom, Abraham Wirin, the ACLU attorney who had represented the strikers at the fact-finding commission hearings, defended Chambers as an ordinary union leader trying to bring the New Deal into the California fields. Two workers present at Chambers's Pixley speech refuted the district attorney's contention that the union leader had advocated violence. Instead, they insisted he had counseled *against* violence. In her testimony, Decker presented the CAWIU's cause as part of a New Deal–era struggle for workers' rights. On December 5, the jury surprised everyone by deadlocking 6–6 on a verdict, and the judge declared a mistrial.[73]

Chambers was out of jail, but he did not feel free. Shadowed by the awful knowledge of what had happened in San Jose, he decided he needed to disappear for a while. His whereabouts for the next month are unknown. But there is compelling evidence that he hid in an enclave of California Bohemians—and thus found the opportunity to influence the greatest novelist of the Depression, and, by extension, America's memory of the farm strikes.

4

BOHEMIANS

Sometime in the winter of 1933–34, John Steinbeck and his friend Francis Whitaker drove to the coastal village of Seaside and interviewed two men who had helped lead the cotton strike. One was a young man, a cousin of Bill Hammett, who went by the name Cecil McKiddy. The other was slightly older and clearly the leader of the two; he called himself Carl Williams. Those were not their real names. Because of the blacklists, spies, and threats of lynchings, all union organizers used aliases.

After hearing their stories, Steinbeck sat down to write the novel that would change his politics and his future. At the suggestion of his agent, he fictionalized the story, turning the cotton into apples, the women into men, and the Mexican Americans into Okies. His strike novel, *In Dubious Battle*, would vault him into the highest ranks of American authors and put him on the path to *The Grapes of Wrath* and the Nobel Prize.[1]

Although historians know a lot about the younger man in the Seaside attic, the older man, "Carl Williams," is more mysterious. Williams was an important leader of the cotton strike—so important that he had been forced to flee the Valley. He was familiar with the details of Pat Chambers's life and his role in the strike—so familiar that Steinbeck initially thought of writing the story from Chambers's perspective. He talked to Steinbeck at precisely the time when Chambers was in hiding—after the end of his trial in early December and before the start of the next big farm labor strike, in

Imperial Valley in early January. And Chambers's real name was John Williams—the same last name Carl Williams used.

When historians tracked him down in the 1970s, Chambers would not admit to being Steinbeck's source for *In Dubious Battle*. He conceded that he had met Steinbeck, but was deliberately vague about the circumstances.[2] On another occasion, when a farm labor organizer asked about Steinbeck, Chambers responded simply with a "cascade of swear words."[3]

But Chambers never explicitly denied that he had been the man Steinbeck interviewed in Seaside.[4] And all of the evidence—the last name, the timing, the man's position in the strike leadership, Chambers's nonresponsive answers to specific questions—points to Chambers as Steinbeck's source.[5]

Why would Pat Chambers, one of the most important farm labor organizers in U.S. history, refuse to acknowledge being an inspiration for the foremost novelist of American farm labor organizing? The answer lies in the ways that Steinbeck changed the story of the strike to reflect what he believed were universal truths. In the process, he recorded the farmworkers' struggle for history, but he also rearranged the narrative in ways that fundamentally altered its meaning—a meaning very different from the one Chambers would have wanted.

The early winter of 1933–34 was a crucial moment for the union organizers because it was then, between strikes, on the central California coast, that they rested briefly and searched for allies with influence. In Ella Winter and Lincoln Steffens, they found journalists who would try to alert a national audience to their problems. In Steinbeck, they found their historian and publicist, the man whose telling of their story would shape—and distort—Americans' views of labor, California, and the Great Depression.

That winter, Decker, Chambers, and other union leaders also met artists, poets, and art patrons—men and women with guilty consciences and deep pockets who could help finance their cause. The question remained, though, how much real help these allies could or would give the farmworkers, and how much they would use them to salve their consciences and push their own agendas.

Bohemia-by-the-Sea

A handful of poets and painters first built shacks on the beach in Carmel early in the twentieth century, attracted by the natural beauty of the crescent-shaped bay and a developer's offer to give free lots to any artist who could contribute to the Bohemian ambience. The village was a success despite— or perhaps because of—its remoteness from California's urban centers. Until 1937, when a New Deal highway project linked the Monterey peninsula to the rest of the world, no good road connected Carmel with San Francisco, some 120 miles to the north, or Los Angeles, 320 miles to the south.

Playwrights, sculptors, and novelists bought weekend retreats in this "environment as near paradise as you will ever find in the present world," as one Carmel newspaper claimed.[6] Others put down permanent roots amid the pine trees and cypresses and succulent-covered dunes. Jack London, Robert Louis Stevenson, and Sinclair Lewis found themselves inspired by the landscape. Reclusive poet Robinson Jeffers built a distinctive tower of sea-battered boulders, Tor House, where he wrote verse about the futility of life and from which he occasionally descended to entertain artists and intellectuals from around the world.

The founders of Carmel-by-the-Sea fought hard to protect their community from what they saw as the horrors of modern technology while endowing it with the cultural advantages of a modern metropolis. In the 1930s, the village's three thousand residents had no public utilities, sidewalks, house numbers, or mail delivery, but they did support an art gallery, lecture forum, music society, Bach festival, and the state's first open-air public theater.[7] Artists and idlers could attend plays written and performed by New York's theater elite and then gather for cocktails at the eccentric beachfront homes of internationally renowned writers.

Carmel's architecture was eclectic, with arts-and-crafts bungalows interspersed with rustic shacks, Spanish-style adobes, and whimsical faux-Tudor cottages. Its society was libertine, with much alcohol consumption and sexual experimentation. And its politics—at least until the 1920s—were decidedly left of center, ranging from progressive to Stalinist. By the 1930s, wealthy tourists and small shopkeepers had begun to outnumber the original settlers, and these new Carmelites grew increasingly discomfited by the artists' radicalism.

An unusual May/December couple helped to make Carmel a center of political activism. Lincoln Steffens was already in his fifties when he met twenty-one-year-old Ella Winter at the Paris Peace Conference after the Great War. A Californian—he grew up in the gabled Victorian house that later became the governor's mansion—Steffens made his name as a muckraker in the early twentieth century, when his *Shame of the Cities* awakened middle-class Americans to the squalor of inner-city immigrant life. By 1919, his politics had evolved from moderate progressivism to ardent communism, after an exuberant postrevolutionary trip to Russia. "I have seen the future," Steffens proclaimed after his visit to Moscow, "and it works."[8]

His young wife, who was German Jewish by ancestry, was born in Melbourne, Australia, moved to London as a child, and later graduated from the London School of Economics. She attended the Paris Peace Conference as a secretary to future Supreme Court justice Felix Frankfurter, who had come to lobby the peacemakers for a Jewish homeland. At the time, Winter was a Wilsonian idealist, hoping that the conference could bring about a new world order of harmonious coexistence and liberal democracy.

Winter and Steffens met when she delivered an official invitation to him in his hotel room and he greeted her at the door in his bathrobe. "A love letter?" the aging journalist teased the pretty, dark-haired college student at his door.[9] She was not impressed by his middle-aged attempts at flirting, but she did agree to wander the streets of Paris with him while discussing history and politics. When they rested and talked philosophy by the Seine, he reached over and put his hand over hers, and she thought, "So you're a rotter like all the other men."[10] But gradually she warmed to this slender, good-looking man, with his black velour Homburg, intelligent face, and very blue eyes.[11] Given her ambition, his fame and connections probably did not hurt his chances with her.

Like many of the delegates and supplicants, Winter came to Paris an optimist, but the many disappointments of the conference shook her faith in the possibility of attaining peace and justice under capitalism. She listened with increasing eagerness as Steffens told her of the world being built in Russia. "I've seen some answers to the questions that plagued me all my life," Steffens assured her.[12] Winter soon fell in love with the Soviet system as well as with the man who convinced her of its virtues. Steffens, in turn, loved Winter's enthusiasm and youth; he saw her as a joyous, hopeful "young genius."[13] They broke up for a time after the conference while she studied at Cambridge, but she soon decided to rejoin him in Paris.

In 1924, Winter found herself unexpectedly pregnant with Steffens's child, and the couple could not decide what to do. Steffens viewed marriage as an outdated, bourgeois institution, but their friends argued that they would have trouble with passports and inheritances and other legal issues unless he married the mother of his child. He finally agreed to wed her in Paris. Their son, Pete, was born soon afterward. But Steffens suggested before they got married that they should divorce in five years, even if they both felt the marriage was working; that way she could feel free to pursue other relationships as he aged.

They lived for a time on the Italian Riviera and then traveled the world, their lives eased by Steffens's considerable income from his stock market investments. "It was all romance, and Wall Street paid," the old Marxist noted with satisfaction in his autobiography.[14]

Winter and Steffens moved to the central California coast by chance. On a tour of the state, which Steffens arranged to show his bride the favorite places of his boyhood, the newlyweds stopped for a time in Carmel. A real estate agent persuaded them to look at a house on San Antonio Avenue that had been owned by Dutch artists and was filled with handcrafted furniture. The main room had high windows fronting the beach; above, a balcony provided views of the cypresses and spectacular white sands along the shore. There was a study in which Steffens could work—he was setting down his life story at the time—and a small table outside where his wife could write and smell the sea. He wanted to buy it immediately.

Winter was not persuaded. She was a cosmopolitan woman, not at all interested in living in a remote village. Yet Steffens never put much stock in his young wife's opinions. Against her wishes, he put an offer on the house, and Winter was astonished when it was instantly accepted. Suddenly she found herself stuck, as she explained later, "quite a distance from Westminster."[15]

They named their home the Getaway, and Steffens invited his many literary and artistic friends—or "any s.o.b. in a jam"—to come get away from it all, with them.[16] At first, they socialized mainly with their illustrious neighbors and fellow Bay Area residents, like Colonel Charles Erskine Scott Wood, a lawyer, poet, and philosopher, who visited from his Los Gatos home with his wife, poet Sara Bard Field. George West, the editorial page editor of the *San Francisco News*, the only large liberal newspaper on the West Coast, loved to talk with Steffens and his intriguing guests for hours. West's wife, poet Marie de Lisle Welch, was a good friend to Winter, while photographer Edward Weston and mythologist Joseph Campbell lived nearby.

Soon, Steffens's literary and artistic acquaintances from around the country and Europe came to call, along with journalism students from Berkeley and Stanford who longed to learn from a man they regarded as the greatest living American reporter. At the Steffens/Winter cottage, these novice writers might bump into Jean Harlow, Charles Lindbergh, or Charlie Chaplin; make small talk with H.G. Wells or Sinclair Lewis; attend a wild party on the beach thrown by socialite Mabel Dodge Luhan, as her unhappy Native American husband, Tony, thumped drums in the background; or meet someone intense and impressive who had not yet made his mark, like the intriguing, edgy young writer from Salinas named Steinbeck, who attended the Carmel soirées but always seemed to stand apart from the crowd. Thus the Getaway, a home chosen for its remoteness, became a cultural center of the West.

Despite the intellectuals and artists in the neighborhood, Winter felt trapped and bored in her "eccentric village." She alternated between depressive moods and periods of intense energy. She found little in Carmel to lighten her depression or focus her passions. Moreover, her marriage to a much older man presented its challenges: Steffens slipped frequently into "black moods," in which he was unable or unwilling to communicate with other people. He suffered a series of strokes, with the last one, in the fall of 1933, crippling him until his death in 1936.[17]

In 1929, Steffens suggested a clandestine divorce, as he had vowed he would do before they married. Winter could see other men, while remaining in their home as her ex-husband's partner and caretaker. Although they wanted to keep the split secret, an enterprising reporter discovered the divorce decree, and it became the subject of much speculation. Winter was angered by the gossip about her unorthodox relationship, but Steffens seemed to revel in it (later, when the local paper reported that she had twenty-nine black lovers, he responded drily, "Why not thirty?").[18]

Winter tried to find fulfillment in Carmel's Bohemian culture. She joined the "God circle," which met weekly in a local woman's Victorian living room to cultivate enlightenment through Authentic Experience; she strove to appreciate the beauty of nude dancers among the attic rafters; she watched as Luhan threw mescaline parties where couples were encouraged to switch partners, just for the fun of "making trouble." In her red velvet housecoat with its sable trim, thrown casually over her jeans and sweatshirt, Winter listened intently to the swamis and seers who drifted through town. "Mr. X will now explain to us what we do not know in a language we do not understand," one local woman said as she introduced an Indian spiritual leader. But Winter could not shake the feeling that Carmel was too lightweight, a fantasy world.[19]

Then, as the Depression continued, she found a new sense of purpose. All over the country, artists and intellectuals were suddenly, passionately interested in the problems of ordinary Americans. "There has never been a period when literary events followed so close on the flying coattails of social events," critic Malcolm Cowley wrote.[20] The international Communist Party responded to Nazi saber rattling in Europe by reversing its longtime policy of spurning intellectuals (because of their lack of proletarian credentials) and instead recruiting them in an effort known as the Popular Front. The term referred to the coalition that fought on many fronts in the war on fascism, including the cultural one.[21] Most Popular Front artists never signed Communist Party membership cards, but they joined Communists in using their art to celebrate the dignity of working people and the power of collective action. Steffens, who had seen the future in Russia in 1919, felt vindicated and exhilarated. "Things are happening," he told his wife, "everybody is listening, and the world is aware of Russia, acutely."[22]

In 1930, Winter leapt at the chance to learn about Russia firsthand by traveling to the Soviet Union with a group of American dignitaries. Sherwood Eddy, a Protestant missionary and national leader of the Young Men's Christian Association, invited her to join several prominent Americans, including Senator Alben Barkley, the future vice president, on a guided tour.

So many Western intellectuals, writers, and ministers visited the Soviet Union during the 1930s that historians and cultural critics afterward called it the Red Decade. Shocked by the failure of unregulated capitalism after 1929, these liberals yearned to find a better alternative in the socialist utopia. Giddy with excitement over Stalin's Five-Year Plan, they were willing to overlook the human costs of achieving it. British journalist Malcolm

Snapshot of Ella Winter in the 1920s. Ella Winter Papers,
Rare Book & Manuscript Library, Columbia University
in the City of New York.

Muggeridge wrote of his amazement that American progressives could believe the lies of their official tour guides. The Stalinist propagandists de-
ceived earnest clergymen, civil libertarians, and social justice crusaders
alike. "It was as though a vegetarian society had come out with a passionate
plea for cannibalism," Muggeridge wrote.[23] Like the liberals whom Muggeridge

mocked, Winter minimized or dismissed the evidence of Stalinist repression because she was so determined that communism should succeed. "Oh Steff," Winter wrote from Moscow, "never will I have such a thrill again as this first view of Soviet Russia—a thrill as nowhere on earth." Consciously echoing Steffens, she concluded, "It is idealistic and logical and it works."[24]

Winter spent months away from her aging partner and her active young child, enthralled by the unlimited "impossibilities" of the new order. "People were poor, certainly," she wrote later, yet "millions of children, workers' children who before had had nothing and could hope for nothing, were eating, singing, dancing, holding hands in the new nursery schools, freed from squalor and disease and neglect."[25] She returned to the United States to embark on a lecture tour extolling the virtues of communism, which, in her telling, included gender equity, civil rights, sexual freedom, and psychological health.

As Winter finished her lecture tour, her ex-husband's *Autobiography*, describing his career triumphs and conversion to communism, was published to great acclaim. "There are one or two books a season which no intelligent person can afford to miss," the *New York Times Book Review* said. "Mr. Steffens's is one of them."[26] Winter was elated by the success of the book that she had helped to guide and edit: "It was a little my baby, too," she explained.[27] But she dreaded leaving the Manhattan book parties to return home. And so she was thrilled when her husband's publisher, Alfred Harcourt, agreed to fund a six-month trip so she could research her own book, an examination of love in the USSR.[28]

The result, *Red Virtue*, as its title implied, was a celebration of psychological and sexual liberation under communism. Winter argued that communism completely transformed society and culture. It improved not just work, leisure, and gender and interracial dynamics, but supposedly universal aspects of human psychology. Everything changed, even "the words the young man whispers to his girl under the moon, the temper tantrum of the child crossed by its parents—these are different from what they formerly were in Russia, from what they are in our societies."[29] The Soviets liberated women in particular. "For the first time in the history of the world," she wrote, "a country is abolishing all discrimination on the ground of sex between women and men."[30]

These changes, she argued, flowed naturally from the abolition of capitalism. In chapters on sex (better under communism), crime (dramatically reduced), and mental illness (virtually nonexistent), she told of the cultural, social, and psychological benefits of a communal economy. When her publisher's money ran out, she returned to the United States and began another long lecture tour, speaking of the Soviet future to packed halls across the country. She went back to Carmel briefly to finish her book—"a Moscow *Middletown*," the *New Yorker* called it—and then spent three glorious months in New York promoting it.[31] Finally, she reluctantly returned, once again, to her bedridden, elderly, sort-of husband and her coastal village. It could not contain her ambitions.

"I Am Mrs. Lincoln Steffens!"

Winter first learned of the farmworkers' strike from a Carmel waitress. Just an hour away, near the town of Watsonville, Filipino lettuce pickers were refusing to work, hoping to raise their wages to 20¢ an hour. The sheriff responded by arresting the pickets for vagrancy, even though they lived and worked in the community. Shocked at the brazen mendacity of the local officials, and eager to see the American class struggle up close, Winter jumped in her little green sports car and drove as fast as she could to the courthouse in Watsonville. She began making daily pilgrimages to the vagrancy trials. She tried to help the strikers in their legal battles by raising money for bail and by using her (ex-)husband's famous name to get better treatment from the local officials. At one point, when a judge tried to discourage her by ordering her back and forth between courthouses in Palo Alto and San Jose, she said, "I am Mrs. Lincoln Steffens and you are not going to send me out *one more time!*"[32]

As the Santa Clara Valley strikes continued, Winter met Caroline Decker at a conclave of concerned liberals in San Jose. Like many people, she was impressed by Decker's beauty and self-assurance. "She looked like a dancer," Winter remembered later, "but she talked like an economics instructor."[33] Decker took her to visit the striking workers in jail, while her husband, Jack Warnick, helped Winter raise bail money from local ministers, lawyers, and social workers.

Winter quickly spread the word in Carmel about the uprisings in the fields, focusing her boundless energy on supporting the workers. Her friends had long known that when she wanted to do something, help people, or find a purpose, she could not be stopped. As Nora Sayre wrote, "she could be criticized for rashness, for inaccuracy, for running off the road, but not for indecision."[34] When she embraced a cause, she devoted her life to it. In 1933, the Cannery and Agricultural Workers Industrial Union became her cause.

Many Carmelites were stunned to discover that California suffered from violent labor disputes, that workers could be oppressed in a land of "sun and scented trees and bright fields."[35] Under Winter's guidance, politics replaced psychosexual angst, pharmacological experimentation, and pseudo-philosophical blather as the topics of the day among the Carmel Bohemians. As Winter remembered, "The question 'Is the universe conscious?' gave way to 'Can we make our social system work?' "[36]

Steffens believed he knew how to make it work: through revolution. After the publication of his autobiography in 1931 and before his last stroke in 1933, he lectured all over the country, at Rotary clubs and universities and churches, about the virtues of the Soviet model. In packed halls, he debated others on the question of "Can capitalism be saved?" always taking the negative. Steffens conceded that Communist governments might be oppressive at the beginning, but he insisted that social justice and liberty would thrive in the end. "Communism, when it is ripe and ready," he wrote, "will be a basis upon which will be erected such liberalism as the world has never seen but always has longed for; naturally."[37] If there was ever a moment in American history when seemingly rational liberals could consider communism as a viable option for the future, 1933 was that time.

At Winter's urging, the artists' colony began rallying to help the Communist union organizers and members. The Carmel chapter of the John Reed Club—the intellectuals' auxiliary of the Communist Party—took on the cause. The thirty chapters of the club throughout the United States encouraged their twelve hundred members to use their artistic talents for the class war. In the view of club members, the purpose of art was not transcendence or beauty. Instead, comrades were supposed to wield art as a "class weapon" for revolution, as the club's slogan said.[38]

Carmel's John Reed Club was one of the smallest chapters, with only nine members—Steffens called it "a near-Communist organization for near-writers and near-artists"—but Winter poured her considerable energy into organizing them to help the farmworkers.[39] In November, after the end of the cotton strike, she brought Decker to Carmel to speak to the club and its supporters. She was forced to hold the event at her home after unsympathetic local officials padlocked the club's building, alleging it was a firetrap.[40]

At the meeting, Decker's good looks, dynamism, and "unswerving conviction," in the words of the local newspaper, impressed the audience, which included James Cagney, everyone's favorite movie gangster.[41] Decker and Warnick stayed frequently in Carmel during the next few months, and Winter arranged for them to live in a cottage near her house. They attended parties at the Getaway, where Cagney taught Decker to tap dance.

Cagney gave money to the workers' cause, as did other well-meaning and well-heeled Carmelites ("nice people who don't do a thing," Steffens cynically called them).[42] One movie star (whose name Winter declined to disclose) handed her $150 in cash as he headed back to Hollywood after a weekend in Carmel spent learning about farmworkers. "Use it any way you want," he told Winter, "for any purpose, I never want to know."[43] She kept the money safe for a few months until new crises in 1934 provided an opportunity for her to distribute it.

Steffens contributed by waging a letter-writing campaign to raise money to buy Decker a typewriter. It pleased him to solicit $1 contributions from Republican officials and ranchers for the typewriter fund, as part of his "unpromising experimental probing for humor in high places." He asked Governor Rolph and prominent growers to help buy a machine for "the tiny little labor agitator who is doing what no big A.F. of L. leader has ever dared to undertake; to organize the migratory workers of the lovely orchards and vegetable ranches of California." Actually, he said, he planned to raise money for two typewriters, so that he could keep one in reserve in case the first was destroyed in a raid.[44]

Steffens and Winter's most critical contribution to the farm labor strikes, though, was to persuade two particularly talented writers to document the struggles. One was a white, native Californian with a background in ranching; the other was a celebrated poet of the Harlem Renaissance. John Steinbeck and Langston Hughes would both use the cotton strike as raw material for literary inspiration, but come to very different conclusions about what it meant.

Blood on the Cotton

Langston Hughes was already famous when he arrived in Carmel in 1933. A Midwesterner from a black, middle-class family, Hughes had first moved to New York to become a professional writer after the end of the Great War. He worked on a freighter, traveled the world, and visited Europe and Africa before returning to Harlem to write poems and short stories on the politics of race in America. In 1926, he published in *The Nation* a widely noted essay, "The Negro Artist and the Racial Mountain," which was a manifesto for cultural nationalism and black pride. "The younger Negro artists who create now intend to express our individual dark-skinned selves without fear or shame," he wrote. "If white people are pleased we are glad. If they are not, it doesn't matter." African Americans "build our temples for tomorrow," he proclaimed, "strong as we know how, and we stand on top of the mountain, free within ourselves."[45]

A cultural radical since the beginning of his career, Hughes became a political one in 1931, after a trip to Haiti, a country "poor, ignorant, and hungry at the bottom, corrupt and greedy at the top," where inequality was supported and enforced by U.S. Marines.[46] He began to write for the *New Masses*, the cultural magazine for American Communists. The following year, he traveled to the USSR at the invitation of the Soviet government, which was producing a film about American racial conflicts. Hughes believed that the Soviets had succeeded in banishing racism. Although he never officially joined the Communist Party, he supported many CPUSA-affiliated groups after his return home and spoke frequently about the injustice of American race relations. As he moved left, Hughes became convinced that race and class oppression in America were linked, and that capitalists deliberately exploited racial divisions to split the working class.

In 1933 and 1934, in the depths of the Depression, Hughes, a cosmopolitan African American, spent a year in the overwhelmingly white rural village of Carmel, courtesy of an eccentric patron. Noel Sullivan, the heir to a San Francisco banking fortune, liked to sponsor struggling young artists and support them while they created their art. Sullivan enjoyed an enviable lifestyle, with a cream-colored Cadillac driven by a liveried chauffeur, a mansion on San Francisco's Russian Hill, and a weekend cottage in Carmel. But he felt embarrassed by his inherited wealth. "Deep down in my heart, though grateful for the many unsought blessings that have come to me," he wrote once, "I have always been ashamed of privilege."[47]

After he returned from the Soviet Union, Hughes visited Sullivan at his home in San Francisco, and during a leisurely lunch of sparkling wine, abalone, and strawberries with cream, told him of his desire to find a retreat where he could concentrate on his writing. Sullivan immediately offered the use of his Carmel home, complete with houseboy, groceries, and a companionable German shepherd, for the next year. Hughes thus began "the first long period in my life when I was able, unworried and unhurried, to stay quietly in one place and devote myself to writing."[48]

While in Carmel, Hughes wrote short stories examining race, love, and longing in America. Fourteen of those works appeared the next year in a collection titled *The Ways of White Folks* (after W.E.B. Du Bois's *The Souls of Black Folk*), a sort of anthropological examination of the cultures of white America. Many of the stories featured shallow, condescending white people who professed to love blacks for their musical talents and primitive sexuality. Hughes's bitter renderings of these idle, wealthy characters, with their delight in Paul Robeson records and African tribal dances, and their horror of any signs of blacks' genuine independence of mind, may well have been inspired by his California neighbors. He gave Sullivan a copy of the manuscript for Christmas, along with a note thanking him for giving him "the shelter of your roof, and the truth of your friendship, and the time to work."[49]

Despite his comfortable circumstances, Hughes was initially isolated and somewhat uneasy in Carmel. There were only three black families in the village in 1933, and none of them traveled in the literary-artistic circles of the beachfront.[50] But by the spring, he also felt oppressed by the constant activity in the town. "Seemingly there are too many people in my life," he wrote. "Carmel is not at all a remote village on a rocky and wind-blown coast. It is 59th Street and Fifth Avenue. And every hour somebody from London, Paris, Chicago, or New York arrives and a cocktail party is given for them."[51]

Ella Winter made certain that Carmel would not stay isolated from the wider world. As the fall of 1933 continued, she learned more about the San Joaquin cotton strike and decided she could not remain in Carmel and "merely read about it." She and Steffens became close friends with Hughes, who courageously accompanied her to antilynching rallies and Party-sponsored protest marches. When she began to help the strikers, Hughes caught her enthusiasm. The two young writers—both political radicals, both misfits in the upscale, increasingly touristy village—began to work together to raise money for the farm laborers and to publicize their troubles.

At the peak of the cotton strike, Winter and Hughes gathered their friends and organized a caravan of three cars, led by Noel Sullivan in his Cadillac, to Visalia, some two hundred miles to the south and east. The well-dressed group arrived at the courthouse and demanded to see the district attorney and the sheriff. The officials were not happy to see "Mrs. Lincoln Steffens."

"How long you bin in this town? One afternoon?" the sheriff asked her, according to Winter's own account. "What could you find out in one afternoon? I bin here all the time and I see what them agitators do, nothin' but a bunch o' troublemakers—the more trouble, the better pleased. But not here in my county, *no, sar.*"[52]

Rebuffed by the local officials, Winter and the group visited the strike camp near Corcoran. Despite their experience with workers in the Santa Clara Valley, they were not prepared for the squalor of the campsites, or to see, as Hughes wrote in an unpublished story, "the cost of profits in terms of blood and terror."[53] Caroline Decker, tense, on the verge of tears, told the activists that without money for pipes for a sanitation system, the camp would not be able to pass an inspection by the county health department. The strikers would have to leave the tent city and lose their solidarity.

As Decker spoke, Sullivan took out his checkbook. He scrawled some numbers and his signature. "For the pipes," he said, handing her a check. "I hope that will be enough."[54] The activists returned to Carmel, content in the knowledge that they had been able to help the workers in a tangible way.

Winter returned from the San Joaquin Valley determined to raise awareness of the California labor troubles. In the *New Republic*, she wrote of the pickers' brave attempts to unionize in the face of repression by those she called "California's little Hitlers."[55] Just like in Nazi Germany, she argued, local government officials encouraged vigilante attacks on alleged subversives. She also emboldened her literary friends to support the strikers with their pens. Marie de Lisle Welch wrote poems for the *New Republic* about the strikers' camps, and *San Francisco News* editor George West sent sympathetic reporters to cover the strikes.

In the spring of 1934, Winter and Hughes decided to dramatize the workers' struggles by writing a documentary-style play about Caroline Decker. Radical artists in the Depression often turned to documentary theater to publicize workers' struggles. Basing their scripts on real events, and sometimes decorating the sets with huge photographs of contemporary newspaper headlines, the writers hoped to agitate and activate the audience members—to encourage them to participate in the production and feel inspired to get up and do something after the show was over. Hughes and Winter sought to draft a script that would lead Americans to help the farmworkers. Hughes wanted the play to be "a sound and provocative drama of the actual struggles of agricultural and migratory workers in California (and, in a sense, all America) today."[56]

Their play—called "Blood on the Cotton," then "Blood on the Fields," and finally "Harvest"—was the first dramatization of the racial and class struggles in the California fields. The script follows the events of the San Joaquin Valley cotton strike, ending with the Pixley massacre, and includes white, African American, and Mexican characters. Living in tents, unable to buy food for their families, the farmworkers divide initially along racial lines, until a strong, Irish American organizer, Mack, and a lovely young female leader, Jennie, help them see their common class interests.

The play features know-nothing growers ("Don't you know where they get their money—what's that furrin town in Russia?" one grower asks another), arrogant New Deal officials, schoolmarmish social workers, obtuse professors, selfless pickers, and heroic organizers. When a worker named José proclaims his love for Jennie in the last scene, just before he dies from gunshots, she tells him that romantic love is nothing compared to the passion of the class struggle. "We were comrades, José. Compañeros," she says. "That is the greatest love."[57]

They never found a producer for the play. Although Hughes later wrote successful scripts for black theater companies in New York, this attempt to tell the story of the racial and class conflicts in California fell flat. "Harvest" showed Popular Front culture at its weakest: a turgid, didactic attempt to use art as a weapon in the revolution.

Despite its flaws, though, Hughes and Winter's play grapples directly with racial divides among California workers. The Okies start out by blaming the "greasers" and "niggers" who compete for their jobs, but come to see that the growers deliberately pit the workers against one another to stop them from organizing. One Okie woman explains the problem this way: "I ain't blamin them pickers. I'd as soon blame them farmers livin in big houses and eatin the fat o' the land and me out here breakin my back in the sun."[58]

Their approach—especially their willingness to analyze race—contrasted sharply with the work of the man who would bring the attention of the world to the California strikes. However clunky the effort, Hughes and Winter sought to present uncomfortable truths about the farm labor battles of the 1930s. But it was Steinbeck who told these epic stories to a mass audience.

"History While It Is Happening"

In the fall of 1933, there were few signs that Steinbeck would become the definitive writer of the California experience, let alone a Nobel Prize winner. He and his wife, Carol, lived in a tiny, gloomy wooden house down a dirt lane in Pacific Grove, a working-class village less than ten miles from Carmel, on the northern side of the Monterey peninsula. Steinbeck's parents gave their son and daughter-in-law the use of the cottage and $25 a month, showing their confidence that John's writing would eventually provide a living.

Steinbeck had grown up in nearby Salinas, an inland market town and the Monterey County seat. His father had been a businessman before becoming a county official; his mother, a schoolteacher before she was married, had inherited a sixteen-hundred-acre ranch near King City, some fifty miles to the south. When Steinbeck was young, the Salinas Valley was checkered with sugar beet and alfalfa fields. By the 1920s, when changes in health education and diet prompted Americans to become a nation of salad eaters, Salinas became "the Valley of Green Gold," with its multimillion-dollar lettuce crop driving the local economy.[59]

Steinbeck studied creative writing and literature at Stanford and published short stories in the college magazine, but soon decided that the professors had little of value to teach him. He dropped out and worked occasionally in the Salinas Valley as a farmworker and a ranch hand—jobs that provided him with ideas and details for his future books.

Success did not come quickly or easily. In the fall of 1933, Steinbeck was thirty-one years old and had published a handful of novels that had sold few

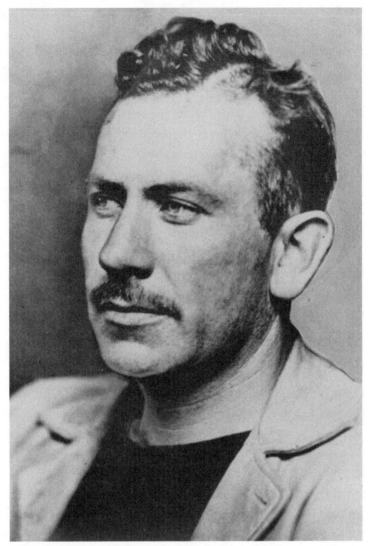

John Steinbeck in 1939. San Francisco History Center, San Francisco
Public Library.

copies and attracted little attention. He was writing short stories for literary
magazines at $50 apiece and starting a comic novel about Mexican Ameri-
cans. This novel would become *Tortilla Flat*, published in 1935, and would
help win Steinbeck a national reputation. But in 1933, a thriving, professional writing career was still an aspiration, not a reality.

Steinbeck had not shown much interest in politics or in social or economic problems while he was in his twenties. But the Depression awakened him to the suffering of people around him. And some of his friends were determined to help him see this suffering as a political problem.

Steinbeck drove to Carmel frequently to visit his friend Francis Whitaker, a carefree, rebellious man who worked as a blacksmith and a sculptor of decorative metal works. The two men and their wives frequently spent their evenings relaxing with friends in Pacific Grove or by the beachfront cabins in Carmel.[60] They did not have much money, but they knew how to enjoy life. Once, when they were visiting Los Angeles and the sun was hot and the booze plentiful, Whitaker stripped naked and sunbathed on the top of a friend's car, clinging to the roof when Steinbeck decided to drive away. "Anything at all was an excuse for a party," Steinbeck remembered later. "When we felt the need to celebrate and the calendar was blank, we simply proclaimed a Jacks-Are-Wild Day."[61]

Whitaker was more than a libertine: he was also a committed Communist and a leader in the Carmel John Reed Club. He helped arrange speakers and panel discussions for the club on the major social issues of the day. He also wrote and printed a newsletter for striking lettuce pickers, and began to encourage his middle-class, previously apolitical friend from Salinas to empathize with struggling California agricultural workers.[62]

As part of his campaign to convert Steinbeck to his political views, Whittaker introduced the writer to the radical luminaries of Carmel, Steffens and Winter. During the cotton strike, Steinbeck began to visit the couple regularly. He greatly admired Steffens, who, thanks to his autobiography, was now viewed as one of the country's most important living journalists, and Steinbeck enjoyed spending his afternoons chatting with the old man in his home.

Steffens and Winter saw Steinbeck as a native son who could use his gifts as a storyteller to alert the rest of the world to the miseries in the West.[63] They promoted and praised his writing, and invited him to wild parties at the Getaway.[64] There, he seemed intrigued but reserved, always analyzing people he met as potential characters in a story.[65] A rangy, handsome man, he listened as the visiting literary stars from San Francisco and New York—men far more accomplished than he, at the time—loudly debated potential solutions for the economic crisis, raising their voices over the pounding of the surf.

At Whitaker's request, Steinbeck began attending meetings of the John Reed Club, where he heard speakers debate the racial and economic inequalities of America and the current labor disputes. Although he did not accompany Winter on her missions to the strike camps, he listened to her reports, and he wanted to learn more.

After the cotton strike ended, Steinbeck heard from his friends in Carmel that two union organizers were hiding in an attic in nearby Seaside. He and Whitaker decided to visit them and record their tales.[66] Soon he was writing In Dubious Battle at a frantic pace.

In the midst of this hectic period, Steinbeck made the creative, narrative decisions that would so infuriate Pat Chambers in later years. In Steinbeck's novel, the main protagonist, Mac, the Chambers character, is an older, cynical organizer willing to sacrifice anyone, even his friends, for the goal of Communist revolution. Mac frequently explains his views and strategies to Jim, an idealistic young organizer based on Decker. Jim, a new convert, travels with Mac to the apple orchards of an inland valley, where they find pickers angry at recent cuts to their pay. Mac greets the news of the wage cuts with enthusiasm: "If we can get a good ruckus going down there," he tells Jim, "we might be able to spread it over to the cotton fields. . . . And then we *would* have something."[67]

Mac begins to organize the workers to demand more pay, but he does not care whether they get their raise—and actually prefers that they do not get one, at least not immediately. "A strike that's settled too quickly won't teach the men how to organize, how to work together," he tells Jim.[68] In fact, Mac hopes that the strike will provoke the employers to violence: "Every time a guardsman jabs a fruit tramp with a bayonet a thousand men all over the country come on our side," he says. "Christ Almighty! If we can only get the troops called out."[69] This was the growers' line: that the union leaders actually hoped for violent confrontation. Yet Decker and Chambers insisted that they wanted to avoid violence, and neutral observers like George Creel and Norman Thomas agreed.

Steinbeck's Mac is a true believer who has few regrets about hurting people if suffering is necessary to heighten the contradictions and bring on the revolution. Near the start of the novel, when he and Jim encounter a migrant woman in labor, he pretends to be an expert on childbirth, in hopes of ingratiating himself with the workers. Fortunately, mother and child survive the experience. "That was a lucky break," he tells Jim. "We simply had to take it. 'Course it was nice to help the girl, but hell, even if it killed her—we've got to use anything."[70]

In the same way, Mac sees the strike as a tool to use in a bigger cause. "If the thing blew up right now it'd be worth it," he says. "A lot of the guys've been believing this crap about the noble American working-man, an' the partnership of capital and labor. A lot of 'em are straight now."[71] The novel ends with poor Jim's murder—and Mac's cynical exploitation of his dead body to provoke the workers into a vengeful rage.

Despite his research and interviews, and despite his professed intention to write history, Steinbeck claimed not to care about the causes of the strike. "I'm not interested in strike as a means of raising men's wages, and I'm not interested in ranting about justice and oppression," he wrote to a friend as he finished the book. Instead, he wanted to use the conflict to investigate the psychology of mobs and to meditate on "man's eternal, bitter warfare with himself."[72]

Women and people of color play no significant roles in Steinbeck's version of history. Decker was the main leader of the strike after Chambers went to jail, yet the author changed her gender in his fictional tale, and eliminated the women strikers altogether.[73] Steinbeck's workers are Okie or native-born American migrants, while the Mexicans and Filipinos of the cotton strike have vanished.

Moreover, the federal government does not make an appearance in Steinbeck's version of the cotton strike. There are no federal officials present, and thus no food relief for the strikers or government-enforced mediation. George Creel, the State Emergency Relief Administration, the National Labor Board, and the National Recovery Administration are all absent. The New Deal does not exist as part of *In Dubious Battle*'s fictional California.

At times, Steinbeck protested that the book was intended as metaphor, yet he also tried to have it both ways by insisting he was writing "history while it is happening."[74] By this latter standard—judged as a history, as an attempt to capture the complexity of life in the fields, to examine how race and capitalism created obstacles to justice and social mobility in California—*In Dubious Battle*, despite its vigorous prose, was inferior to Hughes and Winter's leaden agitprop play.

After finishing the manuscript in a productive frenzy, writing thirty thousand words in longhand in the last eight days alone, Steinbeck sent off the book to Covici-Friede, his publisher in New York. The company had just released Steinbeck's first popular book, *Tortilla Flat*, and founder Pascal Covici was eager to read more of his work. But the *In Dubious Battle* manuscript arrived while Covici was on vacation. One of his editors rejected it, saying that the Communist characters were little more than caricatures. Mac, the editor said, was "Mr. Hearst's idea of a Red."[75]

Steinbeck was sure that the critical editor was a Communist "of the Jewish race."[76] The rejection just confirmed his view that Communists were intolerant of views other than their own. He wrote his agent that the editor's response was "a perfect example of the attitude which makes the situation in [*In Dubious Battle*] what it is."[77] Covici apparently agreed; when he returned from vacation, he fired the editor and offered to publish the book.[78]

In Dubious Battle appeared in January 1936 to ecstatic reviews. It was "one of the most courageous and desperately honest books that has appeared in a long time," wrote one *New York Times* reviewer. "It is also, both dramatically and realistically, the best labor and strike novel to come out of our contemporary economic and social unrest."[79] Another *Times* reviewer called it "wildly stirring" and brilliant, while the *Washington Post* pronounced it "a dynamic and enthralling novel" as well as "a report from the economic front line which is filled with honesty and empathy."[80] The *Los Angeles Times* put Steinbeck on a list of twelve living American writers who would be remembered a hundred years in the future.[81]

Most reviewers praised the book for its evenhanded condemnation of both Communists and growers. In the critics' opinion, the author did not push any particular ideology. There was "no editorializing or direct propaganda," one *New York Times* reviewer said.[82] Yet Steinbeck's essential conservatism—his insistence on centrism and avoidance of conflict—*was* a political position, and it shaped his editorial stance. His decision to erase brown-skinned people and women of all colors from the story revealed a political point of view. But to the mainstream reviewers of the time, Steinbeck's anticommunist populism—a populism for white men only—was just common sense, not a political stance.

There were a few critics who shared the views of the unfortunate editor at Covici-Friede who had rejected *In Dubious Battle*. In a blistering review in *The Nation*, Mary McCarthy called the book wooden and pompous, with "infantile" digressions about crowd psychology. It might have been a good novel, she said, if the author "confined himself to the facts and refrained himself from ponderous comment upon them."[83] The models for Steinbeck's characters also despised the book. "When you're heart and soul and up to your ears involved in something as important as we were doing," Decker explained to an interviewer years later, "you get very emotionally disturbed when someone has set forth a view that you think is inaccurate."[84] Chambers's opinions were unprintable.

Steinbeck clearly did not like the Communists whom he met and did not think that they were sincere. His reasons for eliminating people of color from the story are more obscure. In part, he might have genuinely believed that there were more white men involved in the strike than there actually were. The leaders he encountered in Carmel were all white, and the San Francisco newspapers highlighted the Anglo strikers in their coverage. He also might have believed that the overwhelmingly white reading public would be more interested in reading about fictional characters with whom they could identify.

Moreover, he shared the racial views of many white Californians of his time. He viewed Jews as belonging to a different, inferior race, as his letter to his agent demonstrated. He claimed to feel a special affinity for Mexican Americans, yet when he did write about them, as in *Tortilla Flat*, he reduced them to caricatures he meant to be amusing.

Most important, though, Steinbeck wanted to explore what he saw as the mythic meaning of the strike—and he apparently thought that racial and gender diversity would complicate that story.

Steinbeck was not alone in focusing on white men in the struggles of the 1930s. Much as he expunged the women and Mexican Americans from his stories on the strikes, the New Dealers in Washington also slighted the contributions of women and people of color to the nation. The Depression prompted Americans to worry about their country's social problems, but even the most concerned artists and political leaders were reluctant to address inequities of race and gender. This reluctance shaped the culture and politics of Depression America: it helped determine how we remember the Depression, and it helped inspire—and limit—the government's responses to American poverty.

As Steinbeck, Winter, and Hughes worked out their fictional representations of the California strikes, Pat Chambers continued to live the struggle. His rest—his period of interregnum, of respite from the threats of
lynching—had ended, and he did not have time to consider how the young
novelist who had so eagerly listened to his story would interpret it for future
generations. In late December he received word that the Party needed his
services again. Down in the southeastern corner of California, a new battle
over power and pay in the fields was beginning. In Imperial Valley, Chambers and the CAWIU would once again discover the promise and the limits
of Franklin Roosevelt's policies for the farmworkers of the West.

During the first year of the New Deal, agricultural laborers had organized
in unprecedented ways. Now, the growers would follow suit, organizing themselves against the workers and their ostensible New Deal allies. In the process, they would develop new techniques of mass persuasion and mobilization
that would transform the nation's political landscape.

5

IMPERIAL

On the afternoon of March 23, 1934, six thousand Californians attended
what the local newspapers called a "monster mass meeting" at the Imperial
County Fairgrounds. Their purpose was to chase the Bolsheviks from the
vegetable fields of southeastern California. Although the event was sponsored by a group called the Growers and Shippers' Protective League, its
leaders tried to appeal to all citizens. "This is not a growers' and shippers
fight," explained Charles Nice, commander of the newly founded Imperial
Anti-Communist Association. "But it is every true-blooded American's
fight to rid Imperial Valley of the 'red' menace. It is the fight of the farmer,
rancher, home owner, business man and every laborer who wants to see his
conditions improved."[1]

The rally at the fairgrounds was only the first step in the Imperial anticommunist campaign. The leaders of the new association sponsored dozens of civic programs over the next few months, with twenty-five to one
hundred residents attending each event. Local farm operators lectured
the Elks, Rotary, and Kiwanis Clubs about the Communist invasion of the
fields near Brawley. Two growers went to a Veterans of Foreign Wars meeting in Calexico and signed up 150 new members in half an hour.[2] All the
speakers at these anti-Red events discussed the proof, according to the
Brawley News, that agricultural union leaders were advancing the goals of
"the third red international of which Dictator Stalin of Russia is the grand
mogul."[3]

The large growers created this extensive anticommunist campaign in reaction to Pat Chambers's unionization drive and the help he received from his alleged New Deal allies. By the spring of 1934, agribusiness leaders realized that before they could get even, they needed to get organized. Soon they would apply the lessons of their antilabor campaign far beyond Imperial Valley.

Redeemers

Better than any other place in the country, Imperial County demonstrated how completely people could transform their environment. As they drove from San Diego, 110 miles to the west, or Los Angeles, 200 miles to the northwest, visitors to the Valley in the 1930s passed through towering rock canyons, with purple, scarlet, and gold in their veins, before gazing in awe at a moonscape of bubbling mud pots and shooting geysers. They traveled past mile upon mile of flat, bright sand. And then, suddenly, when it seemed the desert might stretch on forever, they came upon California's Imperial Valley: lush alfalfa fields, melon vines, and thousands of rows of citrus trees.[4]

Sunk below sea level, bounded by barren mountains to the east and west and the Mexican border to the south, the Valley had been isolated and mostly uninhabited until 1901, when developers dug a canal and shunted the muddy waters of the Colorado River into the basin. Almost overnight, the land of tumbleweed, snakes, and jackrabbits became a nursery for honeydew and vegetables and blue-green alfalfa. Without water, it would have remained the Colorado desert; now it was reborn as an empire. In the 1930s, the men who made it were immensely proud of their achievement—and worried it could all be swept away in an instant.

Because once before, it had been. In 1905, the Colorado River slammed through the shoddy canal gates and turned Imperial Valley into an inland sea. The Southern Pacific Railroad, which had laid tracks through the Valley, paid an army of men to shore up the banks and force the Colorado back into its channel. The chastened Imperial farmers formed a quasi-governmental irrigation district, nominally democratic but in fact controlled by the wealthiest growers, to raise and manage the enormous sums needed to keep the river in check and the desert in bloom.[5]

The mythmakers of Imperial attributed the Valley's success to individualism, family values, and the manly pioneers who had conquered the desert. *The Winning of Barbara Worth*, a wildly successful 1911 novel by Harold Bell Wright about the founding of Imperial County, celebrated the men who "transformed a vast, desolate waste into a beautiful land of homes, cities, and farms." In the book, Barbara, an attractive daughter of Imperial, must choose among several suitors, all of them dedicated to "redeeming" the desert. Wright's novel and the subsequent 1926 movie based on it came to symbolize the Imperial story for many Americans, a "moral fable of the ministry of capital," as Wright called it—a tale of tough, spirited men who brought civilization to a wasteland.[6] As the inscription over the main doorway at the Valley's opulent Barbara Worth Hotel said, only the bravest men could conquer the forbidding territory. "The desert waited silent, hot, and fierce in its desolation, holding its treasures under the seal of death against the coming of the strong ones."[7]

In truth, it was not the strong ones but the strongest one—the federal government—that prevented the desert from wresting its treasures back from Imperial agribusiness. In the 1920s, the growers welcomed the federal government's Bureau of Reclamation to help them maintain and expand the water projects that were the Valley's lifeblood. The landowners remained resentful that they had given up local control in return for federal protection and government involvement in their affairs. But the government demanded that the Imperial growers submit to centralized management in return for federally subsidized water.[8] Without the government canals, no crops would grow. It was because the growers depended so thoroughly on the federal government that they protested so vehemently against it.

Because irrigated land was costly, the Valley attracted investors with lots of capital. Imperial Valley agriculture was, to paraphrase Wallace Stegner, like the rest of California only more so: more expensive, intensive, and corporate. A government report concluded that "the entire farming area is controlled by a relatively small number of growers," including the Southern Pacific Railroad, the Times-Mirror Corporation (owner of the *Los Angeles Times*), Security First Bank of Los Angeles, and Equitable California Holding Company.[9]

Because fruits and vegetables are sensitive to the weather and extremely perishable, Imperial agribusiness was risky and speculative, with

Mexican workers headed to melon fields in Imperial Valley, 1935. Photograph by Dorothea Lange. Library of Congress, Prints & Photographs Division, FSA/OWI Collection, LC-DIG-fsa-8b27001.

the grower-shippers often gambling on the future price of lettuce, tomatoes, and honeydew. Most of the corporate owners were based in Los Angeles, Pasadena, or San Francisco; they hired superintendents to run their farms, and the superintendents in turn paid labor contractors to manage the workers.

The white people of Imperial County lived mostly in the pleasant market towns of the Valley. Brawley, with its wide streets, adobe city hall, and comfortable ranch houses, sat in the middle of the basin. El Centro, the rapidly expanding trading center and county seat, lay to the south. Visitors commented on the charm of the Imperial cities, which boasted downtowns with shaded patios, tropical flowers, and air-conditioned hotels.[10]

The men and women who harvested the crops lived outside the towns, in fetid, crowded colonies. Mostly from Mexico, these migrants in the shantytowns drank the water from the irrigation ditches, and as a consequence sometimes watched their babies die of typhoid fever. During the long sum-

Homes of Mexican farm workers in Brawley, 1935. Photograph by Dorothea Lange. Library of Congress, Prints & Photographs Division, FSA/OWI Collection, LC-DIG-fsa-8b27213.

mer months, the children swatted away the swarms of flies and flopped down under the tents to seek relief from the temperatures, which soared up to 125 degrees. Some of the workers made permanent homes in the Mexican colonies, but most followed the ripening crops north after the harvests, or retreated back across the border.[11]

The proximity of the border ensured cheap labor for Imperial farmers, but it also heightened their sense of anxiety. The local Anglos tried to separate themselves from Mexicans, with "Whites Only" signs in the downtown businesses. Growers often described the workers as childish foreigners who needed a firm hand and little pay. A local judge was known for saying, "One dollar a day is enough for a Mexican."[12] The porous border admitted not only Mexican nationals, but also criminals and smugglers.[13] The uncertainty of the economy; the harshness of the environment; the closeness of the border, with its bootleggers and drug dealers and dark-skinned peoples:

all of these elements contributed to the bloodshed to come. "Violence," wrote Carey McWilliams in 1934, "is what one somehow expects from the place."[14]

Outside Agitators

Imperial's labor troubles began in 1928, when workers refused to pick crops until they received higher wages and basic amenities like toilet facilities. Growers and local law enforcement quickly ended this leaderless revolt, but they faced a tougher challenge two years later when Communists became involved. In 1930, angered by continued wage cuts, five thousand farm laborers stopped work and demanded higher pay and better working conditions. After reading about the strike in the newspaper, three Los Angeles–based Communist organizers—including Eugene Dennis, later the leader of the American Communist Party—shoved a mimeograph machine in the backseat of their car and raced to Imperial County. The organizers set up local committees, helped the workers draft lists of demands, and printed and distributed handbills about the strike throughout the Valley.[15]

Although the Communists helped the workers keep the strike alive a little longer, the ultimate result was the same as before the Party got involved. Local authorities demolished the fledgling union by deporting Mexican strikers, importing Mexican strikebreakers, and arresting scores of workers for "illegal" meetings. The organizers were convicted of criminal syndicalism and sentenced to up to forty-two years in prison.[16] The repression ended the strike, but the problems that prompted it—wages below subsistence level, corrupt labor contractors, and pestilential shantytowns—continued to fester in the subsequent years.

The growers, too, suffered during the Depression, as crop prices plummeted. In January 1934, lettuce sold for 75¢ per crate, while growers said that they needed $1.50 per crate to break even.[17] The Roosevelt administration tried to help Imperial farmers restrict their production of vegetables, thus raising their prices. The average price for fruits and nuts increased 19 percent in the first six months after the implementation of the Agricultural Adjustment Act.[18] But the growers said they were still unable to make a profit unless they slashed workers' pay. By the winter of 1933–34, as the average wage in the Valley plunged to 15¢ an hour, workers once again began organizing.

In late 1933, in a bid to avoid the terrible conditions that could enhance the appeal of Communism, the local Mexican consul helped lettuce pickers set up a union and negotiate a wage of 22½¢ per hour. As in the San Joaquin Valley, the Mexican consular representative believed he should help the growers avert strikes and destroy the Communist-led union. But although the agreement was specifically designed to benefit landowners, some growers refused to abide by it, saying that the price of lettuce was too low to justify the wage. In response, the workers called wildcat strikes and began seeking out more confrontational leaders.[19]

After hearing of the CAWIU's victory in the cotton strike, a group of lettuce pickers traveled to Los Angeles to ask for the union's help. Sensing an opportunity, the Party leadership agreed to intervene.[20]

Darcy first ordered Caroline Decker to send organizers from the union's headquarters in San Jose, but Decker wearily reminded him that her small staff was already committed to other strikes. Darcy rebuked Decker for her impertinence ("It would be well, if, instead of writing very superior letters to everyone, you would remember the Party directives and carry them out more carefully," he wrote her), but he could not make her send organizers she did not have.[21] Instead, he recruited two young Party loyalists with abundant enthusiasm but little relevant experience.

Twenty-five-year-old Stanley Hancock was allegedly the senior member of the duo, but he had no experience in labor organizing and had never picked crops. As circulation director for the Pacific Coast Communist paper, the *Western Worker*, Hancock's sole qualification for organizing the strike was that he had been born in Imperial Valley.[22]

Hancock's partner in the strike, nineteen-year-old Dorothy Ray, did have a little organizing experience. A member of the Young Communist League in Los Angeles, Ray had helped lead a brief cannery workers' strike earlier in the year. Like Hancock, though, she had never worked on a farm and did not speak Spanish, the language of 95 percent of the workers she hoped to organize.[23]

Ray accepted her orders from the Party leadership with some trepidation, in part because she needed an abortion soon, and only the Party could help her. She was married to another Party member, but she did not want the baby, and there were no safe places for an abortion in Imperial. The leaders assured her that they would bring her back to Los Angeles in plenty of time.

Perhaps because she had little time, Ray threw herself into the dispute. She and Hancock decided to seize the moment by calling an immediate strike, rather than trying to organize the workers first. On January 8, 1934, under their leadership, five thousand Imperial Valley lettuce pickers announced that they would stop work unless the growers paid them 35¢ an hour and recognized the CAWIU as their bargaining representative.

The union leaders tried to organize picket lines on the ranches and daily marches through downtown Brawley. The police responded by arresting strikers for vagrancy. When vigilantes set upon the workers with tear gas and clubs, local law enforcement officials joined the attack.

Ray felt inspired by the workers' determination to fight despite the violence used against them. She was also impressed by their willingness to overcome their biases and join forces across racial and ethnic barriers. The overwhelming majority of the pickers were Mexicans, but there were also some Filipinos, Okies, African Americans, and a few Chinese, Japanese, and South Asians. At first, the different groups were reluctant to work with one another, but their prejudices began to lessen over the course of the strike. And regardless of their race, the men respected the leadership of this teenage brunette, who was barely five feet tall and had never worked in the fields. "If you seemed to know what you were doing, then the workers had respect for you, even if you were young and female," she remembered.[24] Because there was a warrant for her arrest, she had to sleep at a different worker's house every night, sometimes sharing the floor with more than a dozen men. But like Decker in the cotton strike, Ray said she never felt threatened by the other workers.

The growers did not need to struggle to overcome divisions: they were unified from the start. And they had many official allies. The head of the local California Highway Patrol, along with his brother, the police chief of El Centro, were growers, as were the police chief of Brawley, the sheriff and undersheriff of Imperial County, and local judges.[25] They were authorities in the borderlands, men who knew how to mete out frontier-style justice to outside agitators.

The growers also controlled the local media and used the ten Imperial County dailies to spread their message. Unlike the San Joaquin strikes, which were covered by several large newspapers, the labor disputes in Imperial got

Mexican farm worker picking melons in Imperial Valley, 1937. Photograph by Dorothea Lange. Library of Congress, Prints & Photographs Division, FSA/OWI Collection, LC-DIG-fsa-8b31916.

coverage from only one urban paper. Unfortunately for the strikers, it was Harry Chandler's *Los Angeles Times*, whose parent corporation owned hundreds of thousands of acres in the Imperial Valley and neighboring Mexico.[26] The labor activists knew they could not hope for sympathetic coverage. "The most horrendous things could go on, and did go on," Ray later wrote, "and all you could expect was that perhaps months later the news would gradually leak out to the people who read the *Nation* and kept up with such things."[27]

The large growers also intimidated the strikers' potential allies among the small growers and businessmen. Shop owners reported to government officials that grower-backed vigilantes threatened them if they showed any sympathy for strikers.[28] Small farmers also received threats.

Still, a few independent farmers let strikers camp on their land. After growers began evicting strikers from their company housing, a farmer outside Calipatria allowed some three thousand workers and their families to set up tents on his property.[29]

A few days into the strike, Sam Darcy decided that Hancock and Ray needed more help. He ordered his top organizer, Pat Chambers, to travel to Imperial. It was mid-January, and Chambers had been hiding somewhere since December 6 (most likely, as we know, near Seaside, where he met Steinbeck). Darcy also ordered another CAWIU leader, Elmer "Pop" Hanoff, to meet Chambers there. The two older men were supposed to provide strategic advice while Ray and Hancock managed the day-to-day operations.

Acutely aware of the potential danger, Chambers and Hanoff led from the shadows. They used aliases, relied on the workers to hide them, and shifted from house to house and camp to camp. Chambers and his comrades knew they could be killed at any moment. "If you checked into a hotel in Brawley, no matter what name you used," Chambers remembered later, "you were sticking your neck in a noose."[30]

Bolsheviks and Other Troublemakers

On January 12, as hundreds of workers and their families gathered in a Mexican social hall in Brawley, a posse of about 150 policemen and armed volunteers surrounded the building. The police chief banged on the door and yelled that he had arrest warrants for the leaders.[31] The workers tried to hold the door closed against the officers. The police and vigilantes began lobbing tear gas bombs through the windows and then barricaded the doors so that the strikers would choke on the gas.[32] The workers and their families, desperate to flee the fumes, broke windows and climbed, gasping for air, through the shattered glass. Some men lifted Ray and Hancock through a skylight, where they fell into the outstretched arms of strikers below.

As the police smashed through the hall, chasing workers with clubs and wrecking typewriters and mimeograph machines, Ray and Hancock dashed to the Mexican colony, where a striker dug up the dirt floor under his bed and hid them in the hole.

The workers reached out to President Roosevelt, just as they had done during the cotton strike. On January 12, just after the police attack on the meeting, the strike committee wired the president: "Local state officers ranchers attack peaceable meeting union hall striking lettuce workers club gas men women children confiscate relief kitchen reign of terror searching all homes we hold you responsible," they said, in the unpunctuated style of telegrams of the era. The president asked an aide to give the telegram to Senator Wagner, in his role as head of the National Labor Board, but neither man took any action. They decided to watch and wait.[33]

Meanwhile, law enforcement officers in Imperial received tips about the union leaders' hiding places. A reporter learned Ray and Hancock's location in the Mexican colony and told the police. When they saw the cops coming, the frightened organizers ran to hide in an irrigation ditch, where a young state patrolman found them. Ray was astonished to see that he was more afraid of the "terrible Bolsheviks" than they were of the armed officer.[34] The union posted bail for both organizers, in part because Ray needed to get back to Los Angeles in time for an abortion.

On the same day, the sheriff cornered a more important quarry. He surprised Pat Chambers, the man that the *Brawley News* called the "kingpin" of the union, in a hotel room in El Centro, and arrested him for inciting to riot and organizing a meeting without a permit.[35]

The newspapers reported the arrest on their front pages: the infamous Pat Chambers was in town! "The same old gang that was cast for the lead in the San Joaquin cotton fracas three months ago is on hand, using the same methods of intimidation," *Los Angeles Times* reporter Chapin Hall told the *Brawley News.*[36]

Chambers's presence convinced the growers and their supporters that "the enemies of order" had conspired to ruin their community.[37] Law enforcement officers quickly locked up dozens of strikers on charges of vagrancy, trespassing, and resisting arrest.[38] Many more were arrested but never charged with any crime. The sheriff, still worried that the strikers had the upper hand, begged the governor without success to send in the National Guard.[39]

Representatives of the federal government decided to take a different approach than the sheriff and the growers demanded. Instead of sending soldiers, they would find facts. In Los Angeles, the executive secretary of the
regional office of the National Labor Board, Campbell MacCulloch, concluded that the violence in Imperial Valley threatened the economy's recovery, and he decided to order an official investigation of the dispute.[40] Like
Creel in the cotton strike, MacCulloch had no power to force the employers or local law enforcement to do anything. But he did believe he had the
power to investigate, and he planned to use it.

MacCulloch dispatched two experienced men to represent the federal government in Imperial. O.C. Heitman and John Lester both worked
for the state Department of Industrial Welfare—Lester in the El Centro
office and Heitman in San Diego. Both were affable men and well known
in the area, and both had worked for the National Labor Board in the
past.[41]

But they did not get far. As soon as they began their investigation in
El Centro, an officer ordered them to the police station, where they were
promptly arrested. The police chief explained that they had been "detained"
for their own protection and they should leave immediately—or else. "We
don't want conciliation," he warned. "We know how to handle these people
and where we find trouble makers we will drive them out if we have to 'sap'
them."[42] The men followed instructions and left the Valley. Local officials
later whispered that both men were secret Communists.[43]

In the view of Imperial officials, the role of the government was to help
the growers maintain existing power relationships in the Valley. The sheriff
requested state troops to help him maintain order in his county, while the
police chief arrested federal officials who dared to investigate labor conditions. Certain types of government intervention (agents with guns and batons) were welcome in Imperial, while others (investigators with notebooks)
were decried as Stalinist enforcers.

As MacCulloch planned his response to the local officials' flagrant disrespect of federal authority, another group of Southern Californians prepared
to intervene. The American Civil Liberties Union decided to bring lawyers,
ministers, and civil rights activists from San Diego and Los Angeles to Brawley to encourage the strikers. Their goal was to force a showdown between
federal law and Imperial agribusiness.

Do-Gooders

Since its founding during the first Red Scare in 1920, the ACLU had provided counsel for striking coal miners, Communist Party leaders, anarchists Nicola Sacco and Bartolomeo Vanzetti, and John Scopes, the teacher accused of breaking the Tennessee law against teaching evolution, among other, less famous clients. Author Upton Sinclair established the first regional affiliate of the ACLU in Los Angeles in 1923.[44]

Some of the region's most distinguished lawyers volunteered their services to the Los Angeles ACLU branch. These men included Grover Johnson, a native of South Dakota who had worked for years as a district attorney in Montana; Abraham Lincoln Wirin, a Russian-born Harvard graduate whose parents had fled the pogroms; and Ernest Besig, a Cornell graduate originally from New York City. These lawyers would enjoy long, storied careers in civil liberties law. Besig, for example, would later defend Fred Korematsu's challenge to Japanese internment and Lawrence Ferlinghetti's defiance of obscenity laws.[45]

The Southern California ACLU also counted among its members a man who would become more famous as an author and historian than as a lawyer. Carey McWilliams was a freelance writer and an attorney for a conservative Los Angeles law firm when he became radicalized by the labor strife of the Depression. He began representing striking farmworkers in court and writing about their struggles.[46] In 1934, he alerted a national audience to the violence in Imperial Valley with an article in the *American Mercury*, "The Farmers Get Tough." The region's growers were blatantly ignoring the Constitution and had "virtually seceded from the union," he wrote.[47]

In addition to left-liberal lawyers like McWilliams, the ACLU enjoyed support from a number of liberal Christian churches in Los Angeles and San Diego. Although evangelical megachurches dominate the Southern California religious landscape today, in the 1930s many congregations in the area still subscribed to the "Social Gospel." They worked toward a world without exploitation—a heaven-on-earth without capitalism. The Plymouth Congregational Church in San Diego, along with Florence Avenue Methodist and Mt. Hollywood Congregational in Los Angeles, joined with the local YMCA and YWCA to vigorously support the farm laborers' cause.

Jerry Voorhis, later famous as Richard Nixon's first political opponent, was one of these California Social Gospelers who helped the farmworkers in 1934. The only son of a wealthy auto executive, Voorhis used his family money to start a school for homeless boys in San Dimas, east of Los Angeles. As a Christian, he believed that the "Gospel is to be taken seriously and that needless poverty and suffering on the one hand and special privilege and inordinate power on the other are entirely contrary to its precepts."[48]

Along with lawyers, ministers, and other reformers, Voorhis made plans to travel to Imperial Valley to attend an ACLU rally in Brawley. At the event, ministers would speak about the workers' moral right to a living wage, while lawyers would lecture on the First Amendment and the new federal protections for strikers.

As the local law required, ACLU officials applied for a permit for the meeting from the chief of police. He promptly denied it. The sheriff supported the police chief, saying the meeting would be used only for "inflammatory purpose."[49] So the ACLU decided to bring its case to the federal government. Wirin asked the federal court in San Diego for an injunction against anyone who would try to interfere with the ACLU's meeting. And, to the growers' astonishment, the court granted the order.

The federal injunction against interference by local authorities was a pivotal moment for some Imperial County citizens. In the past, courts had mainly used injunctions against strikers; now they were using them against landowners. In the growers' view, the federal government had taken the side of their un-American enemies.

On the day of the scheduled meeting, the *Brawley News* editors ominously called the injunction a federal attack on "real Americanism" and predicted that the "enraged citizenry" might take matters into their own hands. "The 'red' flag of rebellion is not going to supplant the Stars and Stripes in Imperial Valley," warned the *News*.[50] The newspaper approvingly quoted a county supervisor who urged mob violence. "If this thing must come to a show down, let us have it and get it over once and for all; I do not believe the American Legion and Veterans of Foreign Wars are going to stand by and see the valley torn to pieces by communistic or subversive elements."[51] A pro-grower inquiry later concluded that the federal injunction "unquestionably . . . prompted the citizens of Imperial Valley to take steps designed to protect themselves and their property."[52]

Wirin, the main speaker at the planned ACLU event that evening, was scheduled to appear along with Voorhis, other ACLU attorneys, and liberal pastors from coastal cities. But an hour before Wirin's lecture on "The Constitution, the NRA, and the right to strike in Imperial County," a group of armed men, including a uniformed officer of the California Highway Patrol, made sure the speaker would not be able to attend.[53]

As he ate supper at a Brawley hotel, the men grabbed Wirin, dragged him outside, shoved him into a car, beat him repeatedly, and then drove him to a deserted area, miles from the nearest town, where they beat him some more. They tied his hands behind his back and pinned him on the ground with a coat over his head. When he pleaded that he was suffocating, they hit him. Then he heard someone say, "Let's get the branding iron before we drown him."

After more beatings and threats, the men robbed Wirin of his wallet and shoes. They drove his Ford roadster over an embankment and smashed it. Then they drove off and left him.[54] The battered attorney walked barefoot through the desert until he surprised a group of partying teenagers who drove him to a telephone, which he used to call his worried colleagues waiting in Brawley.

After receiving Wirin's call, three of his friends—Voorhis, a YMCA official, and a Congregationalist minister—drove from Brawley to the Barbara Worth Hotel in El Centro to wait for him there. As they stood nervously by the main door of the elegant, Spanish Renaissance inn, in front of the murals celebrating the taming of the desert by the "strong ones," they saw armed men emerging from the shadows of the building. The vigilantes, many of them drunk, shined flashlights in the eyes of the visitors and poked at them with revolvers.[55] The labor organizers thought they would be lynched. The sheriff finally arrived on the scene and brusquely told Wirin's friends that he would protect them—if they agreed to leave the Valley immediately and never return. They accepted a police escort to San Diego.

The local newspapers praised the kidnappers and denied that they were part of a "mob." Indeed, throughout the conflicts in the Valley, growers and their supporters insisted that there were no mobs or vigilantes—nor, for that matter, any strikes. "It was not mob rule or mob violence that removed from Imperial Valley Tuesday night the menace of active agitation among the valley's lettuce workers," said an editorial in the *Brawley News*. Instead, "it was a studied, organized movement of citizens seeking the only way out of difficulties threatening the community's peace, when the hands of the land had been tied by the law itself." The federal government had sided with the agitators rather than "those working for peace." In response, the Valley had delivered a message: "Imperial Valley is not San Joaquin Valley. Stay out!"[56]

The words the editorialists in Brawley used to describe the vigilante group were similar to Southerners' defense of the Ku Klux Klan. Indeed, just as the Klan would operate hand in hand with White Citizens' Councils two decades later, the growers' protective organizations in the San Joaquin and Imperial Valleys worked with vigilante groups in the shadows. The respectable organizations—the citizens' council or the growers' association—provided daylight cover for the terrorist wing.

Wirin's kidnapping was a brazen act. The federal government, through the injunction, had guaranteed his right to speak; yet local officials had conspired with vigilante groups to kidnap and beat him and force him to leave. They had tied his hands, yet they said it was their hands that had been bound. Although CAWIU organizers often endured this sort of treatment, Wirin was neither a foreigner nor a Communist. He was a lawyer with prominent friends, who now demanded federal action.

The ACLU first asked the Department of Justice to charge the members of the mob with violating federal law. But Justice officials nervously asserted that they could intervene only if the kidnappers crossed state lines. All intrastate kidnappings should be handled by the local district attorney—who made clear that he would never indict the vigilantes. Federal authorities also refused to prosecute anyone for violating the court order that had protected the strikers' right to assemble. An assistant attorney general made the ingenious argument that the vigilantes had abducted Wirin *before he could reach the meeting*, and therefore had not technically interfered with the meeting itself.[57] There was no federal crime, the Department of Justice decided, and thus no federal responsibility to investigate.

Although the Department of Justice was too skittish to intervene, the National Labor Board was not. Campbell MacCulloch, the Los Angeles labor board administrator, was stunned by the series of events. First, he—as the representative of the federal government on labor issues in Southern California—had sent two agents to investigate the labor dispute, and local officials had arrested and threatened them and chased them from the county.

This was an "indignity to the president," MacCulloch believed; it should not stand.[58] And now these same local officials were encouraging mobs to kidnap and assault labor lawyers in direct defiance of the law and a federal court injunction. MacCulloch recommended a formal, federal investigation of the labor disputes in the Valley.[59]

The combination of MacCulloch's recommendation, the kidnapping of the lawyer, and the earlier vigilante attacks on strikers finally convinced the national government in Washington to act. In his role as National Labor Board chairman, Senator Wagner agreed to launch a high-profile federal investigation into the Imperial disputes, similar to the state's cotton strike commission. He appointed a three-man board to study the situation in Imperial Valley and recommend long-term solutions.

The three men Wagner picked were, like the senator himself, anticommunist progressives: J.L. Leonard, an economics professor at the University of Southern California and chairman of the Los Angeles Regional Labor Board; Will French, the former director of the California Department of Industrial Relations; and Sacramento merchant Simon Lubin, the director of the state Bureau of Commerce and the owner of the Weinstock's department store chain. Back in 1913, during the farm labor organizing battles led by the Industrial Workers of the World, Lubin had helped create the state's Commission of Immigration and Housing, which tried to make the farm labor camps somewhat safer and more sanitary places to live.[60]

The three men took their charge seriously. To the surprise of everyone, including the New Dealers in Washington and the growers in the Valley, the commission conducted an extensive, ten-day investigation and then issued a stinging, thirty-page indictment of Imperial County growers and officials.

The workers in the Valley lived in "primitive, even savage" conditions, the commission concluded, in camps characterized by "filth, squalor, and entire absence of sanitation, and a crowding of human beings into totally inadequate tents or crude structures built of boards, weeds, and anything that was found at hand to give a pitiful semblance of a home at its worst."[61]

As dismal as the camps were, however, the commissioners found the lawlessness of the Valley law enforcement officers even more horrifying. "Freedom to assemble and to speak our thoughts and convictions must not be interfered with," the report concluded, "especially by those who, as peace officers, are sworn to uphold the law."[62]

Given the squalor and the violence in the valley, what could the federal government do? The National Recovery Administration did not regulate agricultural labor, but the strikers did not understand this, the investigators said: "The Mexicans have heard of the N.R.A., they believe that the Federal Government is going to protect them and improve their economic status, but they do not know that the N.R.A. does not apply to agricultural pursuits."[63]

Although the federal government could not use the NRA to protect the strikers, it could take concrete steps to help the farmworkers, the commissioners concluded. Rather than urging the president to send federal troops to break the strike, the commissioners suggested that the federal and state government safeguard the workers' constitutional rights to speech and assembly. Even more controversially, they urged the Department of Labor to encourage the workers to form unions and even send Spanish-speaking representatives to help them. The commission also recommended that the government regulate conditions in the labor camps, set up a labor disputes board, and establish subsistence farms for unemployed workers.[64]

The federal commission was anti-grower, but it was not pro-Communist (a distinction lost on the region's growers). Instead of recognizing the CAWIU, the commissioners urged the government to begin a vaguely defined program of "social and economic education" of the migrants, apparently to help turn them against Communism. They also recommended the deportation of "undesirable"—that is, Communist—aliens. Finally, the report suggested the appointment of a federal mediator.[65]

Two members of the commission, Leonard and Lubin, infuriated the employers by further criticizing them in speeches to civic groups. Imperial farm owners were so angered by Chairman Leonard's comments that they petitioned his employer, the University of Southern California, and urged the university to fire him because of his alleged communistic beliefs.[66] But the growers reserved their greatest contempt for Lubin. In San Francisco before the Commonwealth Club, Lubin declared that the growers had manufactured a Red Scare to divert attention from their oppressive labor practices. "They blame the constant disturbances upon 'Communism' and 'Moscow'!" Lubin said with amazement. "Though the cause is immediately beneath their eyes—a cause which in part they themselves create—nevertheless they seek it ten thousand miles away!"[67]

Like the president, Lubin was a prosperous capitalist. He had no desire to expropriate the expropriators. But he believed that the growers' refusal to pay a decent wage and provide proper housing created just the sort of appalling conditions in which Communism would thrive. He saw no credible threat from the few actual Communists in California. "But," he said, "there is genuine ground for fear in the greed and selfishness, the intellectual sterility, the social injustice, the economic blindness, the lack of political sagacity and the mock heroics and hooliganism among ourselves"—in other words, among capitalists like himself.[68]

At the time, Communists denounced the federal commission as a sham investigation. Since then, scholars have dismissed it as paternalistic and typical of New Dealers' opposition to truly independent unions.[69] Yet the growers and their supporters saw the federal commission's report very differently. It proved their worst fears: the federal government was honeycombed with traitors like Lubin and Leonard, men of "pink tendencies" who were willfully blind to the dangers of the Communist conspiracy and who prevented real Americans from protecting themselves.[70]

The *Los Angeles Times* found it "amazing" that the commission would criticize the growers for "defending life and property by the only means they had; that is, by arresting the treason-preaching 'comrades' and throwing them in jail."[71] The *Brawley News*, the only English-language newspaper in Imperial's largest town, went even further (and it was quite something to go further than the *Los Angeles Times*), calling the report "an abominable thing" that was "being broadcast by 'red' organizations as a part of their propaganda to destroy, if they can, the agricultural industry of this great commonwealth of California, to say nothing of the plan mapped out to tear the government down."[72] The associated chambers of commerce in the Valley denounced the "false and defamatory statements" made by the commissioners.[73]

The Roosevelt administration quickly backed away from the commission's report. Alarmed by the investigators' candor, the National Labor Board in Washington rebuked its own commission and told the members that the state government could "take every important action recommended by you without the assistance of the federal government." This was disingenuous and untrue. Even if he could, there was no way that Governor Rolph would implement any of the suggestions. The federal government was telling its own investigators to shut up and go home.[74]

Despite the administration's repudiation of its investigators' report, the growers responded on their own in two ways: with force and with guile. First, in blatant defiance of the report, they sent the sheriff to condemn and burn the makeshift tent city outside Calipatria where some three thousand strikers lived.[75] In a scene reminiscent of the burning of the Bonus Army camp in the nation's capital eighteen months earlier, state and local police doused the tents and shacks with gasoline and then set them afire. Local officials also stepped up their campaign of legal intimidation. Attorneys who dared to defend the strikers found themselves in jail on vagrancy charges within hours of setting foot in the county.

The labor organizers were terrified. In jail, Pat Chambers, who worried that he might be snatched by a mob at any moment, accepted a plea bargain the district attorney offered. In return for pleading guilty to a minor charge, Chambers promised to leave town and never come back.[76]

But the growers did not rely on threats and force alone. They realized that vigilante violence could sometimes backfire and elicit sympathy for the injured workers.[77] Instead, they needed to turn public opinion against the strikers—and against the New Dealers who seemed to help them.

The Businessmen Unite

The idea for a "citizens' committee" to represent growers emerged out of secret businessmen's meetings in San Francisco and Los Angeles after the end of the cotton strike. Representatives of the largest corporations in California—Pacific Gas and Electric, Southern Pacific Railroad, Bank of America, and twenty-one others—attended the northern meeting. Many of these corporations had invested in agribusiness; others understood that their economic fortunes depended on agribusiness. These banks, shippers, and utilities would fund the group.[78]

The new organization's concern with image began with its name. In the past, California growers had bristled at the term "farmer." Effectively anticipating Carey McWilliams, one grower lobbyist insisted at an agricultural conference in 1926, "We are not farmers. We are producing a product to sell."[79]

But in 1934, these agribusinessmen understood the cultural appeal of the word "farmer" in a nation steeped in the mystique of the Jeffersonian ideal. The first local anticommunist agricultural group was called "American Institutions," but the agribusiness and industrial leaders who set up a statewide organization wanted a name that resonated with the public. After considering ten different names, the founders decided to delegate the final selection to the Executive Committee "in conference with the publicity man of the organization, since the publicity factor will be an important one." The committee chose to call its group the Associated Farmers.[80]

Later, the Associated Farmers would claim tens of thousands of members in California. But at the beginning, it did not have local chapters. Instead, the organization mobilized civic groups to spread its message of the twin dangers of Communism and Rooseveltism. They aimed to break the farmworkers' union and, at the same time, to persuade Californians to reverse the president's pro-worker policies.[81]

The Associated Farmers published anticommunist leaflets and distributed antilabor propaganda to newspapers, radio shows, local civic groups, and schools.[82] Father Charles Leahy of the diocese of San Diego and Los Angeles ensured that the Associated Farmers' literature was used in textbooks and teaching in all Catholic schools and colleges in Southern California.[83] The organization's publicists worked with patriotic and veterans' societies, business groups, and women's organizations, including the League of Women Voters and the Parent-Teacher Association.

The group also encouraged individual growers to spread the word about the Communist threat. In Imperial Valley, grower/officials like District Attorney Elmer Heald and Judge Vaughn Thompson addressed the American Legion, the Rotary Club, and the Brawley Women's League, among others, and alerted them, as Heald told the Calexico Rotary, to "the [Communist] propaganda now being used to upset our whole governmental and social fabric."[84] In Kern County, growers sponsored a speakers' tour by the Los Angeles police chief and the head of his "red" squad, Captain Hynes, and invited service clubs, churches, fraternal orders, and law enforcement officials to come hear them.[85]

The large corporations that gave money to the Associated Farmers wanted to ensure that their hand remained hidden, out of fear that the targets of the publicity campaign would dismiss the message if they knew who was funding it. As Arthur Arnoll, secretary and general manager of the Los Angeles Chamber of Commerce, explained in a private memo, the employers' role "should be kept a deep, dark secret. This is the only way you can win the fight."[86]

The Associated Farmers argued that strikes were not about higher wages; instead, they were Communist tools to promote revolution, to plant the "red rag of sedition" on American soil. These alien agitators, foreign in ideology and origin, wanted to turn America into the Soviet Union, a land of unimaginable horrors—a land, according to one Soviet expert brought to Imperial Valley by the anticommunist association to speak to civic groups, that was rife with promiscuity and drug addiction and even cannibalism, where "droves of wild homeless children live in sewers."[87]

The growers designed their propaganda to exploit anxieties about challenges to racial, gender, and sexual norms. According to anticommunist speakers, Reds menaced more than democracy and capitalism: they taught poor (mostly brown) people to be ungrateful, children to disrespect their parents, preachers to ignore the Gospel, and men and women to stray from their proper roles.

The California anticommunists were particularly concerned about gender inversion and transgressive sexual behavior. Communism sometimes made men gay: they became "pinks," or "pussyfooters," or "busybodies."[88] But it also released a man's "innate savagery" and freed his inner rapist. It transformed women into whores who haunted dance halls in search of sailors to seduce—except when it turned them into lesbians.[89]

According to the anticommunists, the Reds began their attack on the family by teaching women to challenge traditional gender roles, by leading marches and strikes, when really a woman should "stay at home and use her talents more constructively, instead of applying them towards a cause detrimental to American liberty and national stability," as the *Brawley News* explained.[90] If these women refused to stay at home, then the state needed to confine them. As one Sacramento judge said when he sentenced an organizer to prison for an inflammatory May Day speech, "When a gibbering petticoat on a soap box incites men of a low-grade mentality to defy the police, she becomes a public nuisance and there is only one place for her, and that is jail."[91]

The existing gender hierarchy in the United States provided stability and safety, the anticommunists argued. When Helen Marston, a San Diego department store heiress and ACLU member, joined the farmworkers' picket lines in Imperial Valley and found herself menaced by vigilantes, the *Brawley News* blamed her for placing herself in jeopardy.[92] Moreover, the Party leaders, by putting her in that position, showed their contempt for gender norms and for their duty to protect a white woman's safety.

Marston was among many women who played key roles in the Imperial Valley strikes. Dorothy Ray helped lead the workers; San Diego and Los Angeles ACLU members like Marston and attorney Emma Cutler went to jail to show their support for the strike. Working-class women harvested fruit and vegetables alongside the men, and they patrolled the picket lines, marched in demonstrations, and served time in jail like the men.

But women also provided much of the grassroots organizing power for the growers' movement. The Brawley Women's League hosted anticommunist speakers and helped spread the word about the Red threat. In Los Angeles, several women's groups, including the Friday Morning Club, the Women of the Pacific, the Daughters of the American Revolution, and the Neutral Thousands, issued public warnings about the menace to hearth and home throughout Southern California.

Conservatives also worried that the Reds were brainwashing men of the cloth and—in a perverse and sneaky twist—using the pulpit to spread their anti-God platform. Nothing angered conservatives more than the knowledge that "so-called ministers" of the coastal communities were helping their enemies.[93] To counter these Social Gospelers, conservatives asked fundamentalist preachers to use their sermons to spread the word that Communism and liberalism were against the word of God. The Imperial Valley growers pioneered the technique of using the churches to disseminate the antigovernment message; later in 1934, during the fevered battle over who would be the next governor, other business leaders would perfect it.

But ultimately it was not the rebellious heiresses, the "half-baked" preachers, or even the rabid Red organizers who posed the greatest danger to American institutions, in the conservatives' view: it was the government officials who sympathized with them. The growers were especially upset that the Roosevelt administration supported these professional agitators by providing federal food aid to pickers during the farmworkers' strikes. The *Los Angeles Times* claimed that the union organizers assured would-be strikers that "the 'government is with us' and 'Roosevelt will feed you.'" Bums throughout the West were heading to Imperial to fatten themselves on the "good government grub." Although the state and local governments knew how to deal with the strikes, "there are Red spots all along the official line," the reporter explained, especially among federal relief officials.[94]

William Randolph Hearst's Los Angeles paper, the *Examiner*, blamed the man at the top. "It is," the paper reported, "after all and to some degree, Mr. Roosevelt's own fault that these extremists are in a position to speak as dignified advisers of the administration." The *Brawley News* agreed that the Roosevelt administration had made a "grave error" in "flirting too much with fanatic radicals and appointing men on boards who have known sympathies with Communists and affiliated organizations."[95]

For proof of federal Red sympathies, the growers pointed to the National Labor Board report, which had found filth and squalor in the Valley and encouraged the government to help the workers form unions. The *Brawley News* suspected a sinister plot behind the report, especially after NLB chairman Senator Robert Wagner endorsed an unrelated proposal for 5 percent national tax on payrolls. The *News* weighed the evidence: Wagner favored taxes on employers; his three commissioners criticized employers and praised unions. The paper concluded that the Valley had been treated unfairly because the Labor Board was filled with Reds.[96]

In reality, the New Dealers on the Labor Board had no sympathy for Communism. The local Labor Board representatives despised the CAWIU, and agreed with the Communists on only one point: that the workers should have the right to organize collectively so that they could get more money for their labor. The New Dealers in Washington did not even go that far. They just wanted to make sure the crops were harvested so that the economy could continue to recover.

But many California businessmen believed that the Roosevelt administration was too fond of unions and too tolerant of Communists. And the presence of the Reds on the farms gave the growers the opportunity to discredit the whole idea of unions, and of liberal reform. The employers could paint the union leaders—in some cases, with justification—as traitors who worked for a foreign power.

Especially when the organizers made it easy for them. Back in Imperial, a couple of bored union leaders were about to hand the agribusiness propagandists a great gift.

Workers of the World Unite

In San Francisco, Communist Party leaders were disgusted when they heard that Pat Chambers had accepted the district attorney's plea bargain and fled Imperial Valley. No comrade should ever plead guilty in "the courts of the bosses," they explained. A contrite Chambers returned to the Valley to serve out the balance of his six-month sentence.[97] At a time when the CAWIU was desperately short of skilled organizers, the Party leaders found it more important to maintain ideological purity than to keep their best organizer out of prison.

Back in jail in El Centro, Chambers and his cellmate decided to score ideological points by defacing the capitalist prison with Communist graffiti. Alone in their cell, the two men chiseled and painted a hammer and sickle on the wall. The insignia, which appeared on the Soviet flag, symbolized the unity between agricultural and industrial workers. In case anyone missed their point, they wrote "Workers of the world unite" above the image.[98] Ironically, Chambers's knowledge of Marxism did not extend much beyond that phrase. "As far as having a theoretical concept and what all it entails . . . very few individuals actually knew," he said later. The carving was simply an act of defiance.[99]

But the sheriff realized the image's emotional power. He immediately called the newspapers and posed next to the painting for photographers, his body casting an ominous shadow on the wall. "Here's one of the things which fired Imperial Valley's citizenry into organizing an anti-Communist organization," the *Los Angeles Times* crowed. It was "conclusive proof" that Communists were trying to "gain access to school and churches" and tear up the foundations of American society.[100] As he watched the media circus, Chambers began to realize that he had made a mistake.[101]

The violent reaction was not long in coming. Days later, San Bernardino attorney Grover Johnson, working pro bono for the ACLU, arrived at the Imperial County courthouse to represent Chambers and his cellmate. Judge Roy McPherrin agreed to grant a writ of habeas corpus, which meant that

the two men—the most unpopular people in the Valley at that moment—
would be released on bail after the jailers completed paperwork.

As their attorney walked down the white marble steps of the courthouse,
in the shadow of its imposing Corinthian columns, he was ambushed by
about forty men. "You red son of a bitch, arguing constitutional law; we'll
give you a taste of our constitutional law," one man said as he slugged Johnson and knocked off his spectacles. The gang included several prominent
citizens and local officials, among them a county supervisor, the head of a
New Deal public works agency, and the chief executive of the county hospital. The Imperial County sheriff watched the beating and did nothing to
stop it. Later, he said he needed to stay at his post to protect Chambers from
lynching.[102]

Johnson, who was severely nearsighted, could barely discern the shapes
of the men beating him, but he could hear them making plans to force him
into a car. Then his wife screamed. Mrs. Johnson grabbed a pistol from the
glove compartment of their car and brandished it in the air, trying to frighten
off the lynch mob. When some of the men ran, deputy sheriffs quickly arrested the Johnsons and took them to the adjacent jail.

The couple spent a terrifying afternoon watching through the bars
on their cell windows as hundreds of men milled about on the courthouse
lawn. They listened as the city fire whistles screamed, which they learned
was a signal for vigilantes to gather. The sheriff refused to disperse the mob
or arrest those who assaulted the attorney, but he did allow Johnson to call
Judge McPherrin and plead with him to come to the courthouse and help
protect him. The judge rushed over and began arguing with two leaders of the
mob: "I took an oath to uphold the law and the Constitution, and I'm going to
live up to my oath as long as I am Judge." McPherrin then gave an impassioned
speech to the crowd on the need to respect the Constitution. Finally, the vigilantes began to drift away, and the Johnsons were safe.[103] McPherrin would
soon throw out the charges against both men and release them for good.

It was the second vicious attack on a civil liberties lawyer—and this time
the assault came on the steps of the courthouse, the symbol of justice and
the rule of law. Secretary of Labor Frances Perkins decided she had to do
something to stop the mobs in Imperial County. She was appalled by the
workers' living conditions, the growers' violence, and the state government's
inability to keep order.[104]

So Perkins decided to intervene in a California agricultural strike, just as George Creel had done a few months earlier—except this time federal officials would encounter a more experienced and canny adversary. The agribusiness leaders in Imperial Valley had learned how to use the cultural threat posed by a presumed radical/liberal alliance to create grassroots resistance to New Deal labor policies. In the cotton strike, the growers were unprepared and defensive. They would not make the same mistakes again.

Perkins chose to follow the recommendation of the National Labor Board commission and send in a mediator, or really an authority figure—a sort of "old Aunt Susan," she said later, a disciplinarian who "knows where she's going and what she intends to have"—to solve the problem.[105] And because the growers were not actually children but powerful, grown men, she did not send a no-nonsense maiden aunt but a very manly army commander. General Pelham Glassford was about to fight the battle of his life.

6

CROOKS OR TOOLS

General Pelham Glassford stood three inches over six feet, and his military bearing made him seem even taller. Lean, dynamic, and handsome, he was known to his many friends as "Hap" or "Happy" because he was always smiling. To his supporters, he projected confidence and amiability; to more skeptical observers, he seemed self-satisfied. But everyone agreed that the Army's youngest brigadier general in the Great War was fearless. In France in 1918, at Chateau-Thierry and the Marne, he rode his big blue motorcycle into no-man's-land to scout enemy positions and inspire his artillerymen; in 1932, in a new career as superintendent of the Washington, D.C., police, still on his motorcycle, he tried to keep order among the Bonus Army, the thousands of Great War veterans who encamped near the nation's capitol to demand immediate payment of their military service bonus. Neither foreign war nor domestic protest seemed to sully the reputation or darken the mood of Happy Glassford.

That is, until 1934, when Frances Perkins sent him to Imperial Valley to solve the labor disputes there. Enemy riflemen or rioting veterans he could handle. But the Imperial Valley Growers and Shippers Protective Association would test General Glassford's courage and equanimity—and the New Deal's commitment to workers' rights.

Another Federal Intervention

In 1934, Glassford, in his late forties, was a most unusual army general. Although he served with distinction in the Philippines, Hawaii, and France, where he was decorated for gallantry, he also had a restless, creative side. After the Great War, when he was stationed in Washington, D.C., he lived in a house with murals on the walls and children underfoot—"a combination of Bohemia and military discipline if you can imagine it; but you can't," *Harper's* magazine explained. It was a "delightful, ridiculous" place, but the general was not there much to enjoy it. He liked to save up his leave and take long motorcycle trips to the West, where he worked sporadically as a circus barker, a reporter for the Hearst newspapers, and an artist.[1]

Glassford retired early to devote his time to painting and to horse breeding on his family's ranch in Arizona, but he was tempted back into public service in 1932 when the District of Columbia police department tapped him to serve as superintendent. Glassford knew little about policing. (When a newspaper reporter asked him about his relevant experience, he said, "Well, I've been arrested. Once for driving through a red light and once for speeding on a motorcycle.")[2] Yet he proved a popular peace officer known for his talent for charming, rather than confronting, protesters. Hap Glassford was a West Point graduate "who never acted like one," a friend remembered later; he believed there was always a peaceful solution to apparently irreconcilable conflicts.[3]

It was his competent handling of the Bonus Marchers that drew the attention of Secretary of Labor Frances Perkins. Fifteen thousand veterans descended on the nation's capital in 1932 to demand the early payment of their service bonus, which had been promised them in 1924 but was not due until 1945. Hungry and jobless in the Depression, the veterans wanted their money immediately, and were prepared to camp out until they could persuade Congress to give it to them.

Rather than seeing the veterans as the enemy, Glassford arranged for hot meals, cots, and tents for their encampment on the Anacostia mud flats, and he personally donated some of his own money to start the marchers' commissary. He consistently tried to engage, rather than threaten, the protesters. His former comrades-in-arms responded with gratitude and elected him the secretary-treasurer of their group.[4]

The Bonus March ended disastrously, but not owing to any fault of Glassford's. When some of the marchers refused to leave Washington, General Douglas MacArthur routed them with tear gas and ordered his men to torch their tents. Glassford denounced the use of force, resigned in a dispute with his superiors, and emerged as a national hero.[5] In handling the Bonus Army, Glassford gave the country "a remarkable demonstration of mob management without benefit of tear gas, riot club or machine gun," in the opinion of *Time* magazine.[6]

Perkins heartily approved of Glassford's handling of the Bonus March.[7] He was compassionate yet professional. Moreover, throughout his term as police superintendent, he strongly supported protesters' right to free speech. Although fiercely anticommunist, Glassford defended Communists' right to demonstrate, and had once even led a Communist parade himself on his blue motorcycle.

When Perkins sent him to Imperial Valley, she made clear that she wanted him to use federal power to bring order to the lawless West. "Now, you know, we are the federal government," she told him. The farmworkers were Mexicans and had "Latin blood," which in the secretary's opinion included inherent childishness and lack of self-control. But the strikers were in the United States of America, and they were entitled to certain basic rights. "They've been having some awful treatment by the local governments out there," she told him. "We have to somehow or other straighten that out."[8]

The growers' groups protested the appointment. There was no need for a mediator, the employers explained, because there were no real labor disputes, just disturbances fomented by outside agitators who were exploiting ignorant foreigners. "I feel quite sure," said Alvin Jack, the president of the Growers and Shippers Protective Association, "that Mr. Glassford will find nothing to conciliate when he gets here April 5 for there are no strikes and have been none."[9]

The *Los Angeles Times* editorial board saw Glassford's appointment as another sign of the Roosevelt administration's inability to comprehend the dangers Communism posed. "The idea of 'conciliating' the differences between patriotic American taxpayers and alien Communists seeking to overthrow the government is one that could occur only to official Washington," the *Times* concluded. "Unless Gen. Glassford is to be supplied with a sharp stick for the Communist disturbers he can find no useful occupation."[10]

State government officials agreed that Imperial Valley did not require federal intervention. Governor Rolph's director of industrial relations, Timothy Reardon, told Secretary Perkins that state negotiators had already settled all strikes throughout the state, and there were "no labor or agricultural disputes in the Imperial Valley or in California at this time."[11] The state government endorsed the growers' definition of a strike: if Communists led pickers out of the fields, then the work stoppage should be seen as part of the Red plan to "get the public at their mercy and pave the way for a Red dictatorship." Therefore these disputes were revolutionary acts, not strikes, and the local law enforcement officials did not want or need federal mediation.[12]

To counter what they saw as confusion about the situation in the Valley (after all, some people were calling it a "strike"), two business organizations— the state Farm Bureau and the California Chamber of Commerce—formed their own commission of inquiry. This was the third investigation of the violence in Imperial County (after the regional labor board's aborted inquiry and the National Labor Board's report). The grower commission included Claude B. Hutchison, dean of agriculture at the University of California; W.C. Jacobsen, an official with the state department of agriculture; and John Phillips, a member of the board of directors of the Associated Farmers and an aggressively right-wing grower and assemblyman (and later congressman) from Banning, just north of Imperial Valley.

The "Phillips report," as it became known, attacked the federal government's interventions in the Valley. Both the National Labor Board investigation and the Glassford mission were misguided, the report said. Imperial Valley growers should be left alone to handle outside agitators in their own way. "There is no strike," the report insisted. "Therefore there can be no 'mediation' and no intervention by State or Federal authorities until the situation changes."[13]

But the New Dealers refused to allow the growers to render the strike invisible. As Secretary Perkins said, "It had all the aspects of a strike. It was called a strike. The police called it a strike." And if it was a strike, then the federal government had a duty to investigate whether the strikers' rights were being violated. "It seemed up to us to handle it," she concluded.[14]

The Roosevelt administration did not want Glassford to walk down the dangerous path blazed by the National Labor Board commission, which had condemned the growers for violating the strikers' rights and paying so little that workers lived in "filth" and "squalor." The Department of Labor warned Glassford that it disapproved of the NLB report and did not want him to take a similarly pro-worker stance. As the chief lawyer for the department wrote, "there were many points in the report in which neither the [leadership of the] National Labor Board nor the Executive Departments of the Federal Government concurred." The Department of Labor's leaders in Washington particularly disapproved of the commission's requests for federal officials to organize farmworker unions and for federal marshals to police what Washington considered a "local dispute."[15]

So Perkins did not want Glassford to help the workers form unions or call in federal marshals to protect them. Instead, she charged him with ensuring that the spring melon crop was harvested on time—a relatively easy task because grower-backed vigilantes had already scared the pickers back into the fields—and, more important, recommending long-term reforms that would prevent strikes, violence, and vigilantism from occurring again.

Glassford and Perkins did not ever contemplate reforms that would redistribute wealth in Imperial County. Both the secretary and her emissary had a condescending view of the Mexicans, who they believed were childlike, happy people who did not require and would not appreciate American wages and working conditions. "These Mexicans don't know any other way to live," Glassford told Perkins. "They've got a lot of children, a lot of dogs, a lot of chickens. They're just going to live like that anyhow, live like nomads."[16]

The federal government's job, Glassford believed, was simply to protect the workers from the growers' worst abuses. He did not realize that the growers would interpret this relatively small expansion of federal government power in Imperial County as a threat to their entire social order.

Glassford began by trying to reassure the farm owners that the federal government was on their side. He insisted, loudly, publicly, and frequently, that he agreed with them that the Communist union should be abolished. He conducted joint hearings with the grower-backed commission and socialized with prominent farmers and local officials. After a few weeks of investigation, he condemned the CAWIU leaders as "vile agitators," "un-Americans," and "skunks." He wrote in a bulletin circulated to all workers in the Valley that the union leaders had "no interest in the welfare of the workers. Their only objective is to create dissension, destroy private property and foment a strike."[17]

The general's denunciation of the Communists was calculated: it was part of his strategy for winning the growers' confidence. As he reported to the Department of Labor, "It is absolutely essential at the present time that they believe me to be entirely under their control." He hoped he could cajole the growers into raising wages, "thus forestalling a strike and possible bloodshed."[18]

The Education of Happy Glassford

However, as General Glassford continued his work in the Valley, he grew steadily more alarmed at the growers' violations of civil liberties. In early May, a few carloads of ACLU activists from coastal cities attempted to drive through the Valley on a "goodwill tour." Because of threats to their safety, Glassford begged the ACLU leaders to stop the tour; when they refused, he fumed to the Department of Labor that the organization was "doing everything in its power to foment trouble, and to aggravate the citizens of Imperial Valley."[19] In the end, the twenty-person ACLU delegation stayed only briefly in the Valley before a mob of vigilantes surrounded them and scared them into leaving.

Glassford's attitude toward the growers began to shift. He had not wanted the ACLU to come. He believed that the tour was designed to bait the growers, and the activists were clearly making his mission more difficult. Yet he was astounded by the menacing atmosphere that greeted the harmless, sign-waving attorneys and ministers. Soon afterward, a vigilante viciously beat an ACLU lawyer who was attempting to represent workers who had been arrested. In fact, throughout the winter and spring, every single one of the five attorneys the ACLU sent to defend Imperial strikers was beaten and threatened with lynching.

Glassford was also appalled by the growers' attitude toward the company union they had set up with the help of the Mexican consul. The large growers initially hailed the establishment of the union as a great step forward and negotiated agreements with it. But once the CAWIU leaders were jailed and the threat of a strike receded, they refused to talk to the company union or abide by the contracts they had negotiated with it.[20]

Throughout his investigation, Glassford heard from ordinary citizens who told him they opposed the large growers, but did not dare say so in public.[21] One Methodist minister who witnessed an attack on a lawyer swore out a complaint with the police, then withdrew it after he was pressured by a group of his parishioners; then he filed the statement again, and withdrew it again.[22] Even members of the mobs told him that they participated only because the large growers forced them to do so. A reluctant vigilante told him: "I'd like to be out of this mess, but what can I do? If I don't line up, my business will be ruined."[23]

Many Imperial residents pleaded with the general to find a way to control the grower-sponsored violence. A laborer wrote Glassford that "we working people of this valley have nothing in common with the Communists but we now believe the actions of the leaders of the vigilante movement are not inspired by patriotism but are to protect their pocket book." The workers had expected the federal government to punish the vigilantes. The letter ended with a question: "Are we to be disappointed," he asked, "or will it be done?"[24]

Privately, Glassford told his supervisors in Washington that he found the growers "obstinate and arrogant" men who presented "stolid resistance against concessions or reform."[25] He wrote the U.S. attorney in Los Angeles that he hoped soon to "launch an attack against the shippers and growers on the question of labor domination," and he wanted the Department of Justice at the same time to prosecute the vigilantes.[26]

Glassford also grew increasingly frustrated by the growers' persistent challenges to his authority. The Associated Farmers wondered why he was in Imperial at all, given that the National Recovery Administration "has officially declared that agricultural labor is not subject to code regulation of any kind." They warned Governor Rolph that Glassford's mission was setting "a dangerous and embarrassing precedent" of federal government disregard for California's "statehood rights."[27] The governor, who needed the growers' support in the coming election, publicly decried Glassford's mission.[28]

Glassford worried about the extent of his legal power in Imperial. He diffidently wired the Department of Labor that "it would be helpful if scope and limitations of my authority as conciliator could be clarified."[29] The department's chief lawyer responded by citing a statute empowering the secretary of labor to appoint a mediator in disputes whenever she determined that "the interests of industrial peace" required federal intervention. However, the lawyer cautioned that the general did not have "actual police authority"; Glassford could merely "adjust grievances" when the parties in a dispute required "some impartial intervention in a friendly fashion."[30] In other words, Glassford had no real power at all.

Indeed, every time the general attempted to assert federal authority in the Valley, the Department of Labor privately advised him that there was none—at least in regard to labor disputes. When Glassford proposed that the workers vote on whether they wanted to join a union, the department's counsel responded with concerns, caveats, and skepticism.[31] When he suggested mandating a minimum wage for the workers, the lawyer replied nervously that although his proposals seemed "sound," the general had "no authority to issue them in the form of mandatory standards."[32] Glassford did not press the issue; he said he understood "that the matter is under political fire and that I must use the greatest possible discretion."[33] At a time when conservatives like Herbert Hoover condemned the National Labor Board and National Recovery Administration for exercising tyrannical authority, the general proved remarkably reluctant to offend local officials and businessmen.

From the ACLU's perspective, Glassford's diffidence proved that he was under the control of the bosses. Infuriated by his failure to take bolder steps, the ACLU called on the Roosevelt administration to remove the general "because of his open hostility to the workers and his bitter public attacks on labor organizers." The civil liberties attorneys considered the general "dumb and acquiescent" in the face of the growers' depredations.[34]

For his part, Glassford believed that the ACLU was complicating his mission. "I am convinced," he wrote Abraham Wirin, the lawyer kidnapped by a mob back in January, "that the Imperial Valley situation cannot be corrected through sudden and drastic measures, but that the cure must be accomplished through evolution, in which education gradually will bring about a change in local public opinion." He was trying to encourage this evolution, he said, and he "would appreciate the cooperation (instead of the antagonism) of the A.C.L.U."[35]

Glassford repeatedly warned the farmworkers' supporters that growers needed to be persuaded, not confronted. As Glassford told a leftist maga-

zine on May 15, "I've got to be reasonable. I've got to show a certain parti-
sanship for the purpose of keeping my influence down here. The Growers
and Shippers control the banks, the press, the police, the American Legion—
everything. I can't aggravate them too much. I can't afford to, that's all, and
if I am to accomplish anything, I've got to lean over a little on their side."[36]
He also needed to be careful because the growers were spying on him. An
organization known as the "secret thirty" tapped the phone and telegraph
lines in the Valley.[37]

Yet over the course of his three months in the Valley, Glassford lost faith
in his ability to convince the growers to treat their workers better. In a private letter, he wrote the Department of Labor that he no longer had any
expectation that the farm owners would support reforms, despite his "very
strenuous effort to correct conditions through persuasion."[38] At best, he hoped
that the growers' recalcitrance would provoke the workers to strike again;
then the New Dealers could legitimately blame the growers for the strike;
"AND," he wrote in all caps for emphasis, "THE DEPARTMENT OF
LABOR WILL HAVE AMPLE JUSTIFICATION FOR AGAIN STEP-
PING INTO THE IMPERIAL VALLEY DIFFICULTIES."[39]

The general had come to believe that the growers were no better than
thugs, and he was itching for the chance to expose them. Later, his secretary
confided to an ACLU attorney that the general planned to criticize the employers long before he let on: "I knew all along how he WANTED to open up
and let loose," she wrote, "and yet for a time it looked very much as though
no opportunity to do so would present itself."[40]

Glassford's chance arrived in early June, in the form of another bloody
attack on a civil rights lawyer. On June 7, the ACLU sent attorney Ernest
Besig of Los Angeles to the Valley to monitor the trials of seven Mexican
workers who faced groundless charges of vagrancy. General Glassford, who
had encouraged the ACLU's investigation, met Besig at the train station and
accompanied him to the courthouse. The next day, he put Besig on the
Southern Pacific train to Los Angeles. Then he returned to his hotel, confident that he had protected the ACLU's man in the Valley—by getting him
out of the Valley.

But Besig was not yet safe: he needed to change trains in a small town
called Niland, about thirty miles from Brawley. As he sat on a bench in the
waiting room, a man approached him and suddenly, without warning,

punched him on the side of his head. As Besig tried to protect his face, the assailant continued to pummel him, shouting, "This will teach you to keep out of the Valley." Blood spurted from a deep gash in his forehead. Besig yelled for help. As people ran to his aid, his assailant shouted as he fled, "That's Besig from Los Angeles; he's a Red."[41]

Outraged at the "cowardly and despicable" assault, Glassford helped the attorney get medical attention in Niland, and then brought him to a hotel in Brawley. He smuggled him out through the basement and into an alley, where a car was waiting to drive him to Los Angeles. Glassford followed the car through the desert, with winds sweeping the highway and pounding the cars with sand, until he was sure the attorney made it out safely.[42]

The attack liberated Glassford. Freed from his obligation to kowtow to the growers, the general issued a series of statements denouncing them, each one more uncompromising than the last. On June 13, he declared that the Valley was "governed and controlled by a small group which, in advertising a war against Communism, is sponsoring terrorism, intimidation, and injustice."[43] The next day, he told the newspapers that the charges against strikers were "trumped up," that the growers never intended to improve the conditions of the workers, and that the employers, with their opposition to "law, order, sanity, and reform," had put themselves in the position of "being the most dangerous 'reds' ever to come to Imperial Valley."[44]

In a dramatic public meeting of the Imperial County board of supervisors, Glassford proclaimed that both the district attorney and a local judge were "crooks" who supported the corrupt local power structure. Judge Vaughn Thompson, ashen-faced and trembling with anger, rushed over to Glassford. "Did I hear you say you believed I was a crook?" he yelled. The general paused artfully and somewhat qualified his statement. "I said in my opinion you were a crook." The judge demanded an apology. "I have been in public service for twenty years and no man has ever branded me a crook." District attorney Elmer Heald also insisted that Glassford apologize. "I have been prosecuting attorney for eight years, and I don't believe that even my political enemies would say the things about me you have."[45]

The general conceded that "crook" might be the wrong word. "I admit that this was an unwarranted charge," he wrote in a public statement, "because never for a moment have I entertained the feeling that they would accept bribes or be otherwise financially dishonest." However, he insisted, "they are closely affiliated with the interests and policies of the growers and are so prejudiced against anyone alleged to have radical or communistic beliefs that they are incapable of granting full constitutional rights to such persons in a court of justice."[46]

Glassford decided that "tool" was a better word than "crook" for describing the local officials. In a formal report to the Imperial board of supervisors at the end of the month, he condemned the Valley's rulers as tyrants who manufactured a Red Scare to keep their profits high while their workers lived in "poverty and squalor":

> After more than two months of observation and investigation in Imperial Valley, it is my conviction that a group of growers have exploited a communist hysteria for advancement of their own interests: that they have welcomed labor agitation which they could brand as "red" as a means of sustaining supremacy by mob rule, thereby preserving what is so essential to their profit, cheap labor; that they have succeeded in drawing into their conspiracy certain county officials who have become the principal tools of their machine.

Glassford recommended a state-supervised grand jury investigation of the "organized campaign of terrorism and intimidation" in the Valley.[47] (He did not, notably, recommend a *federal* investigation of the crimes county officials committed, and for this the Department of Labor was grateful.)[48] He suggested that the federal government should try to regulate the wages and working conditions of vegetable pickers, and hoped it would eventually establish a non-Communist union for the workers.

The large growers and their supporters were furious at the general's "strange volte-face."[49] The enraged editorial board of the *Los Angeles Times* declared that Glassford's report and the New Deal's labor policies showed Franklin Roosevelt to be more of a Communist-coddler than Joseph Stalin, because "in fact Communists in Russia are under the iron heel of Stalin and disturbers are sent before a firing squad."[50]

Some growers wished for firing squads or lynching parties in California. Like Creel, Glassford received threats on his life. A county official told him that he could have the general killed for as little as $50.[51] Imperial Valley officials had begun the year by arresting New Deal investigators and threatening them with assault. Now they had progressed to death threats.

The civil libertarians were thrilled that Glassford had finally taken a stand against lawlessness in the Valley. Glassford's report "sounds like a statement from the American Civil Liberties Union," the ACLU declared in its internal newsletter.[52] One ACLU attorney wrote Glassford tartly that he wished Glassford had made such a statement in April, "when the facts on which it is based were as true and obvious as they are today." But it was better late than never, and they were proud to welcome Glassford to the cause.[53] The ACLU begged the New Dealers in Washington to support the general and take a stand against disorder in the Valley. Abraham Wirin wired the Department of Labor: "Please please back up Glassford now that he shows signs of moving in the right direction."[54]

In the end, though, the rest of the Roosevelt administration did not support Glassford. In a marked difference from their attitude during the cotton strike, the other New Deal agencies refused to snatch away federal carrots in order to persuade the growers to stop wielding their sticks. As the general finished his report, the Public Works Administration pledged $27 million of taxpayers' money for an eighty-mile-long canal—the longest irrigation canal in the world—to bring water to Imperial growers.[55] The next month, as the Colorado basin suffered from a drought, the federal government trucked in tens of thousands of gallons of water to the landowners who had just been denounced by its special investigator.[56]

To the ACLU, it was patently ridiculous that the federal government would dispense aid to the lawless rulers of the Valley. Clinton Taft, the ACLU's national secretary, told Washington to stop sending water and building canals until the local officials respected the Constitution.[57] The growers and their allies were livid, with the *Imperial Valley Press* proclaiming Taft's statement to be evidence of mental illness. "Fortunately," the paper's editors concluded, "there is a responsible government in Washington, not swayed by the wild and depraved rantings of fanatics with sawdust where their brains should be."[58]

In the minds of Imperial officials, the "responsible government" in Washington included the Department of Agriculture, which provided subsidies and drought relief despite ACLU protests, and the PWA, which soon began work on the new canal. It did not include the labor investigators who supported striking farmworkers or the relief administrators who fed them.

Retreat

His life threatened, his report published, his mission accomplished, General Glassford decided he would return home to Arizona—"just as soon," he told the Department of Labor, "as this withdrawal can be made without the accusation of fear."[59] In a private letter to Ernest Besig, the lawyer whose attack had prompted his blast against the growers, Glassford was more candid. "Can't stand it here much longer," he wrote. "I do not want to return to Imperial Valley unless it is absolutely necessary."[60] Besig responded that he understood Glassford's desire to flee. The Imperial Valley atmosphere, he wrote, "is so heavy and oppressive with intrigue, hatred and vindictiveness that it nauseates a person." Driving out of the valley, Besig said, was like escaping from prison.[61]

Glassford noted that most of the county officials who supported the growers were Republicans, and suggested that only a Democratic victory in local elections would bring true change to Imperial. "I do not believe," he wrote his supervisors in Washington, "there can be any permanent accomplishment toward righting the wrongs of Imperial Valley without the force of political power." However, he thought it was inappropriate for him as a federal official to endorse local candidates for office. "This is in the hands of the people," he wrote, "and I believe that I have paved the way for the many right-minded citizens of the Valley to themselves correct the existing evils."[62]

And so, after concluding that the growers did not pay a living wage, after investigating the violence and determining that the employers were at fault, after accusing local government officials of ignoring the Constitution and depriving workers of their civil rights, General Glassford simply left. He excoriated the growers, proclaimed himself unafraid of the many death threats he received, and retreated to his horse farm in Arizona. Imperial remained in the hands of the same people, growers and their allies who were free to continue their previous policies—now without even an outside observer. And the New Dealers in Washington let him leave—indeed, *urged* him to leave—without making any substantive changes.

Overall, the general was pleased with his investigation. "This has been one of the most interesting experiences of my life—a veritable education— and I am very grateful for the opportunity to be of service," he wrote the

Department of Labor. "I trust that my efforts here will bring credit to the Administration."[63]

Secretary Perkins agreed that Glassford's efforts reflected well on the administration. He did a "perfect job," she said, and when he left the Valley, "everything was working beautifully." Twenty years later, she remembered the episode with nostalgia and pride, describing how the strapping, nononsense general forced the unruly children to behave and required the bosses to pay a minimum wage and provide clean drinking water to the workers.[64]

The secretary's memory was faulty. In fact, Glassford did not succeed in getting the growers to raise wages or improve living or working conditions for the pickers. His suggested reforms—government regulations, a government-sponsored union—did not come to pass. There was no political or economic transformation of Imperial County. Indeed, three decades later, power and money in the Valley were even more unequally distributed than during the Great Depression.[65] The New Dealers had gestured toward helping the workers in Imperial, but once they saw how little they could accomplish, and how much those meager accomplishments would cost them, they quit. In the end, although the general took a more critical and emphatic stance against the growers than had George Creel during the cotton strike, he accomplished even less than the former public relations agent.

In part, the general's mission failed because Imperial Valley was more remote than San Joaquin Valley. The county's isolation meant that the growers could get away with more violence than would have been possible, or politically viable, in more accessible regions. The anti–New Dealers discovered that in environments where there was no national media presence, where there were few reporters and observers from the cities, they could be as inflexible, and as brutal, as they liked.

More important, though, the Imperial Valley mediation failed because the growers used the months between the two strikes to devise more sophisticated strategies for opposing the New Dealers' limited mediation attempts. Frustrated and angry after the cotton strike, the wealthiest agricultural and industrial interests in the western United States decided that the federal government was no longer their ally in smashing unionism among the working class. Their horror of government-aided unionization catalyzed their movement—and helped them prepare for the future.

In Imperial Valley, the growers responded to workers' organization with collective action of their own. They discovered the value of mobilizing ordinary citizens with cultural issues—and of claiming links between the moderate left and the far left. They tested these techniques in this remote outpost of the far West, but they would find that they worked equally well in the rest of the state—and, indeed, the nation.

Their next step was to gather more information on the union activists who had given them so much trouble. The growers wanted to set up a system to monitor and intimidate the union organizers—and ideally, to find evidence against them that would lock them up for years. Luckily for the employers, one of the most important spies in U.S. military history was eager to help.

7

SEEING RED

Late in April 1934, two men drove up from Oakland to attend the second annual convention of the Cannery and Agricultural Workers Industrial Union in downtown Sacramento. We know quite a bit about one of the men. His name was Wallace Walsh, he took photos for a Communist newspaper, he drove a car with the license plate number 7K9700, and he owned a telephone with the number Trinidad 4946 or possibly 4649. We know little about his companion except that he was very active in several Communist-affiliated groups—and that he took very good notes.

We know this because the second man, identified only as R-384 in his reports, had additional duties besides those required for his official role as a delegate to the union convention. He wrote down the names, physical descriptions, and car license plate numbers of almost everyone he met. He took copious notes on the speeches, resolutions, debates, and financial reports at the convention. He recorded the speakers' accounts of their triumphs, and their warnings about provocateurs and "stool pigeons."

Then he typed up his many pages of notes and sent them down to be indexed, filed, and disseminated by his boss, Ralph Van Deman, a retired U.S. Army general known as the "father of military intelligence," who ran a statewide anticommunist and antiunion surveillance network out of San Diego. R-384, like an unknown number of others in the CAWIU and Communist-affiliated groups in 1934, was exactly the kind of "stoolie" the other delegates worried about: an agent paid to infiltrate their meetings and report on their activities—and perhaps to goad them into breaking the law so police could arrest them.[1]

General Van Deman controlled the most extensive anticommunist espionage network in California, but his was not the only one. The Los Angeles Police Department fielded a "red squad" to infiltrate and intimidate radical groups, as did other law enforcement agencies throughout the state. Employers' groups, most notably the Associated Farmers, also paid spies and informants to insinuate themselves into the CAWIU and other allegedly subversive organizations. Some of these private spy efforts dated back to the First Red Scare of 1919; others started after Roosevelt's election to the presidency and ramped up during the strike wave of 1933 and 1934.

The antilabor spy networks were key components of the employers' response to labor unrest during these years. As the Associated Farmers spread pro-grower and antilabor propaganda, the group also coordinated employers' efforts to monitor and suppress union organization and political dissent. The two approaches—propaganda and surveillance—complemented one another because the growers needed to mobilize public support for their antiunion campaign. As in the cotton and vegetable strikes, their attacks on labor easily became attacks on the New Deal.

The employers' surveillance operations reached their peak in the bloody summer of 1934. When a labor dispute in the Bay Area turned into a citywide uprising, employers already had informants in place to help them monitor and control the workers. Afterward, they were ready to take care of the radicals once and for all.

The File Cabinets of General Van Deman

A tall, lean man whose creased face and piercing gaze reminded people of Abraham Lincoln, General Ralph Van Deman was a legendary figure in U.S. espionage history. An Ohio native and Harvard graduate, Van Deman (pronounced "Van Demon") joined the Army as a surgeon, but it was in imperial military intelligence that he found his calling. In the Philippines in 1899, in charge of the Division of Military Information in the midst of a bloody war against insurgents, Van Deman invented new procedures for cataloging and indexing information on the enemy, and then using the telegraph to send this intelligence quickly to commanders on the battle-field. In this colonial outpost, he revolutionized the Army's intelligence procedures and expectations.[2]

Returning to the United States, Van Deman lobbied to transfer the lessons of empire to the war on subversives at home despite the strong opposition of some of his superiors. When Van Deman proposed the creation of a mammoth military spying effort, the Army chief of staff condemned the proposal. "I think this would be intolerable to our people," General Hugh L. Scott wrote.[3] But Van Deman finally succeeded in convincing Secretary of War Newton Baker to establish the division anyway as the United States entered World War I in 1917. Van Deman became the head of the Army's first stand-alone Military Intelligence Division, or MID.

Van Deman's MID agents searched for enemies abroad and at home. Working with a network of volunteers in patriotic organizations like the American Protective League, the government men sniffed out their fellow citizens who opposed the war, including anarchists, pacifists, socialists, African Americans, East Indians, and Irish Americans. The list of dissidents and potential traitors stretched to include almost everyone who was not a native-born Protestant American of Northern European ancestry, as well as some who were.[4]

All signs of unrest bothered Van Deman, but he was especially upset by challenges to racial segregation—protests, antilynching rallies, and even interracial dating. In his file labeled "Negro Subversion," he reported "several incidents of where [sic] colored men had attempted to make appointments with white women." At first he blamed the Germans for this "general unrest among the colored people." But soon he would fasten on a new and craftier enemy.[5]

In the Philippines and again in Washington, Van Deman learned lessons that would shape his attitudes toward political radicals and labor organizers. He thought that subversives lurked everywhere, and one could identify them by their foreign names, alien ideologies, or dark skins. The best way to anticipate their plots was to spy on them, preferably with the help of enthusiastic volunteers. Then he would collate, index, cross-reference, and disseminate the intelligence.

The general hoped to continue to expand his domestic spying program after the war, but his supervisors apparently disapproved of his bureaucratic ambitions. And so in 1918 Secretary of War Baker replaced Van Deman as MID chief and ordered him to tour European intelligence bureaus.[6]

During his time in Europe, Van Deman came to believe that he had been wrong to see the Germans as the primary foe of America and its values. Instead, a far more fearsome enemy menaced the world: international Bolshevism, directed and bankrolled by Moscow. He wrote a feverish letter to the new head of MID listing all of the countries about to succumb to revolution: "Italy . . . is ready to blow up; Austria-Hungary has practically gone to pieces now; Belgium appears to have been taken over; the conditions in both France and Poland are most dangerous; Holland is honeycombed" with traitors. He concluded that the world was entering a period of "even greater danger" than during the war itself.[7]

Officials in Washington ignored Van Deman's warnings, and he found himself exiled to postings in Asia and then in faraway California. In 1929, Van Deman, now holding the rank of major general, completed his final tour of duty and retired from the Army in San Diego. There, the general discovered that even—perhaps especially—in the land of sunshine, the enemy was preparing for battle. And as before, Americans needed to expose their plots.

In his Spanish-style ranch home on Curlew Street, in the leafy, upscale Bankers Hill neighborhood overlooking Mission Bay, the general read the newspapers with increasing anxiety. In 1932, with Franklin Roosevelt's election to the presidency, Van Deman became concerned that the new administration would not monitor Communist activity with proper vigor. He decided to expand a statewide, public-private anticommunist surveillance network he had created in retirement.

The general began by alerting his friends in military intelligence and local law enforcement to his plans and asking them to send him reports of radical activity in their areas. They responded with enthusiasm. During the cotton strike and Imperial Valley disputes, local sheriffs sent him long lists of union organizers and members, complete with their birth dates and physical descriptions. As the strike wave continued, the general's files expanded to include reports from the San Diego school district, sheriff and police departments throughout California, the state department of criminal identification, the U.S. Post Office, the Border Patrol, the Department of Labor, the Coast Guard, and army and naval intelligence.[8] Van Deman worked with legislative anticommunist committees once they were established: the House

Un-American Activities Committee (HUAC) in 1938 and the California legislature's version of HUAC in 1940.[9] He also shared his information with federal security agencies, including the Federal Bureau of Investigation.[10]

Like many conservatives, Van Deman supported one kind of expansion of federal power while opposing another. Stronger security agencies benefited the nation; stronger labor agencies harmed the economy and undermined business owners' rights. This contradiction would characterize modern conservatism, and it originated in California's farmworker strikes.

Southern California provided fertile soil for Van Deman's fears to take root and grow. His superiors in Washington had dismissed his warnings of incipient revolution. But in California, the Red Scare had begun before the World War and the Bolshevik Revolution with the bombing of the *Los Angeles Times* building in 1910. It had continued with the Preparedness Day attack in San Francisco in 1916 and escalated from there.

Van Deman and his supporters believed that the international Red conspiracy had specifically targeted California. According to Los Angeles Police Chief James Davis, who worked closely with Van Deman, the Communists chose the state "because it is a rich agricultural center and has a great diversity of products; because it produces an abundance of oil; because it has three of the five major ports on the Pacific Coast, which are important points of egress for the flow of commerce into the Orient, the Far East, South America, and Australia." Davis concluded that California provided "an opportunity for agitational activity which is highly gratifying to the Communist agents."[11] Here, as Californians dozed in the sunshine, oblivious to the traitors among them, revolutionaries could seize control of food production and shipping lanes and bring the global economy to its knees.

Besides drawing from a pool of local, state, and federal agents, the general also recruited and managed spies from private groups, especially business organizations and patriotic clubs. Industrial espionage was an increasingly common business practice in the mid-1930s, as employers responded to workers' attempts to form unions. The largest railroad, automobile, and steel corporations hired detective agencies to infiltrate their workplaces and spy on union organization efforts. The Pinkerton detective agency alone employed twelve hundred undercover agents in industry from 1933 to 1935, and it had many competitors.[12] In California, large corporations and small business associations hired spies.[13]

The reports by these spies were not entirely reliable. The *Sacramento Bee's* agent in the CAWIU, for example, missed the joke when he overheard Communists laughing about a Nazi group called the Silver Shirts and calling it a very cleverly disguised Red front. "From the conversation informant gathered that this organization is fostered by the Communist Party. The officials in it are Communists. . . . [They] handle a lot of Communist propaganda," he reported earnestly, apparently unfamiliar with sarcasm as a form of humor.[14] But these agents, or "stool pigeons" and "rats," as the union members called them, were not hired because they were astute observers of the political environment of the 1930s; they were paid to tell their employers where labor organizers planned to go, and when. And later, these agents would provide crucial (if erroneous) testimony during criminal trials.

The general developed a network of agents, identified only by their code numbers. Soon, he received daily batches of envelopes bursting with informants' memos, as well as the flyers and clippings they collected and the photos they took. He and his wife, childless and lonely in retirement, diligently filed these documents in cabinets throughout their home. The Army, whose leaders had overcome their earlier aversion to domestic spying, supported his efforts by giving him filing cabinets and assigning two civilian employees to help him.[15]

The surviving Van Deman files show that his spies had a capacious definition of "subversive." They began by infiltrating official Communist groups: the CPUSA itself, the Young Communist League, and the CAWIU. They moved on to spy on other groups on the left, including the National Student League, the American Youth Congress, the American League against War and Fascism, and the Women's International League for Peace and Freedom. Soon they progressed to spying on non-Communist labor, Social Gospel, or civil libertarian groups, such as the American Federation of Labor, the Young Men's Christian Association, the Young Women's Christian Association, and the American Civil Liberties Union.

Working ten hours a day, indexing, filing, and corresponding with informants he had recruited, Van Deman obsessively amassed a mountain of information. In 1935, he reported modestly to his friends in military intelligence that he had accumulated "rather extensive records covering both [radical] organizations and personnel throughout the country."[16] By the time of his death in 1952, he had assembled files on more than 125,000 allegedly subversive individuals and groups. His home contained a colossal archive of American radical activism.[17]

Van Deman also helped add to the surveillance files of various anticommunist groups, including the American Legion, the Industrial Association in San Francisco, and the Better America Federation in Los Angeles. This last group reported in confidential documents that it had succeeded in compiling *2 million* index cards on subversive individuals and groups ("the enemies of our country").[18]

The Associated Farmers had a more selective filing system. At its offices in the financial district in San Francisco and the heart of downtown Los Angeles, the group's paid staff members created eight hundred index cards that identified "known radicals, fanatics and Communist sympathizers." That last category was elastic—it included, for example, professors and teachers "with radical tendencies or affiliations." The organization also put together a list of all "subversive" groups in the state, naming their leaders and meeting places and activities, and collected a library of Communist literature. Drawing on the resources of the State Bureau of Criminal Identification, the Los Angeles Police Department, the Los Angeles Sheriff's Office, and other local law enforcement agencies, the staff also assembled a rogues' gallery of 250 photographs of California Communists, annotated with their biographies and physical descriptions. As the executive secretary explained to the board of directors, "This 'gallery' should be invaluable in identifying, particularly in agricultural districts, agitators with Communistic connections."[19]

Once they had set up their surveillance networks and publicity campaigns, the employers began to use them in specific strikes. The CAWIU organized several walkouts in the winter and spring of 1934, some involving thousands of workers. Most succeeded in helping the workers win a small raise, often a few cents an hour.[20] But in June, Caroline Decker and other CAWIU leaders ran into trouble when they decided to start a strike in the apricot orchards east of San Francisco in Contra Costa County, which were dominated by three large corporate growers. This time the farm owners were ready.

Back in March, months before harvest time for stone fruit, the California state chamber of commerce arranged a secret meeting for growers, shippers, and businessmen in Contra Costa to "consider the possibilities of renewed labor agitation in the County during the coming season, and to anticipate what preparation should be made to forestall any such difficulty."[21] When the CAWIU called the strike in early June, the growers put their plans into effect.

The growers' campaign in the apricot strike proceeded on two fronts: intimidation and propaganda. The sheriff worked with the California Highway Patrol and a vigilance committee to arrest the picketers en masse and herd them into a corral in a rail yard, where thirteen CAWIU leaders were arrested for vagrancy and the remaining workers were "deported" to the next county. (Decker, however, slipped away before the arrests.)

As the sheriff and vigilantes cooperated to control the strikers, the Associated Farmers worked to shape media coverage of the strike. The group stationed a public relations specialist at the strike area who "assisted the local newspapers and the local correspondents in preparing newspaper copy." The publicists wanted to make sure that these stories "tied in conclusively the Communist party to the agitation."[22] California employers consistently found that they won more support from the public if they branded the labor disputes as Communist agitation.

At the same time, the growers started to work with a powerful new ally in Sacramento. Because the federal government refused to actively support their strikebreaking efforts, the growers wanted to be sure that they controlled the state government. And the new governor seemed keen to help agribusiness—at least as long as agribusiness was willing to help him.

Old Baldy

During the Contra Costa apricot strike, Governor Rolph finally succumbed to his many ailments—strokes, heart attacks, high blood pressure, lung congestion, kidney problems, and physical exhaustion among them. He died on June 2. His lieutenant governor and successor, Frank Merriam, found himself in charge of a state careening toward a massive confrontation between capital and labor.

Although a member of the same Republican Party as Governor Rolph, "Old Baldy" Merriam (as his opponents called him) presented a stark contrast to Sunny Jim—as dour as Rolph had been genial. Born on an Iowa farm some sixty-eight years earlier, Merriam worked his way to the top along several different career paths: from school principal to school superintendent, from newspaper editor to owner and publisher, from salesman to bank president, and ultimately from state legislator to governor.[23] In the process, he became convinced of the inherent fairness of the capitalist system, which, he thought, always rewarded those who worked hard, invested wisely, and foreswore the temptations of the flesh that had given so much pleasure to his predecessor in the governor's office.

Merriam was as pro-business as any governor in the country at the time. On the far right of his party, he supported massive government spending cuts and opposed the end of Prohibition. "By friend and foe alike," wrote journalist Franklin Hichborn, "he was regarded as a reactionary."[24] But as soon as he became governor in early June, Merriam briefly threw a scare into the large apricot growers when he seemed to signal that he might be more sympathetic to the strikers than Rolph had been. On June 8, just six days after taking office, he met with a delegation of workers from the Contra Costa strike and condemned the local authorities' use of vigilantes to help them corral and deport the strike leaders. "I have heard your case," he told the workers. "I do not endorse violation of the law by anyone, be it vigilante committees or groups of farmers who may be without legal authorization to enforce the law."[25]

The alarmed growers asked Merriam to send some of his advisers to the strike so that he could see it from the employers' point of view. The aides traveled to Brentwood, where publicists took them on tours of the orchards.

Merriam's aides reported back to the governor that the growers were right: the walkout was not really a strike, but a dress rehearsal for the revolution. Merriam responded by issuing a tough statement against the union organizers. They were, he said, "public enemies" whose "alien creed of violence and sabotage strikes venomously at the heart of constitutional democracy." The state government "must and will offer uncompromising resistance" to these alien agitators, he pledged.[26]

Privately, the Associated Farmers' executive secretary took credit for the governor's apparent reversal. "It is significant that immediately following receipt" of the reports from his observers at the apricot strike that the governor "defined his position and by this action strengthened the position of the California farmer," he wrote.[27] The staff members believed that their clever public relations techniques were responsible for Merriam's conversion.

Perhaps. But it is also possible that the governor had outfoxed them—that he deliberately fudged his position on the farmworkers' strikes until he was certain that the growers would contribute generously to his campaign for the Republican nomination for governor. Merriam's critics would accuse him of this type of mercenary calculation throughout his governorship.[28]

Cheered by the governor's support, the Associated Farmers staff arranged for dozens of "commendatory letters and wires of appreciation" to be sent to the governor lauding his courageous stand for "Americanism." In one telegram, broker Dean Witter congratulated Merriam for issuing "one of the most constructive and patriotic declarations made in the history of this State."

The pro-grower *Los Angeles Times* reported that the telegrams proved that Merriam had "struck a popular chord with the masses of Californians when he served notice to all alien agitators of his determined stand."[29] The notes in this "popular chord" were not necessarily false, but they were orchestrated by the state's wealthiest and most powerful men.

Later, after the invention of synthetic grass, political observers would call this technique "Astroturf." President Richard Nixon would perfect the tactic, but it had its origins in the grower campaign against the unions.[30] The growers had obtained Merriam's support, solicited telegrams hailing that support, and then provided positive press coverage of the whole affair.

The employers learned other important lessons from the apricot strike. Although it had been limited to one region and one type of worker, the dispute had given them the opportunity to improve the tactics they would use in future strikes: shaping media coverage and public opinion, working with allies in local law enforcement and Sacramento, and deploying vigilantes when necessary. They would use these techniques the next month when they confronted a much more frightening prospect.

The Siege of San Francisco

The biggest general strike in American history began with a dispute over power on the waterfront. In the spring of 1934, longshoremen on the West Coast organized to demand better wages and conditions—and, even more important, control of the hiring halls on the docks. The laborers despised the corrupt employment system, in which workers were forced to pay bribes to get jobs. Led by Australian radical Harry Bridges, the rank-and-file dock-workers decided to fight for their rights under the National Industrial Recovery Act and renew their decades-long struggle to put the unions, rather than the employers, in charge of the hiring process.[31]

Federal officials, including George Creel, tried to mediate a solution, but neither side wanted to compromise. Creel believed that the employers were actually baiting the workers and hoping for a strike. They stood to lose millions of dollars, but they would be "amply compensated" for this loss over the long term if they could use the strike to destroy the union.[32] When the two sides refused to budge on the key issue of control of the hiring hall, long-shoremen in every port on the Pacific Coast, for the two thousand miles of coastline from San Diego to Seattle, walked off the job.

In San Francisco, the employers tried to keep the port open with non-union labor. They recruited several hundred strikebreakers and housed them on ships floating offshore. But their gambit failed when the Teamsters refused to transport the cargo that strikebreakers had unloaded.

Soon, other maritime unions joined the longshoremen on the picket lines. Ships clogged the harbor, unable to receive or discharge their cargo. Trade—and the transportation of California fruits and vegetables around the world—came to a halt.

San Francisco employers described the maritime strike in apocalyptic terms. This was not just a conflict between employers and employees; it was a war between "American principles and un-American radicalism," said the leaders of the San Francisco Chamber of Commerce.[33] Given its significance, business leaders voted to turn control of employers' response to the strike to the Industrial Association of San Francisco, which represented the wealthiest financial and industrial interests of the city.

On July 5, a day that became known as "Bloody Thursday," the Industrial Association tried to open the San Francisco port by force, with strikebreakers driving trucks under the protection of city police. When the replacement workers started to drive from the waterfront to inland warehouses, pickets surged forward, and the cops attacked the strikers. Amid a blinding fog of tear gas, under a hailstorm of bricks and rocks, police outfitted with gas masks lunged at the strikers with batons flailing and guns blazing. They shot two workers to death, and hundreds more were gassed, beaten, and wounded by gunfire.

Reporters struggled to find the best war analogy to describe the scene on the docks. It was the return of "the days of 1917 and '18"; or worse, it was "Gettysburg in miniature," a new civil war in an industrialized, urban landscape, with towering warehouses, rather than the mountains of Pennsylvania, in the background.[34] One of the wounded was Joe Rosenthal, photographer for the *San Francisco News*, who recovered and went on to take the famous picture of Marines raising the American flag over Iwo Jima during World War II. The maritime strike was as dangerous as the battle of Iwo Jima, he later said.[35]

In response to the violence on Bloody Thursday, Governor Merriam sent in National Guard troops to restore order and "protect state property." Two thousand soldiers—outfitted in steel helmets and glistening bayonets, and "armed to the teeth," the newspapers said—marched onto the wharves.[36] Army trucks mounted with machine guns patrolled the waterfront, their gun barrels swiveling and searching for targets. Soldiers huddled on the rooftops of buildings on the Embarcadero, peering through field glasses and aiming their rifles at the enemy—other Americans. San Francisco was under military occupation.[37]

The next day, Merriam sent 2,600 more soldiers and expanded their orders to include guarding the corridors from the coast to interior warehouses and occupying the Oakland waterfront as well. Merriam's political opponents claimed that the governor made a deal with the Industrial Association to send troops in return for tens of thousands of dollars in contributions to his reelection campaign. This allegation was never proved, however.[38]

The governor tried to put down the unions with brute force, but tens of thousands of workers in San Francisco were determined not to let him win. Infuriated by what they saw as the Guard invasion of their city, union after union voted to go out on strike: butchers, laundry workers, auto mechanics, engineers, carpenters, painters, textile workers, actors, firefighters, electrical workers, ferry boat drivers, bartenders, bakers, barbers, and, most crucially, the Teamsters—180 unions in all voted to walk out to protest "the indiscriminate shooting down of strikers and innocent bystanders."[39]

San Francisco's unions voted to close the city with a general strike, only the second such strike—after Seattle's in 1919—in American history. Gas stations, schools, grocery stores, and most restaurants shut their doors. For four days, the city became a ghost town, with few cars, trolleys, or trucks on

National Guard troops in San Francisco during the general strike, July 17, 1934.
San Francisco History Center, San Francisco Public Library.

the streets. Soldiers with bayonets guarded the waterfront, while pickets nervously stood their ground at ominously vacant intersections. Milk and food
deliveries continued, however—the labor council leadership prohibited the
grocery deliverymen from joining the strike—and the phones, lights, and
water taps worked throughout the crisis.

Most California newspapers, which kept publishing thanks to a well-
timed raise to their typesetters, portrayed the strike as the first step toward
a Russian-directed revolution that would sweep the country and wreck the
government, churches, and families. The coverage of five of the six major
Bay Area papers was coordinated by John Francis Neylan, William Randolph
Hearst's general counsel, who huddled in the Palace Hotel with other publishing barons to plot a common strategy. Earlier, after Bloody Thursday, the
Associated Farmers' publicists had expressed dismay that some reporters were
calling the workers "strikers" instead of "Communists." ("It's no secret, why

stop the fine public reaction the repeated word, Communist, brings," one staff member wrote to another.)[40] Neylan made sure that the newspapers spoke with a unified voice during the general strike.[41]

The *San Francisco Chronicle* warned its readers that an army of Communists would soon march down from Washington State to San Francisco, "ready to add terrorism to the strike chaos." In addition, "flying squadrons" of Communists planned to blow up railroads and highways as they made the Bay Area a "focal point in the red struggle for revolution and control of government."[42] (In a front-page editorial, the *Chronicle*, with apparently unintended irony, advised its readers to refrain from spreading "unfounded and unauthorized reports and irresponsible rumors" that came from any source except the "responsible and trained press.")[43] Reading the coverage of the general strike, humorist Will Rogers wryly noted, "I hope we never live to see the day when a thing is as bad as some of our newspapers make it."[44]

To be sure, Communists participated in the strike. Radical leader Harry Bridges was indeed, as the U.S. government claimed, a card-carrying Communist; and during the strike, Sam Darcy and other Communist Party leaders hid in the city and tried to direct strategy. At one point, Ella Winter drove from Carmel to San Francisco to help the Communist cause. When she tried to contact Darcy, she received instructions to go to a specific street corner and wait. At the appointed time and place, a car pulled up in front of her—itself an alarming circumstance, as no one else was out driving at the time. "Get in, quick," she heard a voice inside say. When she jumped in the car, she was astonished to find Darcy in the driver's seat. He took her to a deserted spot near the Cliff House, where she fumbled in her purse to pull out the $150 she'd received from her Hollywood friend. It wasn't Moscow gold; it was paper money withdrawn from a California bank, and precious little of it. The Communists were grateful in any event, and pledged to use the money to print more leaflets.[45]

San Francisco's civic and business leaders were convinced that these scattered radicals with their small wads of cash could spark a nationwide revolt. Western public officials urged President Roosevelt to recognize that America's Bolshevik revolution had begun. California senator Hiram Johnson demanded that national officials wake up to the danger: "Here is revolution not only in the making but with the initial actuality."[46] The governor of Oregon asked the president, who was in the middle of the Pacific on his way to a

Hawaiian vacation, to come to California with the Navy to stop the insurrection, "WHICH IF NOT CHECKED WILL DEVELOP INTO CIVIL WAR."[47]

Roosevelt's advisers dismissed these concerns as the hyperbolic reports of self-interested businessmen. Secretary of Labor Frances Perkins told the president that there was no danger of revolution, and in fact many of the unions participating in the strike were actually quite conservative.[48] Perkins scoffed at businessmen's charge that the strikers endangered "sacred institutions and traditions"; "the only 'sacred traditions' which the strike leaders sought to destroy were low wages and graft-ridden hiring halls," she told him.[49] Perkins and adviser Louis Howe urged the president to remain calm and not to cut short his vacation, because, as Howe telegraphed him, such a move might "start the very panic it is necessary to avoid."[50]

President Roosevelt agreed and decided to continue to press for mediation, not invasion. People "lost their heads" during the general strike, he remembered later, and "demanded that I sail into San Francisco Bay, all flags flying and guns double shotted, and end the strike. They went completely off the handle."[51]

The president's calm approach saw the strike to a swift and easy settlement. After four days, the union leadership declared the strike over and agreed to accept federal government arbitration. Over the long term, the settlement of the San Francisco general strike became an object lesson in the New Deal's recovery strategy. The longshoremen's union won its most important goal: a union-controlled hiring hall. As highly paid blue-collar workers, longshoremen gradually moved into the middle class, and, just as the New Dealers had predicted, became satisfied participants in the capitalist system. They wanted higher wages, not a Communist takeover. Bridges, the Australian Communist who led the strike and fought several U.S. government attempts to deport him, became a proud Republican and supporter of Richard Nixon by the 1960s. The outcome of the general strike eventually created many contented capitalists.

But that was not the case in the short term. Although the National Guard marched out of the city and the tear gas wafted away on ocean breezes, anticommunist panic did not dissipate so quickly. During the strike, newspapers had been screaming that a Communist plot menaced the West. Now that the strike was over, American legionnaires and members of other patriotic groups began to attack the alleged masterminds of the plot. Vigilantes up and down the West Coast turned with fury on the men and women whom they held responsible for the breakdown of their social order.

White Terror

Unhinged by the general strike, mobs formed in Seattle, Portland, Oakland, Richmond, Alameda, Stockton, and San Jose, among other cities. They ransacked Communist Party buildings, smashed furniture, burned books, and beat alleged subversives. Hayward vigilantes built a public scaffold with a noose as a warning to Reds. In Berkeley, a posse of three hundred surged through the city, hurling bricks through the windows of homes of suspected Communists. The bricks had a warning wrapped around them: "This citizens' committee is aware that you are affiliated with Communists, Bolsheviks, or other government-destroying groups. Leave here immediately or face drastic measures."[52]

Although the vigilante attacks appeared to be spontaneous outbreaks of mass hysteria, they were often encouraged and protected by the employers' groups, as well as by local, state, and national officials. The Associated Farmers funded and organized some of the mobs, and county sheriffs and highway patrol officers stood by while vigilantes assaulted, kidnapped, and terrorized their victims. At the height of the violence in San Francisco, the National Guard set up a machine gun nest to protect the crowds who were looting the meeting places of radicals. The newspapers were mostly amused by the vigilante justice: "REDS TURN BLACK AND BLUE," read one photo caption in the *San Francisco Chronicle*.[53]

One hundred and twenty-five miles down the coast, the Monterey peninsula "began to take on the color and tone of Hitler's Germany," according to Langston Hughes. When the members of Carmel's John Reed Club called an emergency meeting to protest the vigilante attacks up north, they heard rumors that the town's "patriotic citizens" would not allow the meeting to take place.

That night, Hughes arrived at the local meeting hall to discover the street blocked with cars, police headlights illuminating the doorway, and the chief of police standing outside. Inside the hall, anticommunist activists, organized by a new chapter of the American Legion, sat grimly among the

The headquarters of the West Coast Communist newspaper after a vigilante raid in July 1934. San Francisco History Center, San Francisco Public Library.

radicals and took notes on who attended and what was said. Hughes was acutely aware that he was the only black person in the crowd.

The next day, some three hundred vigilantes drilled on the village green to prepare for a fight against the twenty John Reed Club members. The radicals received anonymous letters and open, verbal threats of violence. Carmel "bubbled with a kind of hysteria," Hughes wrote.

The conservatives, led by the wealthy capitalists who owned summer homes in nearby Pebble Beach, mobilized the ordinary middle-class and working-class Carmelites by emphasizing the Communist threat to white supremacy. Hughes heard that he was "a bad influence on the Negroes of the town" and that he "aspired to social equality with whites." People said they had seen him walking with white women on the beach and had heard him calling them by their first names.

Then one day he read an editorial against him in the Carmel *Sun* that terrified him. With the generous use of scare quotes, the editor suggested that Hughes did not know his place:

> Langston Hughes has been a very "distinguished" guest in Carmel—not that the town is proud of it. He has been the guest of "honor" at parties. Whites were invited—a "select" few—to bask in his wisdom. White girls have ridden down the street with him, have walked with him, smiling into his face.

This kind of fraternization was "odorous," the *Sun* wrote in another editorial, and not at all American. If he wanted to socialize with white girls, he should move to Russia.

As the threats escalated, Hughes worried that he was in physical danger. He knew that black men accused of seducing white women sometimes got lynched. He abruptly left town and went to visit a friend in Reno. The next month, he returned to Carmel to gather his things, but only for a brief time. The California Red Scare convinced him it was time to return to the safer environs of Harlem.[54]

Lincoln Steffens, confined to his bedroom and unable to flee, angrily warned leaders in Washington about the dangers of extremism on the coast. "There is hysteria here, but the terror is white, not red," he wrote in a public letter to Frances Perkins. "Business men are doing in this Labor struggle what they would have liked to do against the old graft prosecution and other political reform movements, yours included; they are sicking [sic] on the mob, which, mark you well, is all theirs."[55]

Many liberals agreed with Steffens that wealthy businessmen organized the vigilante raids for their own political purposes. George West, editor of the *San Francisco News* (the one Bay Area newspaper that did not entirely cooperate with Neylan), argued that conservatives were using the general strike as an excuse to attack radicals—and, by extension, New Dealers. The

San Francisco Red Scare, he said, was "a piece of real politics by which a group of rather forlorn and for the most part ineffectual individuals were deprived of their rights in a vicarious atonement for the losses and alarms of the general strike." Now conservatives were trying to use the strike to turn public opinion against the Roosevelt administration, with the Hearst newspapers in particular "going to great lengths to identify communism and the New Deal."[56]

Journalist and New Dealer Lorena Hickok also worried that conservatives would unfairly link Roosevelt with the general strike. Near the end of her cross-country trek as chief investigator for federal relief programs, Hickok wrote from California that the New Deal was the real target of the coastal anti-Red frenzy. "It's a whispering affair," she told a relief official on August 15. The state's business leaders tried to "plant in the minds of the conservative, middle class of Californians the idea that all those about the President in Washington are Communist sympathizers, if not actually Communists," she said. Leading newspaper publishers were making plans "publicly to rid the state of Communists, but privately to fight Roosevelt."[57] The New Dealers believed that California businessmen had decided there was profit in selling fear.

But as advertising professionals know, it's easier to sell a product you believe in. In their private meetings, when they spoke honestly with one another, many California conservatives indicated that they bought their own product: they truly believed foreign agitators threatened public morals and social order. In the opinion of these business leaders, even if the New Dealers were not true Reds, they were helping to create an environment in which Communism could flourish.

A week after the end of the general strike, under the vaulted, hand-painted ceilings of the Borgia Room in San Francisco's St. Francis Hotel, a group of the Bay Area's most prominent business and civic leaders gathered to listen to horror stories from the Los Angeles police chief about the social and sexual dangers posed by California Reds. Chief James Davis reported that Communists wanted to enlist black men in the revolution by promising them unlimited sexual access to white women, whose bodies they would "nationalize" and then distribute to loyal Communist men. As he warmed to the subject, he reeled off a list of terrifying Red plots: the Communists planned to infiltrate the armed services and provoke mutinies; blow up water mains, gas lines, and munitions factories; poison the water and food supplies; and then await the arrival of Russian troops. Davis encouraged the business leaders present to work to "develop a national public sentiment" against dangerous radicals and the treasonous liberals who aided them. They needed to tell the unvarnished truth to other Americans. "It is a thing that cannot be handled by soft soap!" he concluded. The men left the meeting more determined than ever to organize and raise funds to fight radicals and those who aided them.[58]

Like Davis, William Randolph Hearst came out of the general strike with a renewed commitment to exposing and destroying the nation's enemies—especially those in Washington. "The revolution in California against stable government and established order," he wrote in a signed editorial, "would never have occurred except for the sympathy and encouragement which the fomenters of revolution were receiving or believed they were receiving from those high in the counsel of the Federal Administration." The qualification "or believed they were receiving" showed that Hearst did not care if the New Dealers *deliberately* abetted revolution; the effect was the same whether they wanted to or not. "The fires of sedition," he concluded, "had been lit by these visionary and voluble politicians."[59]

Roosevelt had done nothing to encourage the general strike. He saw collective bargaining and federal labor mediation as means to recovery and stability, not radical change. Indeed, he believed that his programs helped thwart revolution, not promote it. But no matter how much the president insisted that his policies actually benefited capitalists, Western business leaders refused to believe him. In the next election, FDR would try even harder to distance himself from California radicals—and once again he would find similar, frustrating results.

8

CAMPAIGNS INC.

Clem Whitaker and Leone Baxter worried about their candidate. It was July 1934, and they had recently formed the nation's first political consulting firm, Campaigns Inc. They were hoping to make a splash by helping their first individual office seeker win election. But their client, George Hatfield, was not making it easy for them. As he entered the final weeks of his campaign for the Republican nomination for lieutenant governor, Hatfield lacked two crucial ingredients for success: money and ideas.[1]

What the two consultants did for Hatfield would launch their legendary careers and transform the way politics was practiced in the United States. But at this moment, they had to admit they could not figure out why Californians should vote for their client. It was "mighty hard to write interesting announcements for Hatfield as we are so totally devoid of an issue," Whitaker confessed in late July 1934. He hoped that "we will be able to develop some kind of an issue shortly."[2]

Then, on August 28, voters in the Democratic primary for governor gave them that issue. Upton Sinclair, celebrated author, erstwhile socialist, and current New Dealer, won the Democratic nomination and terrified the political establishments of both parties in California and beyond. To avert what they saw as a potential socialist takeover of the state economy, California's business leaders poured millions of dollars into the campaign against Sinclair. Whitaker and Baxter would continue to work for Hatfield, but Sinclair's candidacy helped them win additional, well-funded clients as well.

The 1934 governor's race in California marked a new era in American political history. The campaign featured important firsts, including the first newsreel attack ads and (in the persons of Whitaker and Baxter) the first professional campaign consultants. When those consultants discovered how to unite middle-class and working-class voters with appeals to religion and family, they helped to construct a new Republican coalition.

Ending Poverty in California

Upton Sinclair was born in Maryland, came of age in New York, and found fame in Chicago. But he discovered his true home when he moved to the Los Angeles area in his forties. A vegetarian, sun worshipper, teetotaler, obsessive tennis player, and enthusiastic practitioner of mental telepathy, the slender, tanned, world-famous author of dozens of books was a Southern Californian at heart. He built a home in a working-class neighborhood in Pasadena in 1916 and began typing his best-selling books on his sunny patio alongside his clapboard house and swimming pool.

Sinclair's books included attacks on journalism ("a class institution, serving the rich and spurning the poor," *The Brass Check*, 1919), the church (the "natural ally of every form of oppression and exploitation," *Profits of Religion*, 1917), and the college administrator ("the most universal faker and variegated prevaricator that has yet appeared in the civilized world," *The Goose-Step*, 1922), among other American elites and institutions.[3] But his masterpiece was his 1906 exposé of the Chicago meatpacking industry, *The Jungle*. With his gripping story of a fictionalized Lithuanian immigrant family whose members were driven to starvation, prostitution, and madness as they struggled to survive in the "wild-beast tangle" of twentieth-century industrial America, where a remorseless capitalist system treated the worker like a hog in a slaughterhouse and "seized him by the leg . . . cut his throat and watched him gasp out his life," Sinclair hoped to convert his readers to socialism.[4] Instead, his grim description of the unsanitary conditions in the stockyards led outraged consumers to demand regulation, rather than abolition, of capitalism. "I aimed at the public's heart, and by accident I hit it in the stomach," he lamented.[5] *The Jungle* prompted the passage of the Pure Food and Drug Act. It also secured Sinclair's fame and financial independence.

In Los Angeles, Sinclair found antilabor politicians and cops who were just as horrifyingly reactionary as the villains in his seldom-subtle books. He first engaged in political combat with the conservative forces of Los Angeles in 1923 when he recited the Bill of Rights in public to show his support for striking longshoremen—and was promptly arrested. The police chief denounced him as "the worst radical in the country" and the district attorney charged him with inciting contempt for the law and the Constitution—which Sinclair had allegedly done by reading aloud the document's first ten amendments.[6] Sinclair beat the rap and went on to found the first local chapter of the American Civil Liberties Union. His arrest confirmed his belief that his adopted state was governed by "a small group of rich men whose sole purpose in life was to become richer, and who subordinated all public affairs to that end."[7] He dedicated himself to exposing their selfish and immoral behavior and turning them out of office.

As a member of the Socialist Party, Sinclair ran unsuccessfully for governor of California twice—in 1926 and 1930—and once for U.S. Senate. But he never won more than sixty thousand of the 2 million votes cast.[8] In 1933, one of his friends persuaded him to switch to the Democratic Party because 50 percent of Americans voted for the party of their grandfathers ("In order to get anywhere," Sinclair agreed, "it is necessary to have a party which has grandfathers").[9] Soon after his re-registration as a Democrat, he filed the papers to run for governor. He made the announcement in characteristic fashion: by writing a book. In *I, Governor of California, and How I Ended Poverty: A True Story of the Future*, Sinclair pretended to look back, in 1938, on his accomplishments throughout his four years as governor, during which he had adopted his program to restore prosperity. He called it End Poverty in California, or EPIC.

Sinclair's EPIC plan envisioned an economy that blended what he saw as the best elements of capitalism with the efficiencies and social justice of socialism. Successful private businesses would be left alone, at least initially, while the state government would sponsor cooperative enterprises in industries still mired in the Depression. The California Authority for Land would purchase idle property and turn it over to unemployed farmers and workers; the California Authority for Production would buy empty factories from their owners and transform them into worker co-ops. The laborers would consume what they produced, either directly—by eating the food they raised or

Upton Sinclair in 1934. San Francisco History Center, San Francisco Public Library.

using the goods they made—or indirectly, by bartering with other co-ops. For people too old or infirm to work, the state would provide a monthly pension of $50.

The EPIC programs would be financed by the California Authority for Money (which would sell bonds, issue scrip, and facilitate barter transactions) and by a steeply progressive tax system. Sinclair proposed to abolish the regressive sales tax along with the property tax for most Californians. Instead, the state would get its money from a tax on the highest incomes (up to 50 percent for those earning more than $50,000 a year, or $889,000 in 2014 dollars), a public utilities tax, and property taxes on the most expensive homes.

Sinclair insisted that his plan was consistent with the New Deal, which he claimed to admire. Certainly a few elements of EPIC were similar to some of Roosevelt's policies, or at least those policies as they would evolve by 1935. With the Civil Works Administration, Public Works Administration, Civilian Conservation Corps, and Works Progress Administration, the Roosevelt administration employed millions of out-of-work Americans; with Social Security, it would eventually provide old-age pensions; with the short-lived and underfunded Resettlement Administration, it would build a few model communities that were, in their infancy, vaguely suggestive of EPIC's rural co-ops.

However, at least at the beginning of his campaign, Sinclair was far more radical than even the most utopian of the New Deal visionaries. His proposed pensions were not, as Social Security would be, funded by a payroll tax, but by income and property taxes on the richest Californians. Sinclair's tax program was much more redistributionist than any of Roosevelt's proposals; as scholars have pointed out, FDR's tax schedule was not very progressive.[10] EPIC's industrial and agricultural proposals aimed to transfer ownership to workers collectively, not to support the existing owners, as Roosevelt's policies did. Indeed, this was the heart of the difference between the New Deal and EPIC: Roosevelt wanted to save capitalism, while Sinclair hoped to tax the rich, empower the poor, and, ideally, someday create a society that would transcend capitalism.

At the beginning, everyone agreed that Sinclair could not win. In March, journalist Oswald Garrison Villard observed in *The Nation* that "no one who is following the campaign carefully believes that Sinclair will get the Democratic nomination."[11] Obviously, the Democrats would choose an establishment candidate. The problem was that the establishment could not agree on one.

State of Instability

California "lacks a political gyroscope" to stabilize its movement, Carey Mc-
Williams wrote in the 1940s; it "swings and sways, spins and turns in ac-
cordance with its own peculiar dynamics."[12] The mass migration to California
from all parts of the country made politics there uniquely volatile. As many
as one-tenth to one-third of the voters in each election were new to the state,
which made it almost impossible to predict election results. Moreover, thanks
to progressive reforms enacted earlier in the century, the state lacked strong
parties or any sort of party discipline.

Republican domination of the state was the one constant in California's
changeable political environment. During the 1920s, Democrats won only
8 percent of state and national partisan elections in California, and regis-
tered Republicans outnumbered Democrats by a four-to-one margin. By the
time Sinclair declared his candidacy, the Democrats' fortunes had improved
dramatically, but they were still in the minority in both houses of the state
legislature. The 1934 election gave them the opportunity to win the governorship for the first time in the twentieth century.[13]

But the Democrats could not settle on a candidate. In the race for the
party's nomination for governor, top Democrats were split between George
Creel, who was well known to voters for his war propaganda and his labor
mediation efforts, and Justus Wardell, the publisher of a San Francisco business newspaper and an early Roosevelt supporter, with neither man garner-
ing much enthusiasm.

The Roosevelt administration could see there would be a battle for the
party's nomination, but decided not to intervene. Creel had done little to
endear himself to Roosevelt's inner circle. A year earlier, he had ostentatiously (but briefly) quit as California's National Recovery Administration
chief in a bid to get more power, and he sometimes wrote self-pitying letters
to White House aides complaining about their lack of appreciation for him.[14]
Moreover, Roosevelt's political fixers did not know if he could win. Privately, the president's aides viewed the gubernatorial campaign as a potential disaster for Roosevelt. Treasury official Jefty O'Connor, FDR's chief
adviser for California, politely termed the primary race a "mix-up," while
Postmaster General Jim Farley called it a "terrible mess."[15] Reporter Lorena
Hickok suggested that the fascists across the Pacific Ocean might be able

to impose order on the state's politics. "God damn it, I think we ought to let Japan have this state," she wrote Harry Hopkins in a report about California politics and relief policies in July 1934. "Maybe they could straighten it out."[16]

Both Creel and Sinclair pleaded for Roosevelt's endorsement. Creel warned FDR's aides that a Sinclair victory would "link the New Deal with socialism." He predicted that Sinclair would lose badly to Governor Frank Merriam in the general election, the state would "swing to the right," and then "the party will be dead for another thirty years."[17]

For his part, Sinclair tried to trade on his acquaintance with Eleanor Roosevelt, whom he had once visited in the White House. Through the mails, he pressed his *I, Governor* book on Eleanor and asked her to endorse him. The First Lady politely demurred. "I have read your book and I have given it to my husband to read," she told him. "Some of the things which you advocate I am heartily in favor of, others I do not think are entirely practicable, but then what is impracticable today is sometimes practicable tomorrow." She told him she would not make any public statement about the race "at present."[18] As the campaign continued, she courteously but sternly warned him to stop implying that she supported him.[19]

To contrast himself with Sinclair, Creel presented himself as the safe, liberal choice in the race—a sane progressive who occupied the middle ground "between cataleptic conservatism and emotional and subversive experimentation."[20] Governor Merriam, of course, was the cataleptic conservative, a political dinosaur, "reactionary to the point of medievalism." But Sinclair was just as bad, Creel maintained—he was a "rainbow-chaser" whose platform was "just about the craziest thing you ever read," he said in a private letter.[21]

But many ordinary Californians wanted to chase Sinclair's rainbows. Nearly one thousand local EPIC chapters sprang up around the state, with an estimated one hundred thousand dues-paying members. The groups sponsored bake sales, parades, rodeos, garage sales, picnics, and barbecues to raise money for their candidate and spread the word about his plan. They sold bars of soap and matchboxes and posters and buttons with his picture or the EPIC symbol, a productive honeybee. They also fielded an EPIC baseball team in downtown Los Angeles, composed songs, and sponsored huge rallies and pageants throughout the state. They published a newspaper, the *EPIC News*, and printed five hundred thousand copies every week (and almost 2 million a week by the end of the campaign).[22]

To broaden his support, Sinclair convinced a mainstream Democrat, Sacramento lawyer Sheridan Downey, to be his running mate. They called their slate "Uppie and Downey."

Most important, Sinclair's campaign launched a grassroots effort to register voters. EPIC volunteers signed up 350,000 new Democrats in the first half of 1934 alone. For the first time in California history, there were more Democrats than Republicans in the Golden State.

On primary election day in late August, these new voters helped to give Sinclair an astonishing victory. He won with more votes—436,000—than his six Democratic opponents combined, and almost 150,000 more than Creel, his closest rival. Even more important, he received 90,000 more votes than Merriam did in securing the Republican nomination. Almost fifty EPIC-endorsed candidates for state legislature also won their primary races. Suddenly, the fantastic seemed possible: Sinclair could become the next governor and put his utopian schemes into effect.

Up to this point, California conservatives had viewed the governor's race with amused detachment. If Sinclair eked out a victory in the primary, so much the better. They thought there was no chance he could win the general election. But the size of his primary victory stunned them. The day after the election, at his home in Palo Alto, former president Herbert Hoover sat down to pen an ominous letter to the man who needed to beat Sinclair. "My dear Governor," he wrote to Merriam. "I want you to know that I am at your service. It is the most momentous election which California has faced."[23]

It was not just California that faced the horrors of a socialist future in the event of a Sinclair victory. Hoover and other conservatives believed that all of America could be imperiled. In a panicky editorial, the *Los Angeles Times* warned of the "maggot-like horde of Reds" who were "eating at the heart of America," or, switching metaphors, termites who were "secretly and darkly eating into the foundations and the roof beams of everything the American heart has held dear and sacred." With this election for governor, the *Times* said, the people of California would decide the fate of America: "Either we take the Red path; or we close that gate right now, forever."[24] As the California Real Estate Association explained in its advertisements, "It's Merriam or Moscow!"[25]

California businessmen, who had organized in response to the labor troubles, now threw their money and energy into the governor's race. Sunkist's Charles Teague coordinated three days of meetings in Los Angeles among the Southland's most powerful business leaders. On the second day, Teague asked the men to pledge $50,000 to start a comprehensive anti-Sinclair campaign, called the United for California League, and he raised the money on the spot. He formed a committee to raise an additional $450,000 for a campaign just in Los Angeles.[26]

As the head of Sunkist, which stamped every individual orange and lemon and grapefruit coming from its farms, Teague knew the value of good advertising, and he engaged his company's ad agency, Lord & Thomas, to run the anti-Sinclair campaign in Southern California.[27]

While a New York ad agency ran the Southern California anti-Sinclair campaign, the northern effort featured a new brand of political professionals. The 1934 race marked the first time that political consultants, rather than party officials, managed a campaign. Clem Whitaker and Leone Baxter would help defeat Sinclair and go on to change the way Americans elected their leaders.

The Lie Factory

Raised in the tiny northern California town of Willits, Clem Whitaker started working for the local paper at age thirteen and began covering the state capitol for the *Sacramento Union* at age seventeen. He became the *Union*'s city editor, a political writer for Hearst's *San Francisco Examiner*, and the creator and owner of a Sacramento news service. After he suffered health setbacks, he decided to sell his successful news service and move into lobbying and public relations. In 1933, Sacramento lawyer (and Sinclair running mate) Sheridan Downey hired Whitaker to defend a huge public water and power program, the Central Valley Project, from a referendum bankrolled by a deep-pocketed private utility, Pacific Gas & Electric. On the campaign, Whitaker met a beautiful, young, redheaded publicist from Redding, Leone Baxter, and together they formed the firm Campaigns Inc. It was the nation's first political consulting company. Four years later, after Whitaker divorced his first wife, Whitaker and Baxter married each other.[28]

The Central Valley Project referendum was the first campaign for Campaigns Inc., and it was one of the few times Whitaker and Baxter would represent the underdogs. When it lost the water referendum, PG&E put Whitaker and Baxter on retainer. Their firm went on to oversee seventy-five campaigns over the next couple of decades, including initiatives and referenda sponsored by utilities, oil companies, and railroads. Whitaker and Baxter would go national in 1948 when the American Medical Association hired them to do to President Harry Truman's universal health care proposal what they had done to a similar statewide plan in California—kill it.

The 1934 governor's race was the first time Whitaker and Baxter managed the campaign of an individual candidate, as opposed to a ballot measure. Despite their later reputation for serving conservative causes, they refused to work directly for Frank Merriam, whom Whitaker viewed as incompetent and reactionary. Instead, they ran the campaign of Hatfield, Merriam's running mate and the Republicans' candidate for lieutenant governor.[29]

Advertisers and press agents had worked for political candidates for decades, but Whitaker and Baxter provided much more than publicity and marketing: they managed every aspect of Hatfield's race. Besides devising and placing advertisements, they wrote his speeches (in five-, ten-, and fifteen-minute and longer increments), his press releases, and his pamphlets; they designed and distributed bumper stickers and signs; they produced and coordinated his direct mail effort; they organized support groups and arranged endorsements; and they raised money and decided how to spend it. Most important, they devised the themes and strategy for his campaign.

After Sinclair's victory, Whitaker and Baxter signed on as consultants for a bipartisan outfit called the California League Against Sinclairism. They quickly decided to focus on cultural issues. Their first task was to skim through all of Sinclair's forty-seven books and innumerable pamphlets for material to use against him. It was not hard to find Sinclairisms to use against Sinclairism.

Over the years, Sinclair had criticized many venerable institutions, including every major university in California (Stanford, the University of Southern California, and the University of California), most religious denominations (including Jews, Catholics, Mormons, Seventh-Day Adventists, and Christian Scientists), doctors, dentists, the movie industry, oil companies, railroads, the Parent-Teacher Association, and the Boy Scouts. As Whitaker explained years later, "Upton was beaten because he had written books." Baxter added, with apparently sincere regret, "But because he was a good man, we were sorry we had to do it that way."[30]

Sinclair's real statements were sometimes shocking enough, but his opponents also picked out quotations from characters in his novels that did not reflect the views of the author at all. The *Los Angeles Times* highlighted these selectively edited, misattributed quotes and put them every day in a special, black-bordered box on its front page ("Sinclair on marriage," "Sinclair on Christ"). One much-repeated statement on marriage ("the sanctity of marriage . . . I have had such a belief . . . I have it no longer") was actually uttered by an embittered Sinclair character in a novel after his wife had left him. In other words, the quotation in context meant the opposite of what it seemed to mean in isolation. Sinclair protested that it was as if the *Times* had quoted Lady Macbeth and then charged Shakespeare with justifying murder.[31]

The anti-Sinclair campaign provided illustrations to accompany the out-of-context quotes. Whitaker and Baxter hired a cartoonist to draw representations of revered institutions—marriage, say, in the form of a bride and a groom—menaced by a big black blob labeled the "blot of Sinclairism." The captions usually featured an alarming Sinclair quotation (for example, marriage under capitalism was "marriage plus prostitution").[32]

The state's newspapers eagerly printed these cartoons and other anti-Sinclair material from Whitaker and Baxter. Of the seven hundred papers in California in 1934, 92 percent supported Merriam, 5 percent supported other candidates, and 3 percent were neutral. Not a single paper backed Sinclair.[33] With the owners and publishers denouncing him, reporters and editors were not inclined to give respectful coverage to his arguments. "It is difficult to get a man to understand something," Sinclair wrote afterward, "when his salary depends upon his not understanding it!"[34] With his characteristic talent for coining a memorable phrase, Sinclair called the campaign against him "the lie factory."[35]

The greatest lies were told by the movie industry. Like many businessmen, Hollywood executives despised Sinclair for his attack on their industry—in their case, *Upton Sinclair Presents William Fox*, a tell-all memoir based on the bitter recollections of a former studio head. They also loathed his progressive income tax and property tax schemes and his proposal to buy their vacant studios and set up film collectives when he became governor. Moreover, most studio heads were Republicans, with Louis B. Mayer of Metro-Goldwyn-Mayer serving as state party chairman. Movie executives vowed to relocate the entire industry to Florida if Sinclair won election. The candidate scoffed at these threats. "It is hard to drive people out of California," he noted.[36]

Sinclair's enemies in Hollywood invented the negative audiovisual advertising that would later come to dominate campaigns in the television age. In the weeks before the election, MGM produced three anti-Sinclair "news" reels. Purporting to show interviews conducted by an "inquiring reporter," the scenes were edited or even staged to convince voters to choose Merriam. Well-spoken, attractive Californians explained that they would vote for Merriam because they wanted to keep their houses, their jobs, or "prosperity." Suspicious-looking, inarticulate men—some with dark skins, shifty eyes, or Eastern European accents—expressed their intention to vote for "Saint Clair" or "Seenclair." One man told viewers that "Upton Saint Clair is the author of the Russian government, and it worked out very well there."[37]

The anti-Sinclair campaign said little about Merriam because the man known as "Old Baldy" was not a very marketable product. The governor was a dull speaker who failed to excite even the most conservative voters. Republican journalists suspected him of being dishonest, and they quietly investigated accusations that he had deserted his first wife and embezzled money in Iowa. (They could find no proof they were true.)[38] Moreover, in a country and a state leaning increasingly to the left, Merriam was, as the *Sacramento Bee* noted with disgust, supported by "a notorious aggregation of reactionaries." The *Bee*, the flagship paper of a progressive Republican chain, protested that "California cannot and must not have such a man as governor." Yet the *Bee* refused to endorse Sinclair, who posed "as great a menace to the state" as did Merriam.[39]

The *Bee* editors solved their dilemma by endorsing a third-party candidate, erstwhile Republican Raymond Haight. A Los Angeles attorney and the relative of a governor, Haight was running on the new Commonwealth Party ticket, which was the creation of a popular Los Angeles preacher, Bob Shuler.

Haight's candidacy frightened the Republican establishment. They thought he might draw enough votes from Merriam to make Sinclair governor. Party officials offered him $100,000 in cash, among other bribes, to convince him to drop out of the race.[40] Haight, who believed he needed to save the state from Merriam's medievalism and Sinclair's utopianism, refused to accept the offers.

Given the third-party threat and their own candidate's lack of charisma, Merriam's managers opted to make their campaign almost entirely negative. The California League Against Sinclairism stressed three main issues: Sinclair's alleged contempt for Christianity, disdain for American families, and sympathy for Communism.

Conservatives had already used these cultural issues in Imperial Valley against an ostensible alliance of labor, Communists, and New Dealers. Now they hoped to use these themes to mobilize their middle-class supporters and undermine Sinclair's working-class support.

Herbert Hoover, for one, believed that religion would be the key to Sinclair's defeat. "It is a melancholy thought," he wrote to a friend, "but the majority of the people of California are probably with Sinclair on economic issues, but enough can probably be divorced upon his religious beliefs to answer the moment."[41] Democratic activists agreed that the election might "hinge greatly on the gullibility of narrow-minded religionists, of which we have a goodly supply in California."[42]

The anti-Sinclair publicists worked closely with evangelical pastors, particularly those in Southern California. They encouraged ministers to spread the message that Sinclair threatened American churches, families, and homes. One pastor, former boxing champion Martin Luther Thomas, used his hugely popular nightly radio show to blast Sinclair for opposing "the Christian religion, its Founder, [and] the Churches of the nation."[43] Another Los Angeles radio minister delivered a sermon on "the Four Horsemen of the Apocalypse, Anti-Christ, and Upton Sinclair."[44]

Sinclair insisted that it was unfair to portray him as an atheist. It was organized religion, not a "personal God," to which he objected.[45] Indeed, many prominent Methodist, Baptist, Congregationalist, and Unitarian ministers endorsed his campaign. Grassroots groups like the United Christian Voters League of California worked on his behalf and sent letters to every pastor in the state, urging them to vote for candidates who practiced the

Christian values of selflessness and generosity.[46] Wendell Miller, minister of
the reformist Methodist Church on Florence Avenue in Los Angeles, pro-
grammed his church's electric signs to read, "I would rather vote for an atheist who acts like a Christian than a Christian who acts like an atheist."[47]

Just as he was not really godless, Sinclair was not actually a Red. Leading
Communists and Socialists despised him for embracing the New Deal. The
Socialist Party disowned Sinclair and ran its own candidate for governor,
while Communists denounced his plans as "wildly insane" and "the most
cold-bloodedly pro-capitalist and reactionary proposals that were offered by
any candidate in any election in the United States in a decade."[48] Sam
Darcy, California's pragmatic Communist leader, wanted to cooperate secretly with Sinclair, but the Party's national officials refused to work with
the man they viewed as an ideological heretic.[49]

"Feminine Bodies" Against Sinclairism

The anti-Sinclair strategists stressed religion and family because they thought
those cultural issues would appeal in particular to women, a relatively new
and somewhat mysterious segment of the voting public. Women had won
the right to vote in California just twenty-three years earlier, but conservative women had not yet played decisive roles in many statewide elections.
Sinclair's opponents believed that female voters could be motivated to crusade against him if they were convinced that he threatened the home.

In San Francisco, Los Angeles, and San Jose; in Oxnard, Santa Barbara,
and Ventura; in San Bernardino, Cucamonga, Redding, El Centro, Yucaipa,
Santa Cruz, and Stockton; in desert towns and coastal metropolises, the
Merriam-Hatfield campaign set up a women's committee—a "feminine body,"
as one newspaper called it—to warn against the menace of Sinclairism.
Sometimes the campaign staffers worked through the local Parent-Teacher
Association or women's club or American Association of University Women.
More often, they set up a new organization of women specifically dedicated
to defeating Sinclair.[50]

At teas, luncheons, and rallies, their speakers emphasized the danger
Sinclair posed to God and country and—most important—the home. The
professional staff of the anti-Sinclair campaign crafted a speech for delivery to women's groups, and then arranged for locally prominent women to

give the speech in their communities. These women alerted "each and every mother and each and every working woman" to the prospect of "wrecked schools, wrecked homes, and wrecked careers" if Sinclair won the election.[51]

The Merriam-Hatfield forces tried to inspire upper-middle-class and middle-class women to become politically active for perhaps the first time in their lives. "At bridge parties and luncheons, where the political conversationalist used to be considered a bore, the sole topic for discussion now is the threat of Sinclairism," said one anti-EPIC speaker, Mrs. William Hayes, in San Jose. "Our religion, our ideals, our very homes are threatened. Our backs are against the wall—and now we must fight."[52] As the San Francisco Hearst newspaper, the *Call-Bulletin*, explained, "Women's place is at the polls." The Hearst reporter claimed that women conservatives "won't content themselves with discussing the situation over a bridge table. They're going out ringing doorbells and shouting their alarm over Sinclair's candidacy."[53]

California Republican leaders were ahead of their counterparts in other parts of the country in marketing conservatism to the voters in religious and gendered terms. These Western conservatives did not stress their defense of private property; instead, they promised to protect the family, the church, and the white race from radical leftists.

This emphasis on cultural threats contrasted sharply with the approach of conservatives in the Midwest and Northeast. At the same time that Sinclair's opponents discussed family and religion, Eastern businessmen were organizing along old-fashioned class lines. In September 1934, some of the country's richest industrialists founded the American Liberty League, an elite anti–New Deal group. The Liberty League's brief statement of purpose mentioned the word "property" three times (government should respect "rights . . . of property," foster the "right to . . . acquire property," and preserve the "ownership . . . of property").[54]

Roosevelt's aides actually welcomed the Liberty League because it proved the Democrats' contention that the Republicans were the party of "fat cats," as Roosevelt said in a private note about the League.[55] Out in California, however, forward-thinking Republicans were crafting more innovative techniques. They were discovering how to link business conservatives with cultural conservatives to create a new, broader coalition.

The President and the Candidate

With all the money and the media against him, Sinclair believed he could win only if the phenomenally popular president agreed to endorse him. As the campaign neared its final weeks, he was still waiting to hear if the president would do so.

Roosevelt faced a difficult decision. On one hand, he did not want the New Deal discredited by its association with an unstable socialist on an impossible quest; on the other, if Sinclair won, then he would help the Democrats take power in California after decades of Republican domination.

Sinclair did his best to force Roosevelt's hand. When he became the Democrats' nominee, he asked the president if he could meet with him. Roosevelt agreed, but his secretary cautioned the candidate that there would be "no discussion of your campaign or politics in your State."[56] Eager and a bit nervous, Sinclair journeyed across the nation to meet with the president at his country home in Hyde Park, New York, on September 4.

Like many men and women before him, Sinclair was charmed—some might say seduced—by the president. "I talked with one of the kindest and most genial and frank and open-minded and lovable men I ever met," he told the press afterward.[57] As their one-hour meeting stretched to two, he was thrilled that Roosevelt seemed interested in his books and his EPIC program. He divulged little to the media about what the two men had said; he had promised the president that much. But he told close friends that FDR had told him he would endorse his ideas in a radio speech in late October.[58] And that would mean Sinclair's election.

Whatever he told Sinclair privately, Roosevelt remained noncommittal in public and refused to discuss EPIC at his press conference the next day, despite many questions from reporters. He stayed silent on the California election through the next several weeks.[59]

Lacking clear direction from their president, Creel and Senator William McAdoo, the two most powerful Democrats in the state, agreed to campaign for Sinclair in the general election. Tantalized by the possibility of victory, Sinclair happily endorsed a vague state party platform that failed to mention many important EPIC points (including the state takeover of empty land and factories, farm cooperatives, state-sponsored scrip, and the end of the sales tax).

While the president delayed an announcement on the race, people on both sides tried to influence him. Roosevelt's mailbag reflected the deep divide within the electorate. Sinclair's supporters often wrote on notebook paper, in pencil, begging the president to stop the "liars," the "Tory machine," "reactionaries," "capitalists," and "fascists" from undermining democracy and thwarting the will of the people. Sinclair's opponents were more likely to send a different type of missive: typed letters, on fancy paper with embossed letterhead, denouncing the "interloper" who joined the party of their ancestors and was now threatening to bring atheism, communism, and chaos, and who would raise their taxes and take their property. Many letter writers included copies of anti-Sinclair leaflets, as proof of either Sinclair's perfidy or the Republicans' mendacity. Almost all the correspondents on both sides predicted calamity, civil war, and/or revolution in November if their man did not win. To all of these writers, Roosevelt's secretary sent the same response: the president did not get involved in "local political party contests."[60]

If ordinary Democrats were divided on Sinclair's candidacy, business leaders in California were not. Senator McAdoo warned the president that there was a "*vast fear* of him among the property-owning class and business and commercial interests," although McAdoo personally found Sinclair reasonable.[61]

Secretary of Labor Frances Perkins, one of the president's most trusted advisers, told Roosevelt that she heard from "sober liberals" that the "fanatic" EPIC program would ruin the state. She was horrified when the president responded that he didn't think Sinclair's victory would matter much. "Perhaps they'll get EPIC in California. What difference, I ask you, would that make in Dutchess County, New York, or Lincoln County, Maine?" he asked her. "The beauty of our state-federal system is that the people can experiment." If Sinclair's ideas worked, others would copy them; if they didn't, well, it was only California.[62] Raymond Moley, one of FDR's former advisers and currently a journalist, pleaded with the president to "dissociate" himself from Sinclair, but Roosevelt waved away his concerns. "Besides," he said, "they tell me Sinclair's sure to be elected." In response, Moley set out to ensure that Sinclair would *not* be elected. In his magazine, *Today*, he published an editorial denouncing Sinclair. Many insiders took the piece as a sign that the Roosevelt administration no longer supported the candidate.[63] Still, the president refused to tip his hand.

As the election approached, the anti-Sinclair forces ramped up their efforts. The United for California League mailed 6 million copies of leaflets that highlighted quotations from his books: "Upton Sinclair's Attitude on Christianity," "The Proof That Upton Sinclair Preaches Revolution and Communism," "Upton Sinclair Discusses the Home, the Institution of Marriage, and Advocates Free Love."[64] They printed fake money in red ink labeled "One Sincliar Dollar," issued by the Uppy & Downy Bank and "redeemable, if ever, at the cost of future generations."[65] They asked Southern California employers to hand out anti-Sinclair literature to their employees and to warn them that they might lose their jobs if Sinclair won.[66]

Sinclair's opponents also tried to prevent likely EPIC supporters from voting at all. Attorneys for the United for California League and the Republican Party argued in court that transient workers and the homeless should not be allowed to vote because they lacked fixed residences. Democratic partisans warned New Deal officials that this strategy could be used against Roosevelt as well. Given the president's popularity, the Republicans' only hope was "to keep as many Roosevelt voters away from the polls as possible."[67] In any event, the California Supreme Court issued a writ prohibiting the proposed purge of the voting rolls on the grounds that it could "have no effect other than to intimidate and prevent eligible voters from going to the polls."[68]

Anti-Sinclair propaganda, 1934. The "Sincliar" dollar was "redeemable, if ever, at the cost of future generations."

Merriam's New Deal for California

Sinclair's race for the governorship took a sudden, irrevocable turn in late September when he made a terrible gaffe. At a press conference at his house in Pasadena on September 26, the exhausted candidate, recovering from a bout with food poisoning, responded unwisely to a provocative question from a reporter: "Suppose your Plan goes into effect, won't it cause a great many unemployed to come to California from other states?" Sinclair smiled and laughed. "I told Mr. Hopkins, the Federal Relief Administrator, that if I am elected, half the unemployed of the United States will come to California, and he will have to make plans to take care of them."[69]

Sinclair was trying to make a joke, but the statement was catnip to the conservative newspapers, which began running dozens of stories on the "advancing hordes of the indigent" who were "lured westward" by the promise of taxpayer support for their profligate ways. The Los Angeles Times described "barefooted and scantily dressed" families from Oklahoma pouring over the borders in their dilapidated jalopies, along with filthy hoboes on train cars, all thrilled at the opportunity to "git some of that free land when this feller Sinclair" won the election. "How does this Utopia thing work out?" was one of the first questions they posed to border officials, the Times reporter claimed.[70] "Every Pauper Is Coming," read the San Francisco Chronicle headline.[71]

Three weeks before the election, the president signaled that he had finally made his decision. He would abandon Sinclair. He communicated his choice through somewhat indirect means, as was typical for him. The president himself said nothing about the race. But he did not stop George Creel from releasing a public letter in which Creel withdrew his endorsement of the author and denounced his "hare-brained, unworkable schemes of social reform."[72] Creel was the first of several key Democratic defections from the Sinclair campaign. Senator McAdoo pleaded ill health and conveniently absented himself from the race. Roosevelt meanwhile sent a message to Eleanor to "(1) Say nothing and (2) Do nothing" on Sinclair's behalf.[73]

As they deserted Sinclair, the New Dealers picked up an unusual supporter out West. Governor Merriam, the man described as a caricature of a reactionary Republican, announced that he was "heartily in accord" with New Deal policies. "President Roosevelt is building for recovery on an

American foundation," he proclaimed. George West, a San Francisco editor covering the campaign for the *New York Times*, saw Merriam's about-face as a political miracle. "When a standpat Republican politician abandons a lifetime of party regularity at 70 to come out in hearty praise of a Democratic President and to appeal for votes on the score of his devotion to Roosevelt policies that have just been denounced by the leaders of his own party," he wrote, "it is time for connoisseurs of the unusual to stand by and take note."[74]

Although West and the public did not know it at the time, Merriam's sudden change of heart came after he met secretly with Roosevelt's political adviser for California, Jefty O'Connor, who flew to Los Angeles at the president's direction. In return for the administration's refusal to endorse Sinclair, Merriam promised that he would present his election as a triumph for the New Deal, and "further said that he would cooperate and work with the national administration."[75] The old conservative insisted he was a born-again progressive who believed reform could stave off revolution. "We must do something for our people," Merriam told O'Connor, "or they will take it away."[76]

Considering all the forces arrayed against him—the movie moguls, the press, industry, agribusiness, the real estate association, the regular Democrats, and, in the end, even his own president—the muckraking socialist from Pasadena did surprisingly well. He won 879,000 votes to Merriam's 1,138,000, while Haight got 302,000. Hatfield beat Downey easily for lieutenant governor as well. If Haight had left the race, or if Roosevelt had endorsed Sinclair, the EPIC ticket might have won. Nationally, the Democrats enjoyed a sweeping victory, with their members controlling 74 percent of the seats in the House of Representatives, 72 percent of the U.S. Senate, and 81 percent of governorships. Outside of the governor's race, California Democrats did extremely well, netting two additional seats in Congress. Two dozen EPIC-endorsed candidates won election to the state assembly, which was now just three seats shy of Democratic control.[77]

Sinclair admitted that he was a little relieved that he had lost. Because of the violent atmosphere in the state that year, he had worried that he might be in physical danger if he won. As he listened to the returns, he thought to himself: "I can drive my own car again! I can go and take my walks! I can sleep with my windows open!"[78] And anyway, he had always known that he was "not trying to be elected so much as to educate the people."[79] He held no grudge against the president. "I had done nothing for him," he said, philosophically, "and he had an election to win, and power to hold."[80] As for Sinclair, he had books to write, starting with the story of the campaign. He called it *I, Candidate for Governor, and How I Got Licked*, and finished it in twenty-two days.

To Sinclair, the 1934 campaign provided a chance to spread his ideas and, in the end, gather material for a great book. To regular California Democrats, the campaign symbolized the dangers of sliding too far to the left. In their view, the party had averted a near disaster—and lost an opportunity to elect a Democratic governor in the national pro-Roosevelt landslide.

To conservatives, though, it did not matter that Roosevelt had spurned Sinclair. They believed that the New Deal had made Sinclair's candidacy possible. As Los Angeles utilities executive William Mullendore explained to a friend, the president had "used his high office to lift out of the gutter and on to a plane of respectability the basic ideas of Socialism and Communism."[81] As with the strike mediation, Roosevelt could not please these conservatives. He could exclude farmworkers from his protective laws; he could abandon his own party's candidate. Yet these Western businessmen still believed that the president threatened their prosperity and their social order.

Although Merriam had agreed to cooperate with Roosevelt for the next few years, the state's business leaders did not intend to follow his example. "These subversive ideas and doctrines must be stamped out in the quarter from which they emanate and where they do the most harm—that is, in the capitol of the nation," Mullendore vowed.[82] He and his colleagues in the Western conservative movement would continue to attack the New Deal by equating it with Communism, an insight they gleaned in the fields of California. First, though, they needed to get rid of the real Communists.

9

MAKING HISTORY

At lunchtime on July 20, 1934, about fifteen men and women at the Communist Party Workers' Center in downtown Sacramento were startled by shouting and pounding on the front door. The workers dropped their books and card games as dozens of police armed with blackjacks, clubs, tear gas bombs, and sawed-off shotguns charged into the building. The police lined most of the men against the wall and trained their guns on them while detectives searched for revolutionary material. They found no weapons but plenty of evidence of dissident politics: picket signs, Marxist literature, and a picture of Lenin.

The cops congratulated one another when they discovered that along with seditious material they had captured Caroline Decker and Pat Chambers, two of the state's most notorious organizers of farmworkers' unions. At the same hour throughout the city, police arrested other Communists who organized unions, taught Marxist theory, or spoke against capitalism in Plaza Park, the preferred place for radical gatherings in the state capital.[1]

Sacramento prosecutors charged Decker, Chambers, and fifteen other Communists with "conspiring to commit criminal syndicalism," or belonging to a revolutionary organization, and put them on trial in state superior court. Reporters from newspapers and magazines throughout the country converged on the California capital to cover what the state attorney general called "one of the most important trials in the history of the state."[2]

Both sides in the Sacramento trial believed that California was the victim of a conspiracy: either a "vicious, reactionary conspiracy to smash unionism," in the opinion of the defendants; or a vicious, revolutionary conspiracy against America, in the view of the prosecutor.[3] According to the government, this handful of California Reds, with their mimeographed flyers and "workers' school" and storefront headquarters in downtown Sacramento, possessed the power to smash the state and "take away from you what you have" in their frenzied assault on American values.[4]

The great Sacramento conspiracy trial was notable for its drama—testimony from "stool pigeons," repeated objections by the bellowing lead defense lawyer, and courtroom battles between the pompous prosecutor and the newspapers' favorite "blonde firebrand," Caroline Decker.[5]

But the trial was more than a good story. It demonstrated the agribusiness barons' success in using fear—fear about changes in race relations and in women's roles—to attack their opponents in the labor movement and to win allies among people who would not have sided with them simply on class interests. It also showed how growers continued to deploy government power for their economic benefit. In Sacramento, employers would use California's judicial machinery to make the union leaders pay a high price for their activism.

The Raid

The Cannery and Agricultural Workers Industrial Union decided to move its headquarters to Sacramento soon after the San Jose lynchings of late 1933. The radical leaders had been unnerved by the spectacle of murderous mobs right in St. James Park, just blocks from their offices. Sacramento was a logical choice for the new headquarters. Although the Party was larger in Los Angeles and more vibrant in San Francisco, Sacramento was in the middle of the great Central Valley and "the nerve center of an agricultural empire," as *The Nation* noted.[6] Moreover, it was the capital city, and protest marches there could capture the attention of the state's power brokers.

In late April 1934, Chambers and Decker arrived in Sacramento to help organize unions, political protests, and Marxist education classes. They presided over the CAWIU's second (and, as it turned out, final) annual conference; they led local parades, including a May Day march; and set up the

Workers' School, which was short on chairs, tables, and blackboards but enjoyed a surplus of idealism. At the school, Decker, Jack Warnick, and other union leaders taught classes on "Principles of Communism," "Communism for Young Workers," "Marxian Economics," "Self-Defense in Court," "Revolutionary Theater," and, in a somewhat more practical vein, English. The Party also organized marches to Plaza Park, where local Communists waved red flags and denounced war, hunger, and the profit motive.[7]

Decker and Chambers took their places in a small but ideologically diverse group of Sacramento radical activists. Some of the local leaders were women who, like Decker, had found their voices in the Communist Party. Lorene Norman, a twenty-three-year-old native of Texas, had picked cotton since she was seven years old. She had recently lost her job at the State Library because of her radical politics. Although young and relatively inexperienced, she became a leader in the city's small Communist movement.[8] She was joined by Nora Conklin, the organizer of the Communist-affiliated Unemployed Council, who had led "dozens of riotous demonstrations" at the county relief office over the previous few years, according to the *Sacramento Bee*. It was Conklin who had been called "a gibbering petticoat on a soap box" by a Sacramento judge when he sentenced her to jail.[9]

Chambers and Decker were also helped by a local leader of the union who was not a Communist, although he was a radical. Norman Mini, a twenty-six-year-old CAWIU organizer and former West Point cadet, had recently broken with the Communist Party for ideological reasons. He announced that he was a follower of Leon Trotsky, who had been banished by Stalin after a leadership struggle in the Soviet Union. True Communists hated Trotskyists more than any other enemy. But Chambers, Decker, and local activists in Sacramento ignored these internecine battles. Mini was a good organizer and a hard worker, and they were happy to have his assistance. Still, Mini's anti-Stalinist views would cause tension among the defendants during the union leaders' trial.

To many liberals, the Sacramento Communist movement seemed pathetic, with its revolutionary theatrics and earnest but lonely soapbox speakers. In 1933, ten thousand Sacramentans had turned out to cheer a parade for Franklin Roosevelt's National Recovery Administration. By contrast, the largest Communist demonstration in the city's history drew two hundred people to see activists wave the red flag in Plaza Park on May Day in 1934. But to many Sacramento businessmen at the time, it was as if Stalin himself were plotting to hoist the hammer and sickle over the state capitol.

To keep tabs on the Communists, local officials and businessmen worked with General Ralph Van Deman's statewide surveillance network to infiltrate the Communist Party and the union.[10] The few dozen participants at CAWIU meetings included spies from the state Bureau of Criminal Identification, the Sacramento police, the district attorney's office, the Associated Farmers, the Chamber of Commerce, and even clandestine agents of the *Sacramento Bee*.

The *Bee* was a somewhat unlikely member of this group of anticommunist zealots. Its owner, C.K. McClatchy, prided himself on his progressivism, and saw his chain of Central Valley papers as "real tribunes of the people, always fighting for the right no matter how powerfully entrenched wrong may be." But McClatchy also believed that constitutional liberties should be restricted to those who respected them, and he did not put the "Benedict Arnolds of the Moscow persuasion" in that category.[11] Alarmed by what he saw as a nest of traitors within his city, he enlisted undercover agents to keep him informed of their plans.

The reports of these informants were quite mundane. The *Bee's* secret agents noted that CAWIU now counted sixteen members in the nearby town of Roseville; that they desperately needed $15 to rent a hall for their convention; and that local Communists expected the parade on May Day to be "a big one." There was no evidence of impending revolution. Moreover, at some events, the informants came close to outnumbering the activists. Indeed, one spy reported that he was the only person to show up at an organizational meeting.[12]

The growers monitored this small band of activists for a good reason: they understood that these union organizers could help trigger a redistribution of power and wealth throughout the state. If the CAWIU succeeded in uniting vegetable pickers, then California workers—in industry as well as agriculture—would be emboldened to fight for more collective bargaining rights. But if officials imprisoned the Communists, then the strikes—and the disruptions to the growers' profits—would stop. The jailing of the Sacramento organizers would leave the CAWIU "without leadership in this section and would result in immediate disorganization and eventual disbandment," as one informant for the employers explained in a private report.[13]

And so the district attorney decided to pounce. At lunchtime on the final day of the San Francisco strike, the city police launched simultaneous raids on the state Party headquarters, the Workers' School, and Sacramento's "Hooverville," the homeless encampment where Communists often recruited members and distributed free food.[14] The newspapers reported that there had been no violence during the raids, but this apparently meant "no violence on the part of the Communists." Unpublished pictures taken by a *Sacramento Bee* photographer showed two workers bloodied and beaten after their arrests.[15]

In all, twenty-four men and women, including Decker and Chambers, were arrested and charged with vagrancy, which was legally defined as wandering "from place to place without any lawful business."[16] In an era

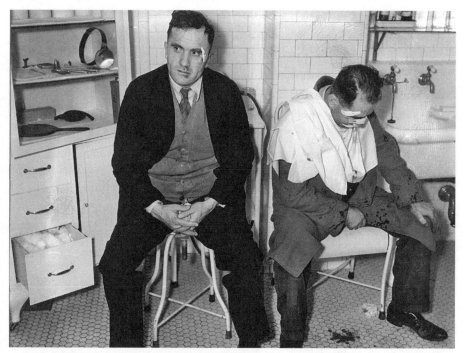

Two unidentified men recover after the police raid on the Communist union headquarters in Sacramento. Center for Sacramento History, *Sacramento Bee* Collection, 1983-001-2421.

when many people were homeless, the police used vagrancy statutes as all-purpose, get-into-jail-free cards. It was clear from the start that the vagrancy charges were cynical ploys by the prosecutor. When he discovered that his men had accidentally caught two actual (non-Communist) vagrants in their dragnet, he quickly set them free. He wanted to detain the Communists, especially Decker and Chambers, long enough to gather evidence to persuade a grand jury to indict them for a more serious crime: criminal syndicalism. If convicted, they could be sent to state prison for decades.

California's legislature had passed the Criminal Syndicalism Act in April 1919, at a time when Americans feared a Bolshevik Revolution at home. Most states enacted some sort of anti-syndicalism or sedition law. California's law made it a crime to advocate violence as a means of "accomplishing a change in industrial ownership or control or affecting any political change."[17] In practice, this meant that people could go to prison for belonging to an organization that the state defined as revolutionary.

In its early years, prosecutors used California's Criminal Syndicalism Act primarily against the Industrial Workers of the World, or Wobblies. By 1924, 164 anarchists had been convicted of violating the law in California. The U.S. Supreme Court upheld its constitutionality in a landmark case in 1927.[18]

Thus Decker, Chambers, Warnick, and their comrades faced two legal proceedings: the first one, the vagrancy trial in police court, included testimony by officers who swore they had seen the defendants wandering around with no lawful purposes; and the other, the inquiry before the grand jury, featured statements by paid informants who recounted revolutionary speeches at Party meetings.

The prosecutors worked with state and local law enforcement and private business groups to secure evidence for the syndicalism indictments. The Associated Farmers was especially eager to help. The organization's officials began by using their connections with government agencies and private surveillance networks to gather information against the defendants. Guernsey Frazer, the executive secretary of the AF, wrote Los Angeles police chief James Davis, Alameda County district attorney Earl Warren, and growers and cotton gin owners throughout the Central Valley to ask for documents that could be used against Chambers, Decker, or any of their comrades on trial. He and his colleagues at the AF emphasized the economic benefits of helping the prosecution. "Obviously, if they can be retained in jail throughout the summer, it will be a great relief to all California agriculture, including the cotton producers," one grower wrote on August 1.[19]

Other agencies and private groups contributed to the effort to destroy the union and the Communist movement. The Sacramento Police Red Squad, the Los Angeles Red Squad, the state Bureau of Criminal Identification, the state Attorney General's office, and city and county prosecutors all cooperated on the case. Beyond the courtroom, business leaders organized to help the state chase the Communists from Sacramento. One group, which included eighty prominent businessmen, formed subcommittees to examine new laws to control communism, raise funds to combat communism, and investigate local schools to root out communist sympathizers.[20]

The Sacramento City Council voted to hire a special prosecutor to conduct the vagrancy trials so that the regular prosecutors could be free to pursue the more serious indictments. When one councilman objected to spending the money, Mayor Thomas P. Scollan argued that the general strike had raised the threat level in California. "Recently they started an unsuccessful civil war in San Francisco," he said. "Talk has given way to action."[21]

Police locked the Communist men in a 25-by-30-foot drunk tank filled with alcoholics and petty criminals. For fourteen days, they inhaled the odors of vomit and filth in the holding cell while they took turns sleeping on the damp concrete floor.[22] When they appeared in court, the prisoners—who had taught classes in "Revolutionary Theater" and "Self-Defense in Court"—tried to score dramatic points by protesting their treatment. At his arraignment, Chambers strode across the courtroom and threw a hunk of moldy bread in front of the judge. "That, your honor," he said, "is exhibit A of the Sacramento city jail."[23] Later, some of the defendants went on a hunger strike and forced the sheriff to serve better food.[24]

The vagrancy trials ended with convictions of eleven of the twenty-four defendants. Caroline Decker was among the thirteen found not guilty. The jury struggled to reach unanimous verdicts, and only succeeded after the judge sequestered them (for the first time in Sacramento police court history) and pointedly reminded them that "much time and money" had been spent on the trial.[25] Despite the thirteen acquittals, the special prosecutor still claimed victory, saying the convictions proved "that Sacramento will not tolerate un-American troublemakers and strike organizers."[26]

The grand jury gave the prosecutor an even bigger victory: indictments for criminal syndicalism.[27] Fourteen defendants faced one count of aiding and abetting criminal syndicalism and one count of conspiring to commit criminal syndicalism. If convicted on both counts, they could be sent to state prison for twenty-eight years.[28]

The Plot Against America

As the trial approached, the newspapers ran almost daily stories on the supposed Communist plots against California and the nation. *Dozens of foreign men reported to threaten prospective jurors! Prosecution witness kidnapped! Young Communist League flyers found at Sacramento High School! Reds plot to kidnap President Roosevelt! Thousands of armed Communists set to invade state Capitol!*[29]

The district attorney grabbed every opportunity to put the case in the headlines. A tall, jowly political veteran, Neil McAllister was running for reelection in November. The case won him unexpected nationwide attention when his agents discovered letters in Decker's apartment that allowed him to link Hollywood stars with the Reds on trial. Police officers confiscated several letters to and from Decker that discussed how to raise money from movie stars, including James Cagney.[30] McAllister distributed copies of the letters between Decker and Ella Winter that discussed Cagney's support of the union. "I have Cagney's money again," Winter said in one letter.[31] In another, Decker said that the actor had promised to pay her bail, no matter how high, if she were ever arrested. "He'd better get a nice lump sum ready," she wrote grimly.[32] Names of three Mexican American movie stars also appeared on a slip of paper in her apartment, without further explanation.

The newspapers ran photographs of the letters in question, complete with artfully juxtaposed photos of Cagney and Decker that made it look as though he wanted to do more than pay her bail.[33] All the actors vehemently denied that they sympathized with Decker or any Red. "I am against all isms except 100 percent Americanism," Cagney protested.[34] Dolores Del Rio, one of the stars whose names appeared on the piece of paper, scoffed that

McAllister was just a publicity seeker. "Why doesn't this man in Sacramento find out about things before he talks so much?" she asked.[35]

If McAllister hoped to use the case to keep his office, Sacramento's voters disappointed him. He was trounced at the polls in November. The new district attorney, Otis Babcock, was a liberal who had campaigned on the slogan that Sacramento needed a New Deal.[36] It seemed that the state's anticommunist public-private alliance had lost the battle. The trial would continue, but with a liberal prosecutor who presumably would focus on the criminal charges, not cultural threats.

The state's agribusiness leaders, however, saw no reason to let Sacramento voters derail their plans. They set out first to overturn the election results, and then to devise the prosecution strategy, pay witnesses, launder money, suborn perjury, and offer the prosecutor a de facto bribe. The growers wanted Chambers and Decker behind bars, and they would leave no aspect of the trial to chance.

Shaping the Case

Immediately after Babcock's election, state business leaders pressured Sacramento's new district attorney to step aside and allow McAllister, his defeated opponent, to run the conspiracy trial. Babcock was obviously conflicted. He first announced that he would let McAllister help him try the case, but then changed his mind and said he would prosecute it himself. The *Sacramento Union*, the capital's second largest daily, and the county board of supervisors praised his decision to save the taxpayers money by trying the case without outside help.[37]

But then California agribusiness leaders took action. Men from the Associated Farmers and other business groups demanded that California attorney general Ulysses S. Webb bypass Babcock and appoint a special prosecutor for the trial.[38] In the November election, California voters had passed a new constitutional amendment that gave the attorney general the right to take over significant local cases.

After businessmen pleaded for his intervention, Webb invoked his new emergency powers and appointed McAllister—the man who had just been turned out of office, presumably at least in part because of voters' disapproval of his pursuit of the Chambers/Decker indictments—as a state special prosecutor in that very case. The attorney general acted after conferences "with a group of Sacramento citizens who have become interested in the prosecution of the case," the *Bee* reported. When Babcock protested, Webb removed Sacramento's new DA from the case entirely. Realizing he had no alternative, Babcock stepped aside.[39]

It was a move that might have come from an Upton Sinclair novel: big business, angry that voters had chosen a liberal to prosecute union organizers, simply nullified the results of the election. If there had ever been any doubt before, it was now clear that McAllister was the dependable agent of California agribusiness.

Having secured the prosecutor, the Associated Farmers set about finding and hiring expert witnesses and consultants for the trial. The organization paid the chief of the Los Angeles Red Squad, the freckle-faced, improbably named "Red" Hynes, to take a leave of absence to assist the prosecution. Hynes received $50 a day for the first five weeks of the trial, for a total of $1,800; and then $25 a day, or approximately $2,000, for the remainder of the trial, plus expenses.[40] This was five times his usual salary of $200 a month. His sideline as a consultant proved quite lucrative for Hynes: the next year, during his divorce proceedings, his wife contended that the police captain had stashed $40,000, or about $700,000 in 2015 dollars, in his savings account.[41] Prosecutor McAllister was not paid by the Associated Farmers, but the group dangled the possibility of lucrative employment after the trial by promising a job to him and to his chief deputy.[42]

The Associated Farmers helped to control the press coverage by providing daily briefings to reporters. The publicity director of the AF, Gilbert Parker, also a Hearst reporter, sat at the prosecutors' table with McAllister and offered to help the other reporters by suggesting angles for stories.[43] The newspapers did not need many suggestions from the growers: the coverage was universally favorable to the prosecution, with the Hearst newspapers and the *Sacramento Bee* competing to publish the most sensationalistic stories.

As usual, the Associated Farmers wanted to keep its role secret. If the Communists' attorneys learned of the growers' help to the prosecution, one staff member wrote, they might use the "sympathy angle" to convince the public that "the bosses and capitalists and their hirelings are attempting to railroad the poor framed up defendants."[44] To ensure secrecy, the AF laundered its money through an employee of the state Bureau of Criminal

Identification. The AF made out checks to Rachel Sowers, the assistant to the chief of the bureau, and she passed along the proceeds to the spies and witnesses.[45]

While the secrecy was strategically necessary, it prevented the growers from taking credit for their efforts. The Associated Farmers staff felt somewhat aggrieved that their fellow businessmen did not appreciate their contributions to the case. "The only organization that has done one single solitary thing in this case has been our organization," Frazer, the AF executive secretary, wrote to George Clements of the Los Angeles Chamber of Commerce. The Associated Farmers had not only directed the case, but "we have had to bear the entire expense ourselves out of our budget," Frazer lamented.[46] McAllister conceded that the trial would have been a "hopeless proposition" without the growers' assistance. In all, the Associated Farmers spent about $14,000 (about $250,000 in 2015 dollars) to put Chambers and Decker behind bars.[47]

The growers also helped McAllister plot strategy for the trial. They knew criminal syndicalism cases could be unpopular with juries. After all, a supposedly grower-friendly Tulare County jury had split 6–6 when Chambers faced similar charges in 1933. So the Associated Farmers decided to consult a man who had successfully prosecuted CAWIU leaders for criminal syndicalism: Imperial County district attorney Elmer Heald, who had won convictions of union leaders back in 1930. Heald traveled to Sacramento at the Associated Farmers' expense to help McAllister prepare his case.[48]

McAllister, meanwhile, assured the newspaper reporters that the upcoming trial would be historic. It was "the most important case in the state and perhaps the United States," he said. Indeed, he insisted it was more significant than murder cases, "because these defendants are trying to bring on conditions similar to those in Russia, where millions can be seen lying dead along the roads."[49] He just needed to persuade a Sacramento jury that this motley collection of labor organizers was in league with these mass murderers.

Conspiracy Theory

In truth, the Communists McAllister had put in jail were not part of a global conspiracy but isolated, lonely men and women who felt abandoned by their

The original eighteen defendants in the Sacramento conspiracy trial. Center for Sacramento History, *Sacramento Bee* Collection, 1983-001-2364.

Party's leaders. As Decker awaited trial, she wrote a friend about her frustration with the Communist leaders—men who, at that point, had refused to put up bond for her $3,000 bail. "So you see—here I am—in jail—ostracized by my own Party," she wrote, "raising a little fuss and being told—this is being done and that is being done and the Party is making every effort to win the case—etc. etc.—and feeling myself the Party is not sufficiently utilizing the case."

Decker was used to tough conditions, but her cell was damp and freezing, and she was faint from hunger. She believed that the union needed her on the outside, making speeches to publicize the injustice of the charges against her. Meanwhile, there was little she could do but stare at the bars on her cell and the gray walls and write bitter letters to her friends.[50] Her husband was also angry and disillusioned with the Party. Jack Warnick took the unusual step of publicly denouncing Communist leaders in the local media when they accused his Trotskyist co-defendant, Norman Mini, of being a government informant.[51]

But the prosecutors did not care about ideological differences or tension among the defendants. McAllister's strategy was simple. He aimed to show that (a) Communists advocated violence; (b) the defendants were Communists; ergo, (c) the defendants posed a violent threat to Sacramento citizens, and should be imprisoned by the state.

McAllister began the trial with what was now a common method for discrediting Communists: emphasizing their radical notions about gender, religion, and race. He read from Marxist pamphlets, newspapers, and books, some of them dating back to the nineteenth century, that discussed the ways that the bosses used race or religion to control the masses. The jurors heard short (and often out of context) selections from the *Daily Worker*, *The Communist Manifesto*, strike flyers, and booklets with titles like "The Road to Negro Liberation." These were all legal publications in the United States, some of them available at public libraries. But McAllister hoped to shock the jurors with these fragments, and persuade them that California would not be safe until the young revolutionaries were behind bars.

The former DA borrowed a technique from GOP strategists in the anti–Upton Sinclair campaign and shifted the focus from economics to cultural scaremongering. He placed particular emphasis on the Party's challenges to racial and gender norms, including its call for a "Negro republic" in the American South and its opposition to laws that banned interracial marriage. Thanks to the increased migration of Southern whites to California, these Southern-style racial appeals had more potency than ever before. He introduced evidence that purported to show the sexual danger that the Reds posed to white women. One witness testified that a Communist speaker in Los Angeles—who was not on trial in Sacramento—had once said his comrades planned to strip capitalist women naked and force them to "come crawling through the mire right on their lily white bellies."[52]

At the defense table, almost a dozen attorneys and jailhouse lawyers jostled for space and supremacy as they loudly challenged the prosecutors (and sometimes each other). Six of the defendants represented themselves, as the Party preferred—all the better for exposing the lies and contradictions of the capitalist state. Mini, the Trotskyist, had his own counsel.

The remaining defendants retained three legendary civil rights attorneys. Two of them were already veterans of labor battles in California. Grover Johnson and Abraham Wirin of the ACLU had represented strikers in Imperial County the previous year. They had been beaten and threatened with lynching, yet now they had returned, undaunted, to a California courtroom to defend equally unpopular activists.

Their co-counsel had not fought the vigilantes in Imperial because he had been busy with an even more daunting task: facing down state-sponsored violence in Nazi Germany. Attorney Leo Gallagher, a renowned defender of unpopular views and people at home and abroad, had been kicked out of Germany in early 1934 for his vigorous defense of Georgi Dimitrov and other Communists charged with burning down the Reichstag, a crime that let Adolf Hitler claim dictatorial powers. Closer to home, Gallagher had been beaten by Los Angeles police when he refused to leave a city council meeting.[53]

Gallagher hated liars, manipulators, and fools. "More than any person I know," wrote Carey McWilliams, one of his great admirers, "Gallagher lacks humor, detachment, tact."[54] He also had a hair-trigger temper and thunderous voice. On one particularly contentious day during the trial, Gallagher spoke so loudly that a juror complained that he was shouting in their ears.

After the juror's complaint, Norman Mini's attorney stalked from the courtroom in disgust and told reporters that Gallagher was endangering the defense. "He is sending my client and the rest of the defendants to the state penitentiary by his attitude," he fumed.[55] At another point, Gallagher referred to opposing counsel as "a bunch of dumb oxen." McAllister dared him to repeat the phrase outside of court.[56]

As the trial progressed, Gallagher became convinced that the prosecutors were worse than dumb. He believed they were hired tools of capital who lied shamelessly when it served their paymasters' cause. When McAllister accused the defendants of funding their union with "Moscow gold," Gallagher demanded that the judge strike the remark from the record. The judge agreed, but Gallagher would not let it go. McAllister, he said, was nothing but an opportunist and a liar. "He knows it is a lie," he added, "but there is no infamy to which he will not stoop."[57]

Gallagher did not think much better of the judge, a pillar of the local establishment who evinced little sympathy for the radical activists on trial before him. Judge Dal Lemmon was a Kansas native, Stanford graduate, and past president of the Sacramento County Bar Association as well as the Rotary Club. He was a member of just about every important civic organization in Northern California, including the Sutter Club, University Club, Commonwealth Club, Pacific Union Club, Del Paso Country Club, and the Elks Club. A Republican, he had been appointed to the bench by Governor Rolph in 1933. Later, in 1947, President Harry Truman would respect him enough to cross party lines and name him to the federal court, and in 1954 President Eisenhower would elevate him to the Court of Appeals for the Ninth Circuit, where he would serve until his death.[58]

The judge was far cleverer and more restrained than the prosecutor, but he still showed clear distaste for the defendants and their attorneys. "Take that sneer off your face, Mr. Gallagher," Lemmon rebuked the defense counsel at one point.[59] Occasionally, however, Lemmon showed impatience with McAllister's prolonged and pointless cross-examinations.[60] Throughout, the judge could barely conceal his contempt for the mad guerrilla theater of the defense and the patriotism-on-steroids buffoonery of the prosecution, and he presided over the trial with an air of "condescending boredom," according to one reporter.[61]

But no one was bored once McAllister began questioning informants, men whom the Communists called "stoolies." The defendants had already suspected that some of these men were spies. Others, though, came as complete surprises. The union activists seemed stunned to see Melville Harris, the young director of the Party's spring membership drive, take the stand to testify against them and admit he was being paid by the Associated Farmers. The defendants representing themselves did not try to hide their disdain as they cross-examined him. The judge rebuked Decker for using the term "stool-pigeon" in her questioning. As Harris left the stand, Nora Conklin and fellow defendant Mike Plesh pronounced their own verdict. "Rat!" they hissed.[62]

The most colorful witness was a disheveled, elderly man named William Hanks who had shown up at the union headquarters a few months earlier and presented himself as an old Wobbly. He had indeed joined the Wobblies back in World War I, but as a spy for the Department of Justice. For the past fifteen years, Hanks had worked as a professional informant for industrial employers and federal, state, and local agencies, infiltrating unions and radical groups and trying to entrap their members into committing violent acts so that they could be arrested. On the stand, he testified that the Reds had kidnapped him before the trial and taken him to Wisconsin in a failed attempt to keep him from bearing witness.

On cross-examination, Gallagher succeeded in shredding Hanks's tale of alleged witness intimidation. Hanks's landlord and the driver who took him to the bus station in Sacramento testified that he had been calm and orderly throughout his departure from town, with no sign of menacing men lurking in the background. Moreover, Hanks's brother and friends swore that he had never mentioned kidnapping during his cheerful sojourn in Wisconsin, where his family lived. Gallagher argued that the district attorney had concocted the tale to make the Reds seem dangerous.[63]

To show the defendants' supposed willingness to use violence, McAllister put growers on the witness stand to tell jurors about Chambers's speech right before the Pixley massacre. Frank Peterson, a cotton farmer from Earlimart, described a frightening scene of angry, mysterious foreigners who threatened the Valley's safety and order. The cotton pickers in Pixley, he said, "were milling around there like a bunch of cattle and talking in Spanish." He did not understand what they said, but he was sure that it "wouldn't have been very pleasant for the white men if they could have understood it." Then, according to Peterson, Chambers got up and said something he could understand: he told the workers to "make the streets as red as Harlan, Kentucky," where workers and security guards had battled to the death. "If they get in your way, put them in a hospital and keep them there; we will show the damned rats," Peterson reported Chambers saying.[64] Peterson was not just any grower. He had been among the group of men who shot the strikers in Pixley.

But strikers testified that Chambers had not threatened violence; rather, he had predicted that the *growers* would attack workers and "make the streets of Pixley run red with blood."[65] Chambers, angry and disgusted, charged Peterson with perjury and murder during his cross-examination: "You was one of the fellows that did the shooting."[66]

After McAllister rested his case, Gallagher put on a flamboyant defense. He began by calling McAllister himself to the stand, as Clarence Darrow had done a decade earlier to William Jennings Bryan in the Scopes "monkey" trial in Tennessee. Gallagher wanted to trick McAllister into admitting that the prosecution team had orchestrated William Hanks's alleged kidnapping. But the confrontation between the two lawyers fizzled when the judge refused to allow most of Gallagher's questions.[67]

Gallagher tried to prove that the farmworkers' union simply wanted to raise wages, not start a revolution. He summoned fifteen cotton pickers to testify about their poverty, desperation, and commitment to peaceful protest. They insisted that Chambers had never advocated violence.[68] The defense also called to the stand small business owners and growers who supported the workers' account of the Pixley massacre. Some farmers told the jury that they had heard Decker and Chambers speak numerous times, but never heard them incite the workers to riot or to attack strikebreakers or growers.[69] As McAllister's narrative unraveled, Gallagher railed against the growers' frame-up of his clients.[70]

Even one man on the growers' payroll came to see the trial as legal entrapment. Gilbert Parker, the Hearst publicity man who worked for the Associated Farmers and McAllister during the trial, found it increasingly difficult to shill for the prosecutors. During McAllister's cross-examination of Big Bill Hammett, the Okie union leader who had helped Chambers and Decker during the cotton strike, Parker shot looks of disgust at the other reporters. Finally, he leaned over to the correspondent for the *Western Worker* and confided, "I'm sorry. This is getting to be too damn much for me." Two days later, he told the reporter good-bye. "I'm through with this dirty business," he said. "I'm going to get myself an honest job."[71]

The defendants did their best to counter the prosecution's propaganda with advertisements of their own. They tried to explain the virtues of a Communist system and to put their radical slogans in context. Nora Conklin defended the Red flag as an emblem of "justice and decent living for all workers; food for children, care for expectant mothers, and elimination of the profit motive in industry and a classless society." Other defendants declared that the American Communist Party had no intention of starting a revolution.[72]

For many of the reporters, the highlight of the trial came when Caroline Decker—called "the Blond Flame of the Red Revolt" by the Hearst papers—testified in her own defense for six hours.[73] She did not hesitate to call herself a Communist and defend Marxist theory. When McAllister asked her if the Party tried to "agitate the people, the dissatisfied people" and persuade them to overthrow the government, Decker retorted that Communists did not create class conflict. "The very nature of capitalism has developed a class society, has developed class hatred, has developed class antagonism," she explained. "The function of the Communist Party is to direct into organized channels, into progressive channels, the energies of the masses of the people instead of permitting chaos and anarchy."[74] She insisted that her comrades, not the government putting them on trial, were the real forces for order and stability.

McAllister, preening in the spotlight, tried to paint Decker as a hardened revolutionary. She repeatedly got the better of him. When the prosecutor called her an "agitator," Decker retorted: "You can call it agitating, I call it educating." Moreover, many great reformers had been agitators, she argued; even Jesus Christ was an agitator. McAllister sneered: "Oh, Jesus Christ was an agitator?" Decker's husband, Jack Warnick, then piped up from the defendants' table: "Yes, he was crucified for it." When McAllister tried to follow up—"Will you tell me in what respect Jesus Christ was an agitator?"—the judge told him to stop. "Well, she brought it out, your honor," McAllister replied peevishly.[75]

Outside the courtroom, city and state officials dramatized the Red menace with anticommunist theater. When Communist sympathizers announced that they would march on Sacramento to demand passage of a state unemployment insurance law, the *Bee* reported breathlessly that thousands of Reds were poised to "invade" Sacramento. To meet the challenge, the city manager deputized five hundred local citizens and drilled them in city parks with axe handles and tear gas bombs.[76] Anticommunist speakers told local groups that the Reds were dedicated to "scrapping all moral standards and erasing the color line."[77]

At the height of the trial, newspapers revealed that General Seth Howard, the head of California's National Guard, had recently begged Washington for more soldiers because of the Red threat to the state. He needed more Guardsmen, he said, "to try to save California."[78]

Avoiding the Problem

The Roosevelt administration had no response to General Howard's request for troops. Nor did it say anything at all about the Sacramento trial. The federal government played no role in the conspiracy case. Sacramento County put the defendants on trial; the state appointed the prosecutor. The fate of Communist union organizers, especially organizers of farmworkers, was of no concern to most federal officials in California and Washington.

One of the few New Deal officials who was sympathetic to farmworkers, Agriculture Undersecretary Rexford Tugwell, confessed in his private diary in late December 1934 that "the problem of agricultural labor is one which is avoided by everyone." Tugwell believed that there were a couple of ways that the New Dealers could start to help farmworkers. Perhaps the Agricultural Adjustment Act could be amended to add protections for laborers, he mused, but he worried that the Senate would never pass such amendments. Alternatively, he speculated, Senator Robert Wagner's new labor relations bill—which proposed to replace and strengthen Section 7a—could cover farm as well as industrial workers. But Wagner needed administration support if his bill were to extend to farm laborers. "The difficulty . . . is that we do not know at present," Tugwell wrote ruefully, "whether or not it will have administration support."[79]

Just two months later, Tugwell became more "disillusioned and cynical" with Roosevelt's policies when a small group of farmworker supporters was suddenly purged from the Agricultural Adjustment Administration.[80] Like Tugwell, other reformers in the early AAA wanted to use government agricultural policy to reshape the American countryside and the rural economy. They hoped that the agency could help preserve small farms, restore the environment, and bring social justice to the nation's rural areas. These idealists had made sure that the AAA codes required the Southern cotton planters to pass along some of their government subsidy payments to their sharecroppers and tenant farmers.

When planters found a loophole in the law and pocketed the payments, the reformers decided to act. The agency's legal division asked one of its contract lawyers, a Harvard Law graduate named Alger Hiss, to draw up a new rule that made it more difficult for the planters to cheat their sharecroppers out of their subsidy payments.[81]

AAA head Chester Davis, an advocate for Southern planters, was furious when he heard about the rule change. He pressured Agriculture Secretary Henry Wallace to disavow the new regulation—and to fire five reformers in the agency who supported it. Wallace and Davis, with Roosevelt's acquiescence, forced several men to resign.[82] The AAA had always benefited the largest landowners, but now it would benefit them exclusively. This part of the New Deal, at least, would have no revolutionary implications.[83]

At a press conference explaining the firings, Secretary Wallace argued that there had been too much leftist sentiment in the AAA. "You know a ship may have too much ballast on the left or right and list in either direction," he said. "We have always tried to steer to the middle."

When a reporter noted that Wallace seemed to have thrown all of his left ballast overboard, the secretary chuckled. He could take more on later if necessary, he said.[84]

That prospect seemed unlikely, though. Those sympathetic to radicalism, or simply to farm laborers, had gotten the message. Standing up for farmworkers could get one fired. It was best—it was essential—to avoid antagonizing the large landowners. The implicit policies of the early New Deal were now explicit: the Roosevelt administration would protect the rights of workers in factories, but not those on factory farms.

Although the purge of the reformers at the AAA quickly faded from the front pages, it later became a favorite subject for historians. For one thing, it showed how Southern planters imposed limits on reforms during the New Deal. Pragmatic federal officials had to accommodate the wishes of the Southern Democrats whose votes were needed in Congress.

For another thing, the name of the lawyer who drafted the new rules would become synonymous with alleged New Deal sympathy for Communism. Twelve years later, when Hiss was accused of spying for the Soviets, the farmers who had opposed him when he was at the AAA would remember what he had done in 1935—and, with great satisfaction, argue that they had been right all along. If Alger Hiss was a Soviet spy, as he appeared to be, then perhaps they could prove that the entire New Deal was a Communist plot.[85]

For his part, Tugwell was despondent. The purge was clearly part of Chester Davis's "studied plan to rid the Department of all liberals and to give the reactionary farm leaders full control of policy."[86] Roosevelt needed Southern Democratic support to get any more New Deal measures through Congress. Farmworkers on Southern plantations and Western factory farms were the losers in this political game, while Republican agribusiness leaders in California were the unintended beneficiaries.

Just because they profited from the New Deal's compromises with Southern planters, though, did not mean that large California farmers became Roosevelt supporters. On the contrary, the proposed rule change confirmed their belief that New Deal agencies were riddled with Communists. They redoubled their efforts to get rid of Reds in government offices and in the fields.

Toward Sacramento, or Moscow?

Back in Sacramento, the conspiracy trial drew to a close after more than four months of testimony. In his concluding argument, Gallagher, true to form, launched a scorching attack on the prosecution, denouncing the state witnesses as murderers and demanding that McAllister be disbarred. He blasted Attorney General Webb—"the iron fist of the ruling class"—for appointing McAllister and his deputy to run the trial "after they had been kicked out of office by the voters."[87]

Gallagher conceded that his own lack of decorum might have hurt his clients' case. "But," he begged the jury, "I ask that you do not convict these people because of some antagonism I have aroused. Do not take it out on these defendants."[88]

When it was his turn to address the jury, Chambers presented the case as a brazen attempt by agribusiness to cut workers' wages and ruin a union that had tried to alleviate "misery, starvation, brutality." The trial was nothing more than an assault on farmworkers' unions, he said. In sentencing the defendants to prison, he told the jurors, "you are sounding the opening gun in an attack on the wages of these workers."[89]

The defendants chose Decker to deliver the two-and-a-half-hour summation to the jury. More than one hundred people were turned away from the packed courtroom that day. Decker did not disappoint her fans. She ignored the criminal syndicalism charges and called on a higher law: the First Amendment of the Constitution. "If you vote for an acquittal," she told the jurors, "you are not voting for Communism. You are voting for the right of the American people to say what they please."[90] Their duty was not to the defendants or even to the community but to something larger: "You are a jury that will make history."[91]

McAllister also appealed to the jurors' patriotism, but his speech was underscored by a very different notion of the meaning of Americanism. So many people had sacrificed to come to California, he said: the pioneers in covered wagons, for example, and the poor, starving members of the Donner Party, who had been forced to eat each other to survive. Now the Reds proposed to destroy everything that the jurors' forefathers had built—"to take away from you what you have, and overthrow this government."[92]

Like Decker, McAllister warned the twelve middle-class men and women in the jury box that their verdict would shape the future of California and the nation. "You are today MAKING HISTORY," the prosecutor thundered. "We stand today on a cross-roads. One road points toward Americanism," he said as he stepped up to the flag at the front of the courtroom. "The other," he shouted, gesturing at the defendants, "points toward Communism."[93] And Communism meant one thing above all: the subversion of the state by agents of Soviet Russia.

McAllister concluded by ostentatiously unfurling the courtroom flag, saluting, and reciting the pledge of allegiance. Then he turned to the jurors. "Ladies and gentlemen of the Jury, I ask you to think of that Flag in your jury room, and I ask you to think of what it stands for, and I am going to ask you to bring in a vote for that Flag—for the good old U.S.A., for My Country 'Tis of Thee, for the Star Spangled Banner, for My Own United States, and God will bless you."[94]

The sharply divided panel debated and deliberated for sixty-six hours, as the anxious defendants, reporters, and attorneys played cards or read in the courtroom. At one point, the jury came back in and asked the judge a question: If they voted for convictions, would that mean the Communist Party was now illegal? The question cut to the heart of the matter. The jurors understood that a guilty verdict would effectively outlaw the Communist Party and Communist unions in California. The judge told them that the question was irrelevant and sent them back to the jury room.[95]

The jury filed back into the courtroom on April 1, finally in agreement after 118 ballots. The spectators began buzzing with excitement as they noticed the sheaf of papers in the foreman's hand: "They've got a verdict!"[96] The longest trial in California history was over.

A crowd outside the courthouse awaits the verdicts in the Sacramento conspiracy trial. Center for Sacramento History, *Sacramento Bee* Collection, 1983-001-2402.

The foreman began by announcing one acquittal after another—the first four defendants were free. But then, starting with Martin Wilson, it became clear that some were headed to prison. In all, the jury convicted eight defendants—Wilson, Chambers, Decker, Lorene Norman, Nora Conklin, Norman Mini, Jack Crane, and Albert Hougardy—of one count of conspiracy to commit criminal syndicalism. Six others, including Jack Warnick, were found innocent on both counts. Surprisingly, the jury acquitted every one of the defendants of "aiding and abetting criminal syndicalism," while still convicting the eight of "conspiring to commit" criminal syndicalism. The distinctions between the two charges were not explained.

As the foreman read the acquittals, some members of the audience sobbed with relief; when he announced convictions, many spectators, and even some of the jurors, wept in sorrow. For his part, McAllister held a triumphant press conference and called the verdict "a step forward for Americanism and all that America stands for."[97]

We do not know exactly how Caroline Decker reacted. According to the Hearst press, she collapsed in tears. Hearst's *San Francisco Examiner* reported that when the sheriff started to lead the convicts to jail, Decker tore away from the officers and collapsed in her husband's arms, where she sobbed. An officer tapped her on the shoulder and led her away.[98]

But the *Western Worker* said she took the convictions "like a good comrade" and grabbed a pack of cigarettes from a reporter as she sauntered off with a matron, "seemingly in good spirits."[99] One paper saw her as Hysterical Woman; the other as Brave Comrade. Once again, she was forced to play a role in other people's stories—stories they told to support their views of women's proper roles.

The evidence against all fourteen was the same, so the decisions to acquit or convict individuals seemed arbitrary. Later, one of the jurors regretted his vote and signed an affidavit swearing that he and a few others, supportive of the defendants but exhausted and intimidated, had wanted to acquit everyone. But they finally agreed to the eight guilty verdicts in return for the six acquittals. "I lost track of things in the jury room," the remorseful juror told the judge. "But a man has got to live with his conscience."[100] Unimpressed, the judge declined to grant bail during the appeal process to anyone except Lorene Norman because she was pregnant.

During their sentencing, Chambers and Decker refused to repudiate their beliefs. "I, as a member of the Communist Party," said Chambers, "who did organize these workers and helped to lead strikes, am proud to say that I go to jail for the reason that these strikes were won, and these workers succeeded for the time being in getting better living conditions." Decker again described the trial as an attack on workers' rights. "We are not being convicted as criminals," she said. "We are convicted for union organization. The verdict is a conviction of thousands of workers, farmers and students with whom we have been associated."[101]

We depend on the journalists present to know what they said. These statements do not appear in the trial transcript. Although the official court reporter recorded at least part of the speeches of the other defendants, the words uttered by the two leaders of the union were dismissed with curt paraphrases in the transcript ("Chambers thereupon proceeded to make a speech expounding the doctrines of Communism . . . and so forth"; "Decker . . . thereupon made a lengthy speech . . . and so forth," wrote the reporter).[102] If the trial was going to "make history," as both sides had claimed, the court was not going to allow the union leaders to write any important part of it.

The judge sentenced the defendants to five years in state prison. Chambers and the other men headed to San Quentin, while Decker and Conklin went to the Women's State Penitentiary in Tehachapi. Lorene Norman was temporarily free on medical leave.

The growers and their allies were jubilant. "State Has Farm Peace," a *Los Angeles Times* headline assured readers. The 1935 summer harvest was "one of the most peaceful and quiet in California in many years," the newspaper said, largely because the farmworkers' union had been "crippled" by the Sacramento trial.[103]

Radicals and liberals agreed with McAllister and Decker that the trial had "made history"—indeed, that it marked a frightening turning point in the history of American labor. Just two years after the government's guarantee of collective bargaining rights, the convictions showed that employers could use state and local governments to limit the reach of federal labor reforms. Carey McWilliams and Herbert Klein wrote in *The Nation* that California had moved from "sporadic vigilante activity to controlled fascism, from the clumsy violence of drunken farmers to the calculated maneuvers of an economic-militaristic machine." No longer would employers need to rely on hired thugs to smash strikes. Instead, they could trust local prosecutors to brand union leaders as "criminal syndicalists" and then send them to prison. McWilliams and Klein suggested that this antiunion alliance between big business and the courts was similar to the state-business partnership in Hitler's Germany.[104]

But these growers and their supporters were not European-style fascists; they were the forerunners of a new, distinctly American movement. These conservatives had won the battle over farm labor in California. Now they would see if they could win the war against the New Deal.

10

HARVEST

The photograph caught George Creel's eye as he flipped through the pages of the *Los Angeles Times* in August 1935. Under the headline "Patriotic Club-women Test Their Prowess at Range," four matronly women, in elegant dresses and fancy hats, smiled grimly and aimed their pistols at an unseen enemy behind the camera. The caption identified the shooters as members of a conservative activist group called American Women, Inc., and noted that their gathering at the Los Angeles Police Pistol Range had drawn three hundred members of their club for "swimming, dancing and dinner"—and, apparently, target practice.[1]

Creel was so amused by the photo that he cut it out and mailed it to President Roosevelt. "These patriotic women are in training to repel assaults on American institutions!" he chortled.[2] The president's reaction is not recorded, but presumably he shared the laugh.

The movement that these women represented, though, was no joke. They truly believed, as a speaker said at one of their gatherings, that Roosevelt's program was "as Communistic a policy as the Russian government's own economic program," and they were prepared to do whatever was necessary to save their country from its effects.[3] They had been politicized by the dramatic events in California over the preceding two years: massive farm strikes, the San Francisco shutdown, the EPIC campaign, and the Sacramento conspiracy trial. They belonged to an alliance of business and social conservatives that

This photograph of Los Angeles clubwomen taking target practice greatly amused George Creel. Copyright 1935, Los Angeles Times. Reprinted with permission.

had grown in response to strikes and radicalism. Now they set their sights on the president and his policies.

The New Deal Revolution

The Western conservatives' political resurgence did not begin immediately after the defeat of Upton Sinclair or the conviction of the farmworkers' union leaders. It had been relatively easy for California's business leaders to discredit Sinclair, a utopian Socialist, and the small band of atheist Reds who led the CAWIU. But Franklin Roosevelt was an infinitely more popular and wilier opponent. Because New Deal liberalism enjoyed widespread support in the mid- to late 1930s, it would take several years—and the coming of a world war and then a cold war—before conservatives could begin to consolidate their gains.

In the mid-1930s, Roosevelt's political coalition and policy goals seemed unbeatable. At the national level, in 1935 President Roosevelt signed the National Labor Relations Act, also known as the Wagner Act, which further protected workers' right to organize. The Social Security Act, passed the same year, guaranteed government pensions to the elderly and insurance to the unemployed. Three years later, the Fair Labor Standards Act established a national minimum wage and abolished child labor.

As before, these New Deal reforms did not cover all Americans, at least at first. Once again, Southern Democrats insisted that the new laws omit domestic and farmworkers; and once again, the New Dealers recognized their need of the Southern Democrats' support and agreed to these exclusions.[4] The Roosevelt administration did begin to help farmworkers with the Resettlement Administration, which for a brief time provided government housing for some of the migrants. Even with their substantial shortcomings, the Wagner Act and Fair Labor Standards Act inspired a wave of unionization and revolutionized the relationship between labor and management in the United States. Thanks to New Deal labor reforms, the number of union members leapt from 2.9 million in 1933 to almost 15 million in 1946.[5]

The voters showed their approval of New Deal policies by reelecting the president by a huge margin. In 1936, Roosevelt won 523 out of 531 electoral votes and enjoyed the biggest reelection landslide since James Monroe had run unopposed in 1820. Conservatives had anticipated Roosevelt's victory, but they were stunned by its extent—and by the shellacking Republicans suffered in Congress.[6] Democrats outnumbered Republicans 334 to 88 in the House and 76 to 16 in the Senate, where four third-party candidates increased the Democrats' margin by voting with the majority.[7]

California Republicans could not even take solace in their home state's electoral results. In 1938, State Senator Culbert Olson, an ally of Upton Sinclair who promised to "Bring the New Deal to California," defeated Frank Merriam with 52.5 percent of the vote and became the Golden State's first Democratic governor of the twentieth century. To the growers' astonishment, Governor Olson appointed Carey McWilliams head of the state Division of Immigration and Housing, thus putting a left-liberal journalist known for his support of farm laborers in charge of monitoring the growers' treatment of their workers. The governor also named union organizer Dorothy Ray (now Dorothy Ray Healey), formerly of the CAWIU, to enforce the state's labor code as deputy labor commissioner.

Progressives dominated California's literary world as well as its politics. The success of In Dubious Battle led John Steinbeck to the cotton fields and eventually to his greatest literary achievement. In 1936, San Francisco News editor George West hired the novelist to write a series of articles on conditions in the California fields. In "The Harvest Gypsies," published in October

1936, Steinbeck described the "filthy, squalid" migrant campsites, where flies landed on open toilets and swarmed around tattered tents that housed grimy, malnourished children. When workers tried to organize, growers responded with riot, mayhem, and murder. "Fascistic methods," Steinbeck told the *News* readers, "are more numerous, more powerfully applied and more openly practiced in California than any other place in the United States."[8]

Like *In Dubious Battle*, Steinbeck's news articles focused on white farmworkers. He stressed that native-born white Americans—a "new race" in the California fields—now suffered the same terrible conditions as immigrants. Indeed, the Dust Bowl migration of the mid-1930s—the movement of an estimated three hundred thousand Americans from the Southwest to California—led to the whitening of the California farm workforce and made the fictive racial landscape of *In Dubious Battle* a reality.[9] These migrants were European Americans—they were "Munns, Holbrooks, Hansens, Schmidts," Steinbeck explained.[10] Unlike, say, Garcias or Chens, the reader could assume, these families would not stand for this treatment. "With this new race the old methods of repression, of starvation wages, of jailing, beating and intimidation are not going to work; these are American people," he wrote.[11] When reformers reprinted the series as a pamphlet, the editors made explicit the racial subtext of the work by titling it "Their Blood Is Strong."

Steinbeck praised the New Deal's Resettlement Administration camps for improving the lives of the relatively small number of workers who could fit into them. He recommended expanding these housing programs, helping the workers buy small farms, and—most radically—protecting their right to form unions. "Until agricultural labor is organized . . . wages will continue to be depressed and living conditions will grow increasingly impossible," he wrote, "until from pain, hunger and despair the whole mass of labor will revolt."[12]

After he finished the newspaper series, Steinbeck traveled the byways of the Central Valley in an old bakery truck to gather more information for the big novel he planned on Dust Bowl migrants. The book would be controversial, he told his literary agent, because "a revolution is going on, and this book is revolutionary."[13]

The result, *The Grapes of Wrath*, would become the best-selling book of 1939 and enter the literary canon as the most important book of the Depression era. Steinbeck alternated chapters of documentary description of the Dust Bowl migration with narrative ones telling the story of one fictional

Oklahoma family, the Joads. Some of the major characters resembled the men who led the cotton strike of 1933. Big Bill Hammett, the Okie lieutenant of the strike, was the model for the Christ-like figure of Preacher Casy, while Cecil McKiddy, the young man in the Seaside attic with Pat Chambers, helped inspire the iconic character of Tom Joad. As in his previous labor novel, Steinbeck marginalized or omitted Mexicans and female strike leaders from his narrative.[14]

The success of *Grapes of Wrath* helped Carey McWilliams find a nationwide audience for his own indictment of California agribusiness, *Factories in the Field*, which came out the same year. Many reviewers saw McWilliams's book as the nonfiction complement to *The Grapes of Wrath*. "Here is the data," wrote one critic, "that gives the terrible migration of the Joad family historical and economic meaning."[15] McWilliams began reporting for *Factories* in 1935 after the Sacramento conspiracy trial. Like Steinbeck, McWilliams wrote of the violent class conflict in the fields. But unlike Steinbeck, McWilliams portrayed a multiracial labor force whose linguistic and ethnic divisions were deliberately exacerbated by the growers.[16]

California agribusinessmen regarded both books as "smear literature and deliberately destructive propaganda."[17] The board of supervisors in Kern County, home of the Joads, banned *The Grapes of Wrath* from school and public libraries, and cotton growers orchestrated a public burning of the book on the streets of Bakersfield, the county seat.[18] Congressman Lyle Boren of Oklahoma—the father of future Oklahoma governor and senator David Boren—denounced *Grapes* as "a lie, a damnable lie, a black, infernal creation of a twisted, distorted mind," while grower and Republican activist Philip Bancroft accused Steinbeck of peddling "straight revolutionary propaganda, from beginning to end" and hewing to "what the Communists call the 'party line.' "[19] The large growers were equally upset by McWilliams's book. In the view of California business leaders, *Factories in the Field* was a "bible for radical labor agitators" (the *Los Angeles Daily News*) that "advocated the destruction of democracy and the substitution of Communism" (*Pacific Rural Press*).[20] The farm owners and their supporters were especially angry that McWilliams held an official post. "He is my employee and your employee, and an employee of the State," wrote one Modesto lawyer to the governor, adding "he has no business to circulate among the people of the State a publication that can and will result in creating class hatred."[21]

The growers endured more bad publicity later that year when economist Paul Taylor and his wife, photographer Dorothea Lange, published their collaborative work, *An American Exodus*. Like McWilliams and Steinbeck, Taylor and Lange documented the human suffering in California's rural valleys.[22] The next year, director John Ford's film version of *The Grapes of Wrath* won two Oscars and brought the Joads' story to millions more Americans. It appeared that Steinbeck was right: there was a revolution going on.

In late 1939, in response to the books on conflicts in the California fields, a U.S. Senate committee journeyed to the West Coast to hold hearings on the farm strikes—and to signal a new federal interest in agricultural workers. Since 1936, a subcommittee headed by Senator Robert M. La Follette Jr., a Republican from Wisconsin, had been investigating employers' violations of the labor rights guaranteed by the Wagner Act. The committee had questioned Southern deputy sheriffs about their beatings of union organizers, Pinkerton operatives about their infiltration of unions, and steel executives about police shootings of unarmed strikers. Now, with the new public concern about California farm labor problems, Paul Taylor persuaded La Follette, his college classmate, to come west to document the farm owners' violations of free speech and labor rights.[23]

In late 1939 and early 1940, in twenty-eight days of hearings, the La Follette committee investigated the sources and results of the California farm strikes. The members heard almost four hundred witnesses, took three thousand pages of testimony, and catalogued more than five thousand exhibits. The staff unearthed memos and compelled testimony about the brutal beatings of ACLU lawyers in Imperial Valley and about collusion between law enforcement and agribusiness to deny workers their rights.

The La Follette committee also heard from supporters of farmworkers, including Governor Olson, who, in a statement written by Carey McWilliams, denounced the growers for ignoring workers' rights and urged Congress to extend the protections of New Deal laws to agricultural laborers.[24]

In its final report, the La Follette committee agreed with McWilliams, Steinbeck, and many other observers going back to the critiques of George Creel and Pelham Glassford: California growers, the committee said, "repeatedly and flagrantly violated" the constitutional rights of farmworkers and their supporters. The farm operators used union leaders' Communist ties as an excuse to attack strikers and keep wages low. By turning the labor conflicts into a struggle against un-American agitators, the committee wrote, "the breaking of a strike and the smashing of a union becomes a patriotic crusade for home, country, property, church, and all that men hold dear." The committee recommended the expansion of key New Deal laws—the Wagner Act, Fair Labor Standards Act, and Social Security Act—to include farmworkers.[25]

The growers were enraged by the La Follette inquiry, with a leader of the Associated Farmers calling the committee "a Gestapo for the Communist Party."[26] At one hearing, grower Philip Bancroft, now an official with the Associated Farmers, accused the committee members of "giving aid and comfort to Communists by trying to smear the farmers and law enforcement officers of California."[27]

In its conclusion, the La Follette committee called for a new economic and political order that would empower all Americans, even the most dispossessed and destitute. The United States, the senators said, must "devise and protect a pattern of economic democracy in which the individual hired wage worker . . . may effectively exercise his civil rights" to organize collectively, or else the country could face "internal decay or the tyranny of small groups vested with great power."[28]

This was not a radical notion. The senators wanted the government to address inequality by protecting workers' right to organize, not by confiscating wealth or nationalizing property. These liberals, as they now called themselves, believed they could promote social and economic democracy by forging a coalition of working-class and middle-class voters who would elect a government that defended collective bargaining rights. Their dream still seemed attainable as the committee wrapped up its work in 1941.

Strong Arms

U.S. entry into the war in 1941 prompted maximum federal intervention in the economy—the kind of intervention that corporate leaders loved. The U.S. government increased its spending in the Golden State from less than $1 billion in 1940 to $8.5 billion in 1945.[29] These federal dollars lined the pockets of ordinary Californians—almost half of their personal income came from the national government—and improved the balance sheets of businesses as well.[30] Cost-plus contracts guaranteed profits for the ship-building industry, which employed 280,000 workers at its peak in 1943, and the aviation industry, which gave jobs to another quarter of a million Californians.[31] The federal government also helped create construction jobs by building or expanding more than one hundred military bases in the state, and by guaranteeing the mortgages of hundreds of thousands of migrants who bought houses in the sprawling new suburbs.[32]

The wartime demand for workers created a tremendous labor shortage on the Pacific coast. Government agencies like the War Manpower Commission and the U.S. Employment Service helped the shipbuilders and aircraft factories comb the country for potential workers. Federal recruiters went door to door, ringing doorbells in an increasingly desperate quest to find able bodies for the war effort. Soon even the most remote mountain counties reported labor shortages. In late 1943, the regional director of the U.S. Civil Service Commission told Congress that the entire state, from the Oregon border down to the southern deserts, had "practically no one left who is available for any particular Federal use."[33]

As the Okies left the cotton fields for the shipyards, growers protested that there were not enough workers to harvest the crops. Governor Olson begged the federal government to bring in "a substantial number of Mexicans" to work on farms, or else the state would face a food shortage that would be "disastrous to the entire victory program."[34] In response, the U.S. government negotiated an agreement with Mexico to bring in guest laborers to pick crops and work on the railroads. The *bracero* program, which was named for the Spanish word for "strong-armed ones," was supposed to serve as a temporary, wartime solution to the labor shortage. About 225,000 agricultural workers came to the United States under the program during the war, most of them from Mexico.[35]

Despite the farm labor program's original purpose as a wartime measure, agribusiness lobbyists persuaded the U.S. government to extend it after the war, even as the railroad guest worker program ended. At first, supporters said *braceros* were necessary to ensure "the orderly transition from war to peace"; and then, in 1951, the Korean War provided a new wartime justification. Almost ten times as many Mexican *braceros* signed contracts in the 1950s as had during World War II and its immediate aftermath.[36] Growers liked the program because it allowed them to replace higher-priced domestic labor with vulnerable foreigners who would be whisked away by government transport after the harvest. As one Central Valley grower explained, "We are asking for labor only at certain times of the year—at the peak of our harvest—and the class of labor we want is the kind we can send home when we get through with them."[37] Although the contracts mandated minimum wages and adequate working conditions, the growers routinely ignored those provisions.[38]

The *bracero* program amounted to a federal government subsidy for big business at the expense of organized labor. Government agencies recruited workers willing to labor for low wages and thus helped corporate agribusinesses increase their profits. The program also killed unionization efforts on California farms. Labor activists could not organize to improve wages and conditions when the workers had no chance of becoming citizens, or even staying in the United States between harvests. Moreover, now that the workers were foreign, temporary, and nonwhite, artists and journalists lost interest in publicizing their abysmal wages and working conditions. With white workers doing so well, no equivalents of *The Grapes of Wrath* appeared in the 1940s.

Intimidation and Counterrevolution

Meanwhile, at the same time as California's agricultural workforce was becoming more visibly foreign and thus less sympathetic, their reformer allies found themselves increasingly on the defensive. Trends in domestic and international politics breathed new life into California's local traditions of Red baiting and union bashing. At the national level, Congress created in 1938 the House Un-American Activities Committee, which investigated radical individuals and groups. Two years later Congress passed the Smith Act, which effectively outlawed the Communist Party throughout the United States and functioned as a federal sedition act. In 1946, Joseph McCarthy defeated Wisconsin senator Robert La Follette—the champion of civil liberties who had condemned California growers—and McCarthy soon began his notorious career as a Red baiter. California established its own un-American activities investigations committee in 1940. California's "Little HUAC"—the most significant of all the state anticommunist committees—helped discredit liberal ideas as Red or pink.[39]

The man who exercised the most power on the California Un-American Activities Committee was not a legislator but a staff member. Richard E. Combs, the Visalia lawyer who had become convinced of the dangers of Communism during the 1933 cotton strike, served as the committee's chief counsel, investigator, and analyst. From 1940 until 1970, Combs monitored, hounded, and blacklisted California radicals and liberals. Trained in surveillance by General Ralph Van Deman, Combs received daily reports on suspected subversives from spies throughout the state.[40] He prompted the committee to launch loyalty investigations that ruined the careers of public school teachers, social workers, actors, writers, lawyers, doctors, and professors.[41]

The state and federal governments' persecution of the left intimidated everyone involved in farm labor organizing in California. Ella Winter and her husband, screenwriter Donald Ogden Stewart, whom she had married in 1939, felt harassed in Cold War America and moved to England.[42] A terrified Langston Hughes proved a cooperative witness before Senator McCarthy's investigations subcommittee in 1953, although he did not give the senator any names. His autobiography, published a few years later, made no mention of his involvement with the Communist union, his fears of vigilante reprisals, or the unpublished play he wrote about the cotton strike during his time in Carmel in 1934.[43] Stanley Hancock, Dorothy Ray Healey's partner in the Imperial Valley strikes, testified against his former comrades.[44]

Healey herself was subpoenaed in 1941 to appear before California's little HUAC, where she sparred with committee members and gave them "such voluminous and irrelevant answers to their questions that by the time I had finished they no longer remembered what they initially asked me." Governor Olson, trying to distance himself from the far left, asked for her resignation as deputy labor commissioner, but she refused to quit and stayed on as a state official for another year and a half.[45]

Healey could afford to defy the Communist hunters at that moment, when the Red Army was battling the Nazis in Europe. But a few years later, during the Cold War, she went into hiding to avoid prosecution under the Smith Act. She was eventually caught, tried, convicted, and sentenced to five years in prison. The U.S. Supreme Court overturned her conviction, but Healey could no longer play any role in mainstream political debate.

Although Healey did not know it at the time, the counter-subversive investigators who prepared the cases against her drew on a massive private archive in San Diego. General Van Deman invited state, federal, and private Red hunters to pore over the files in his San Diego home. On the day he died in 1952, Army soldiers moved into his house to pack up and spirit away the secret material. Army intelligence officers took part of the archive and used it secretly in security investigations until 1971; the other files stayed in San Diego, where private anticommunist groups and state officials mined them for information against their enemies.[46]

The investigations of alleged un-Americans were designed to intimidate anticommunist liberals as well as radicals—and they succeeded in doing so. Combs and the state Un-American Activities Committee pursued Clark Kerr throughout his career as a renowned labor economist. Kerr became chancellor of the Berkeley campus of the University of California, and then head of the UC system. He defended professors who refused to sign a loyalty oath in the 1940s and 1950s and resisted the Un-American committee's attempts to purge UC employees suspected of subversive tendencies.[47] He remained skeptical of Reds and Red hunters alike. The extremist anticommunists were either ignorantly or deliberately "using the Communist threat as a way to attack liberals," he maintained.[48]

Combs and other conservatives thought that Kerr was cavalier about the Red menace and "supercilious and antagonistic" to conservatives' efforts to expose and destroy secret Communists.[49] After the Free Speech Movement protests at Berkeley in the fall of 1964, the state Un-American Activities Committee issued a report blaming the unrest on Kerr's "free-wheeling tolerance" of Communism.[50] The next year, the committee blasted Kerr for what it called the "deluges of filth"—including Communism, homosexuality, and other "unnatural" and subversive ideas—on the Berkeley campus.[51] Kerr fought back and called the report full of "distortions, half-truths, inaccuracies, and statements on situations taken out of context."[52] But the committee's reports fortified Kerr's opponents among the university's governing board, the UC Regents, who would fire him in 1967 when the man in the governor's chair was more receptive to their arguments.

While they intimidated liberals, business conservatives in California also refined the political coalitions and techniques that they had forged during the 1930s. They allied with religious leaders, energized women voters, and created modern campaign techniques to wage war against the Roosevelt revolution. They crafted the institutions and coalitions that would rearrange the American political landscape.

Throughout the late 1930s and 1940s, business conservatives nurtured the alliances they had forged with evangelical Christians during the early New Deal. Pastors like Martin Luther Thomas, the head of a Los Angeles megachurch and a Christian radio broadcaster, pivoted easily from targeting Upton Sinclair to condemning New Dealers. "Our national government today is honey-combed through and through with Communists and nothing seems to be done about it," Thomas told a huge crowd of Christian activists in 1936.[53] Religious leaders in Southern California formed Christian anticommunist groups to protect their churches and families from what they saw as an existential threat.[54] The organization called Mobilization for Spiritual Ideals (later Spiritual Mobilization), for example, sought to "arouse the ministers of all denominations in America to check the trends toward pagan stateism [sic]."[55] This alliance between economic conservatives and social conservatives would continue to grow over the succeeding decades.

So, too, would the coalition between business conservatives and middle-class women who mobilized against what they saw as threats to home and family. After the defeat of Sinclair, Los Angeles clubwomen stepped up their crusade against the individuals and groups who they believed menaced traditional gender roles. American Women, Inc., whose pistols had caught Creel's eye, along with groups like the Friday Morning Club, the Neutral Thousands, and the Daughters of the American Revolution, worked with business organizations to champion conservative causes.

Meanwhile, California's new professional political consultants perfected the direct mail, radio, and film techniques they had used to smear Upton Sinclair. Clem Whitaker and Leone Baxter's Campaigns Inc. earned a reputation as the nation's best political consulting firm. By the late 1950s, the company had managed eighty campaigns and won seventy-four of them. They came up with easy rules for victory: simplify the message, attack the opponent, and entertain the voter. As Whitaker explained in a speech to public relations experts, candidates needed to grab the voters' attention: "Most every American loves *contest*. He likes a good hot battle, with no punches pulled. . . . *So you can interest him if you put on a fight!* Then, too, most every American likes to be entertained. He likes the movies; he likes

Leone Baxter with her husband and business partner, Clem Whitaker, in 1948. George Skadding/The LIFE Picture Collection/Getty Images.

mysteries; he likes fireworks and parades. . . . So if you can't fight, PUT ON A SHOW!"[56]

A 1959 profile of the couple in a national magazine dubbed them "the country's outstanding specialists in political public relations," but concluded that their business would largely be confined to California.[57] In a rather shortsighted bit of prognostication, the writer predicted that politicians outside Whitaker and Baxter's home state would never condescend to employ consultants. "To hire a PR firm to manage an entire campaign would involve an unthinkable degree of abdication for a self-respecting political leader."[58] Yet just a few years later, many self-respecting candidates willingly abdicated their responsibility to Whitaker and Baxter's successors. Scholars would later point to the 1934 California gubernatorial campaign as the moment of "the birth of media politics."[59]

But political techniques, no matter how clever, were not enough to help conservatives win back national power. The movement also needed to find appealing candidates—people who could sell the message of liberalism's dangers to hearth and home, and who could present a populist image while promoting policies backed by business elites. Right after the end of World War II, Herbert Hoover found such a candidate in Southern California.

Tricky Dick

In early 1946, in Orange County, an area that would become a hotbed of right-wing activism, a group of businessmen launched a search for a charismatic candidate who would represent their interests in Congress. The manager of a local Bank of America branch suggested Richard Nixon, a lawyer and Navy veteran. Hoover and his son Herbert Jr. traveled to Pasadena to meet this promising young man and urge him to run for the House of Representatives. Nixon would always remember the meeting fondly and revere the former president for his role in jump-starting his career.[60]

Nixon won his first campaign by ousting Congressman Jerry Voorhis, the idealistic Social Gospeler and former Socialist who, as a supporter of striking lettuce workers, had been menaced by angry vigilantes in front of an El Centro hotel in 1934. Nixon painted Voorhis as a stooge of labor unions and the Soviet Union. He repeatedly denounced him for his supposed alliance with the Political Action Committee of the Congress of Industrial Organizations (CIO) and its "communist principles." It did not matter to Nixon that Voorhis had written a tough Communist registration law in 1940, or that the CIO Political Action Committee had actually refused to endorse Voorhis. "Mr. Nixon *had* to win. Nothing else would do at all," Voorhis wrote later.[61]

Nixon admitted privately that he misrepresented his opponent's beliefs, but he made no apologies for doing so. "Of course, I knew that Jerry Voorhis wasn't a Communist," he told one of Voorhis's aides. But political candidates, he said, needed to play rough sometimes. "The important thing is to win," he explained. "You're just being naïve."[62] Nixon enjoyed support from the same California business interests that helped defeat Upton Sinclair in 1934. Oil companies, movie studios, and agribusiness conglomerates were among his biggest backers.[63] Grower Robert Di Giorgio contributed to Nixon's earliest campaigns, while Philip Bancroft and a friend formed "Farmers for Nixon" to help funnel agribusiness money to him.[64]

The *Los Angeles Times*, a longtime enemy of California liberals and radicals, championed Nixon's career from the beginning. The *Times's* political editor, Kyle Palmer, believed that he saw the potential for national greatness in the Orange County native.[65] Nixon understood that portraying Democrats as dupes and traitors could help put the Republicans back in power.

Once in office, Congressman Nixon served on the House Un-American Activities Committee, where he played a major role in the exposure of an actual Communist spy. Alger Hiss, the one-time nemesis of the growers at the Agricultural Adjustment Administration, was investigated by the committee and ultimately convicted of perjury for denying that he had been part of an underground Communist group in the 1930s. Journalist Whittaker Chambers swore that Hiss had been a spy as well as a secret Red. Much later, documents from the former Soviet Union confirmed that Hiss had indeed passed information to the Communists while working in various government agencies, including the State Department.[66]

The conviction of Hiss, a New Dealer known for his public support of farmworkers in the 1930s and international institutions in the 1940s, gave conservatives ammunition for their charge that the New Deal was, at its core, a Communist project.

Opponents of Hiss from his days at the AAA were thrilled by news of his conviction. "Time has caught up with our enemies," chortled one cotton grower to another.[67] Herbert Hoover felt vindicated. "At last the stream of treason that existed in our Government has been exposed in a fashion that all may believe," he wrote Nixon.[68] After the Hiss case, conservatives recognized Nixon as "AMERICA'S GREATEST ENEMY OF COMMUNISM," according to a flyer advertising one of his speeches.[69]

Nixon continued to battle against real and imagined Communists and their alleged liberal enablers when he ran for a U.S. Senate seat in 1950. In a television commercial for his race against Congresswoman Helen Gahagan Douglas, he promised voters that he would "represent you and your interests in Washington and not the half-baked theories of left-wing intellectuals at pinko cocktail parties."[70] He labeled Douglas the "pink lady"; she called him "Tricky Dick."

Douglas had no idea how tricky Nixon could be. Years later, in 1962, the California attorney general seized General Van Deman's secret files in San Diego, saying they had been used "by unauthorized persons for political purposes." Democrats charged that the unauthorized persons worked for Nixon, and their purposes had been to smear Voorhis in 1946 and Douglas in 1950. These charges were never proven, but left-liberal California Democrats continued to view him as a reckless and sinister Red-baiter.[71]

As Nixon rose from senator to vice president, he fulfilled the dreams of Hoover and other business conservatives who had chosen him back in 1946. When Vice President Nixon won reelection in 1956, Hoover congratulated him and expressed his sense of personal satisfaction. "Ever since our interview in Pasadena years ago when I added my urging that you should run for Congress," he wrote Nixon in a private letter, "I have grown stronger and stronger in my belief in your immense value to the American people. And they have now shown their full acceptance of that view."[72]

Hoover also grew stronger in his belief that the Democratic Party tolerated and even nurtured treasonous ideas. In 1960, as GOP presidential nominee Nixon prepared for a debate against John F. Kennedy, Hoover wrote Nixon that Kennedy's goals were "evil." To left-liberals, Kennedy's policies of tax cuts, increased spending on defense, and indifference (at the time) to civil rights seemed to put him at the center or even slightly to the right on the political spectrum. But to Hoover, Kennedy's agenda was nothing more than "socialism disguised as a 'welfare state.'"[73]

Nixon's top aides, who followed him to the White House, learned their craft in California's culture of frenzied Red-baiting. Murray Chotiner, a protégé of Clem Whitaker and known for his mantra of "attack, attack, attack, and never defend," served as Nixon's consultant or manager for most of his campaigns from 1946 through 1972. His fellow UCLA graduates John Ehrlichman and Bob Haldeman—the latter the grandson of a founder of the anti-Red group Better America Federation—worked on Nixon's unsuccessful 1960 run for the presidency and later became his chief advisers when he won the White House eight years later.

Along with his virulent anticommunism, Nixon's attention to the politics of image marked him as a California product. With its weak party system, fondness for Hollywood glitz, and rootless, diverse residents, the state helped nurture a style of campaigning that emphasized appearance over substance. "What they've got isn't a party," a Democratic official told Theodore White in 1956. "It's a star system, it's a studio lot. They don't run candidates—they produce them, like movie heroes."[74] Nixon was one of the first politicians to "embrace the new tools of political artistry" and "foster

Vice President Richard Nixon visits former President Herbert Hoover in 1960. Hank Walker/The LIFE Picture Collection/Getty Images.

our current image-obsessed political culture," as historian David Greenberg has said. Nixon and his public relations staff created an image of the candidate as a "populist everyman" and helped to unite the wealthy with the disaffected middle classes in a broad, successful coalition.[75]

Reagan's America

Ronald Reagan, who would preside over the transformation of America's political economy in the 1980s, owed his start to the same California business
conservatives who supported Nixon. Reagan's earliest backers included drugstore magnate Justin Dart, oil men Henry Salvatori and A.C. Rubel, steel
tycoons Earle Jorgensen and Leland Kaiser, banker Charles Cook, car dealer
Holmes Tuttle, and entertainment mogul Walt Disney.[76] Some of these men
had close ties to California agribusiness: Kaiser and Rubel's firms had extensive investments in agricultural land, as did Reagan's lawyer, William
French Smith.[77] Strongly opposed to the New Deal from its earliest days,
these Western millionaires saw potential in Reagan, a former actor and corporate spokesperson who shared their loathing of Communism and their
suspicion of the liberals who failed to see its dangers.

The labor struggles in California in the 1940s had shaped Reagan's
hard-line anticommunist views. During his term as president of a relatively
conservative union, the Screen Actors Guild, Reagan grew convinced
that Communists were plotting to take over Hollywood. The Reds' goal, he
wrote later, was "to gain economic control of the motion picture industry
in order to finance their activities and subvert the screen for their propaganda."[78] Publicly, he testified as a friendly witness before the House Un-
American Activities Committee; privately, he worked as an informant for
the FBI.[79]

In 1964, Reagan attracted a national political following when he delivered a televised speech for Republican presidential nominee Barry
Goldwater on the virtues of free-market capitalism and the dangers of
liberalism. "So we have come to a time for choosing," he said. "Either we
accept the responsibility for our own destiny, or we abandon the American
Revolution and confess that an intellectual elite in a far-distant capitol can
plan our lives for us better than we can plan them ourselves."[80]

Like Nixon, Reagan drew on the political vocabulary Hoover and Campaigns Inc. used in the 1934 elections. He castigated the elite on the other
side of a cultural, not economic, divide—an elite of eggheads, not fat cats.
When Reagan ran for governor of California in 1966, he directed his fire at
the intellectual elite at the state's public university system. Candidate Reagan blamed a "leadership gap in Sacramento" that "permitted the degrada-

tion of the once great University of California."[81] He built on decades of populist attacks on the taxpayer-supported university as a cesspool of political radicalism and moral degeneracy, teeming with Reds, pinks, and queers. At Reagan's first UC regents meeting, the majority voted to fire Clark Kerr on the spot.[82]

Given his hostility to unions and support from agribusiness, it was not surprising that Governor Reagan strongly resisted a new organization effort in the California fields. After labor and civil rights groups finally succeeded in killing the *bracero* program in 1965, fruit and vegetable pickers tried to organize collectively for the first time since the Great Depression. The goals remained the same—higher wages and union recognition. But the new, non-Communist organizers aligned their cause with the national, nonviolent movement for racial justice and civil rights for minorities. As a result, the United Farm Workers (UFW) was not just a union; it was *La Causa*. And its leader, Cesar Chavez, knew how to appeal to urban consumers for support.

Chavez helped organize pickers at the largest grape vineyards in the Central Valley and encouraged them to strike for higher wages. When the growers refused to negotiate, he launched a nationwide boycott of the two biggest producers, Di Giorgio Fruit Corporation and Schenley Industries.[83] The grape boycott linked middle-class consumers to the workers and helped Chavez build a broad coalition of backers.

Reagan opposed Chavez and farmworkers' unions from the first day of his campaign for governor. During the speech announcing his candidacy, he held a catsup bottle and predicted that 28 million fewer would be manufactured if the state and federal governments were allowed to "finish their experiments in reform among farmworkers and completely cancel out the Bracero program."[84] Once elected, he helped farm operators break the strikes by authorizing the use of temporary guest workers, chain gangs, and welfare recipients to pick the crops. He filled the top agricultural posts in his administration with growers. The governor also worked with President Nixon to lobby for a federal bill proposed by California senator George Murphy that would have made agricultural strikes and boycotts illegal.[85]

As the boycott gained national and international support, both Reagan and Nixon ostentatiously ate grapes on television. The conspicuous consumption of the fruit became a public badge of honor for conservatives. Growers paid $4 million to Whitaker and Baxter for a nationwide advertising campaign that encouraged Americans to exercise their "consumer rights" and "Eat California Grapes, the Forbidden Fruit."[86] After leaving office in 1974, Reagan would continue to combine populist, visceral appeals to racial and gender conservatism with a libertarian reverence for an unfettered market.

Reagan's vision of a free market still included government support for agribusiness, however. Like most prominent California Republicans and Democrats, Reagan endorsed government programs that benefited the growers, including state and federal irrigation projects and guest worker programs.[87]

Despite Reagan's opposition, Chavez and the United Farm Workers did win some contracts and a few legal, legislative, and moral victories. In 1975, Governor Jerry Brown signed the Agricultural Labor Relations Act, which gave state protection to farmworkers' unions. Chavez became a civil rights icon. The California legislature proclaimed his birthday a state holiday in 1995. And in 1999, city officials in Sacramento renamed Plaza Park, where union organizers in the 1930s had waved the Red flag and denounced capitalism. The new name is Cesar Chavez Plaza.[88]

But the UFW's victories were short-lived, and more symbolic than substantial. The union failed to win the allegiance of many workers, and its organizing efforts were complicated by the increased flow of undocumented workers to the California fields in the 1980s. By 2014, only a few thousand members remained in the UFW, down from more than fifty thousand in 1970.[89]

Reagan's campaign against the UFW was central to his appeal to California voters. His opposition to the grape boycott helped him rally his followers against the mostly Mexican-born workers and the "intellectual elite" who presumed to shame them into giving up the consumption of a favorite food.

The Reagan coalition of Western business elites and social conservatives backed him for his unsuccessful run for the presidency in 1976 and his ultimate victory in 1980. As president, Reagan could now finish the counterrevolution that California conservatives had worked for since 1933.

Seeing the Future

The radical politics of the 1930s did not plant the seeds of a vibrant, broad-based American left, despite the fears of California's conservatives and the commitment and enthusiasm of its radicals. No one in this story moved further left on the political spectrum, and no one died a Communist. Conservatives grew more certain of the truth of their beliefs, many left-liberals moderated their opinions, and radicals lost their idealism and sense of destiny. Despite the New Dealers' attempts to appease the right by distancing themselves from the left, conservatives succeeded in Red-baiting and intimidating liberals and moving the entire country further to the right.

Herbert Hoover lived long enough to savor revenge. In 1945, just weeks after the death of Franklin Roosevelt, President Harry Truman's secretary of state invited Hoover to attend the opening conference of the United Nations. Bitter and suspicious, Hoover rejected the invitation, certain that it was either "evidence of offensive ineptitude—or a foundation for smearing."[90] But in fact the Truman White House wanted to rehabilitate the former president and seek his advice. In 1947, Hoover began chairing the first of two major government commissions, known as the Hoover Commissions, which lobbied for fiscal conservatism and reduced or eliminated many government agencies. His fellow conservatives relished what they saw as new respect for Hoover among "almost all the worthwhile people of our nation," as Philip Bancroft wrote.[91]

In the last two decades of his long life, Hoover raised money to transform his war library and archives on the Stanford campus into a conservative think tank, the Hoover Institution. The Institution contributed to the intellectual revolution that put Ronald Reagan in the White House. Hoover also worked on his magnum opus, a massive history that dated the decline of the United States to his departure from the White House in 1933. The Hoover Institution published it as *Freedom Betrayed* in 2011. Hoover died at age ninety in October 1964, a few months after Barry Goldwater captured the Republican nomination for the presidency, and Western conservatives stood ready to harvest the seeds of the national movement that Hoover had nurtured for four decades.[92]

The Associated Farmers continued to lobby for governmental policies that benefited agribusiness, but it remained a regional rather than national organization. Thanks to the notoriety it won during the La Follette hearings, the group abandoned plans to expand across the United States.[93] Many of its leaders, though, succeeded in winning office themselves. John Phillips, the assemblyman from Banning who chaired the pro-grower Imperial Valley inquiry in 1934, won a seat in Congress in 1942 and represented parts of Imperial, Orange, and Riverside Counties until 1957. The son of Sunkist's Charles Collins Teague, Charles McKevett Teague, represented Ventura and Santa Barbara Counties in Congress from 1955 until his death in 1974. *Oakland Tribune* publisher Joseph Knowland had the satisfaction of seeing his son, William, a state assemblyman, rise to become the majority leader of the U.S. Senate. Senator Knowland brought his father's brand of extremist anticommunism to national policy making. The man known as the "Senator from Formosa"—for his vigorous support of Chiang Kai-shek's Nationalists—used his bully pulpit on the Senate floor to demand war with China, rail against Communist coddlers in the government, and denounce negotiations with the Soviet Union.[94] Through representatives like Knowland, California business conservatives helped steer the national political conversation hard to the right.

Even former New Dealers came to believe that business conservatives and extremist anticommunists might be correct. George Creel shifted so far to the right that he became "virtually a different human being" by the 1940s, according to one historian.[95] Like Hoover, Creel came to equate New Deal policies with treason. "Present-day 'liberalism,' as it has the impudence to call itself, is anti-American," he wrote in his autobiography; "for at its back, as cunning as secret, are men and women who give their allegiance to a foreign power."[96] He spent his last years living in San Francisco's Bohemian Club, the exclusive haven of California's richest and most powerful men, and died in 1953.[97] For his part, the other New Deal labor mediator in the California farmworker strikes, Pelham Glassford, in 1948 tried to convince his former commander Douglas MacArthur—the man responsible for the debacle of the Bonus Army—to run for president.

California agribusiness continued to benefit from the federal government agricultural subsidies begun under Roosevelt. In the decades after the New Deal, the government poured billions of dollars into the pockets of California producers of many commodities, particularly cotton, corn, wheat, and dairy products. In 2012, the value of California's farm products grew to more than $42.6 billion. It was the top agricultural producer in the nation and far ahead of Iowa, the number two state, at $30.8 billion.[98] The increased value of the crops did not result in higher wages. The median annual wage for farmworkers in 2012 was $18,910, compared to $34,750 for all workers.[99]

As agribusiness gave generously to the campaign coffers of candidates for both parties during the 1940s and 1950s, many Democrats joined their Republican colleagues in championing the interests of large growers.[100] Sheridan Downey, for example, the candidate for lieutenant governor on the EPIC ticket in 1934, became a strong advocate in Washington for agribusiness after his election to the U.S. Senate in 1944. In 1947, he wrote a book called *They Would Rule the Valley*, in which "they" were federal government officials who wanted to oppress large growers by denying them taxpayer-subsidized water.[101]

Downey's onetime running mate, Upton Sinclair, never became a conservative, but he did mellow into a mainstream liberal. He remained an unswerving supporter of the president who had abandoned him in 1934. He wrote a successful series of spy novels featuring a secret agent who regarded FDR as "the greatest man in the world."[102] From World War II until his death in 1968, Sinclair drifted away from his radical friends, supported President Truman's containment policy, and admired President Lyndon Johnson's expansion of the New Deal welfare state in the 1960s.[103]

To his critics, John Steinbeck seemed to abandon the ideals of his early career as he aged. His writing became less reformist and politicized over the years, and he astonished some of his admirers with his strong support for the Vietnam War. But in truth, he remained what he had always been: a centrist New Deal Democrat, committed to government jobs and housing programs. He hated Communists, those in America and in Vietnam, but he also despised extremist anticommunist conservatives like Nixon and Senator Joseph McCarthy.[104] Still recognizable as the author of *In Dubious Battle*, he remained contemptuous of manipulators and bullies at either end of the political spectrum. He won the Nobel Prize in Literature in 1962 "for his realistic and imaginative writings, combining as they do sympathetic humour and keen social perception."[105]

The models for Steinbeck's main characters in *In Dubious Battle*, Pat Chambers and Caroline Decker, did not end up serving their entire sentences in state prison. Two years after their conviction, an appeals court overturned the verdicts on technicalities.[106]

They emerged from prison to find that their union no longer existed. The Sacramento prosecutors may have wounded the CAWIU, but it took Party functionaries in Moscow to kill it. In 1935, while the organizers were still on trial, the CPUSA agreed to follow the Moscow line of pursuing a "popular front" with existing unions rather than establishing separate, Communist-led ones. The CAWIU quietly disbanded.

The combination of official repression and the Communists' own failures prompted Chambers and Decker to leave the Party and labor organizing. For Decker, the Soviets' nonaggression pact with the Nazis in 1939 provided the final reason to break with Communism. "I couldn't find the democracy" in the Party's doctrines, she later explained.[107] After her release from prison, she divorced Jack Warnick, married civil liberties lawyer Richard Gladstein, and lived out the rest of her days as a suburban mother and liberal political activist in Marin County. If she saved any papers from her days with the union, her children tossed them out when she died in 1992. Chambers left the Party for similar reasons. He drifted to Southern California, where he became a carpenter.[108]

Chambers followed Cesar Chavez's progress closely in the newspapers. After the UFW won an important victory in a grape strike, Chambers wanted to meet the men and women who had finally achieved the goals for which he had sacrificed so much. He made a pilgrimage to the UFW's headquarters in Delano, not far from where he had led almost twenty thousand cotton pickers in the greatest farmworker strike in U.S. history some three decades earlier.

When he walked into the UFW offices, the quiet carpenter explained to a secretary that he "had done a little organizing in his time." He hoped to talk with someone in the union leadership. Chavez was too busy to meet the visitor—until the secretary told him the man's name. "It couldn't be Pat Chambers," Chavez said. But it was indeed.

Chavez was honored to meet the union veteran who had paved the way to UFW success. The two men had an emotional conversation. The new leader told stories of his victories, and the old organizer kept repeating, "Amazing! Amazing!" But Chavez was bothered by one thing: Why hadn't Chambers come earlier to offer his support? Chambers explained that he feared Chavez would be Red-baited: "I was worried that my coming might hurt you, but now that you won in Delano, I wanted to come."[109]

Chambers was right to worry. The growers might have used his presence to discredit Chavez, just as they had used fear of the Communist bogeyman to destroy farmworkers' attempts to unionize back in the 1930s. The Communists were the only people willing to organize farmworkers at the time. Yet their presence made it easier for the growers to destroy the union.

In Devious Battle

The story of business reaction to California labor activism reminds us that the New Deal—despite its many compromises and disappointments—sought to bring about a dramatic power shift in American labor relations. Roosevelt's labor laws made a new world for the workers who benefited from their protections. Even the agricultural laborers excluded from the laws received attention and help. In response to the bloody conflicts in the California fields, the federal government sent fact finders and mediators, and insisted that the growers stop their violent intimidation of labor organizers. California's agribusiness leaders were so upset by these New Deal efforts—however halfhearted and inadequate they may seem to us today—because they recognized that these policies signaled a remarkable change in the government's relationship with unions, and that this change was a real threat to their control over their workers and profits.

These growers were not angry at the New Deal because they hated big government. Unlike Eastern conservatives, Western businessmen were not libertarians who opposed most forms of government intervention in the economy. Agribusiness relied on the government to survive and prosper: it needed price supports for stability, government dams and canals for irrigation, and state university research for crop improvements. These business leaders not only acknowledged but demanded a large role for government in the economy.

By focusing on Western agribusiness, we can see that the New Right was no neoliberal revolt against the dead hand of government intervention. Instead, twentieth-century conservatism was a reaction to the changes in the ways that government was intervening in the economy—in short, a shift from helping big business to creating a level playing field for workers. Even

Ronald Reagan, despite his mythical image as a cowboy identified with the frontier, was not really a small-government conservative but a corporate conservative.[110] Reagan's revolution did not end government intervention in the economy: it only made the government more responsive to the Americans with the most wealth and power.

The New Dealers did not lose the fights in the California fields for lack of trying. They lost because the obstacles they encountered were so formidable. Agribusiness leaders responded to government-endorsed worker organization with organizing of their own. Before the Moral Majority of the 1970s, before the suburban housewives who mobilized for Barry Goldwater, these corporate leaders pioneered a new style of politics. They formed influential and sometimes secretive groups; they hired publicists, consultants, and Hollywood-style message managers; and they declared culture wars against the radicals and liberals who they said sought to destroy the church and the home. In California during the Great Depression, wealthy businessmen discovered that the language of patriotism, religion, and family could mobilize economic and cultural conservatives into a single powerful bloc.

The New Dealers tried desperately to reassure mainstream voters that they wanted reform, not radical change. But to no avail. The growers and their publicists still branded them as Reds. When these businessmen claimed that New Deal labor laws signaled the death of freedom and the spread of communism, they deliberately distorted the record for their own economic benefit. But their methods worked—and activists at the national level soon adopted them.

Over time, business won the fight against labor. The agribusiness attacks on farmworkers' unions broadened into corporate assaults on industrial unions. Only 11 percent of employed U.S. workers are in unions today, compared to 20 percent in 1980 and 28 percent at the peak of the labor movement in 1954.[111] This collapse of union power helps explain the resurgence of inequality in our time.[112] Since 1980, as the percentage of union members tumbled, the income earned by the top 1 percent almost tripled, and the United States approached levels of wealth inequality not seen since before the New Deal.[113] Meanwhile, conservative billionaires David and Charles Koch and their fellow corporate donors continue the Associated Farmers' tradition of supporting political candidates who strive to weaken labor even more.[114]

In a 1936 campaign speech, Franklin Roosevelt warned against the "powerful influences" that sought to restore a kind of government that was indifferent to the suffering of its people. "We know now that Government by organized money is just as dangerous as Government by organized mob," he argued.[115] The forces of organized money first prepared their counterrevolution against New Deal reforms in the California fields in the 1930s. They are still pursuing their campaign against Roosevelt's legacy today.

ACKNOWLEDGMENTS

This book began with an apparently small request from archivists at the Center for Sacramento History. They were preparing an exhibition of photographs of a conspiracy trial that had taken place back in 1935. Could I please give a public lecture on the historical context of the trial? I had never heard of the case, but I was willing to spend a few days looking into it to help them out. Once I saw the Center's documents on the trial—especially the reports by secret agents who had infiltrated the defendants' labor union—I decided to write an article on the larger political significance of the case. That article, published as "Quelling Dissent: The Sacramento Conspiracy Trial and the Birth of the New Right," in *Boom: A Journal of California* (Summer 2011): 59–74, led me to ask more questions about the conservative groups that fought labor unions and New Dealers in the American West. Soon I was delving into the papers of dozens of activists, from former president Herbert Hoover to Communist union organizers, and tracking down documents in archives and libraries around the country. I want to thank the Sacramento archivists, especially Rebecca Crowther, Marcia Eymann, Patricia Johnson, and Dylan McDonald, whose curiosity about the wider significance of their local history started me on this journey.

I also owe a debt to archivists and librarians at the following places: the Herbert Hoover Presidential Library in West Branch, Iowa; the Franklin D. Roosevelt Library in Hyde Park, New York; the Hoover Institution Archives in Stanford, California; the Special Collections Department in Green Library at Stanford University; the Beinecke Rare Book and Manuscript Library at Yale University; the Legislative Archives section of the National Archives in Washington, D.C.; the National Archives in College Park, Maryland; the Tamiment Library and Robert F. Wagner Labor Archives at New York University; the Rare Book and Manuscripts Library at Columbia University; the Special Collections Department at the University of California, Davis; the Bancroft Library at the University of California, Berkeley; the Southern California Library for Social Studies and Research in Los Angeles; the Special Collections Department at the University of California, Los Angeles; the Brawley Public Library; the Labor Archives and Research Center at San Francisco State University; the Carmel Public Library; the California History Room at the California State Library; the San Francisco Public Library; the Library of Congress; and the California State Archives in Sacramento. I would especially like to thank William Baehr at the FDR Library, Spencer Howard and Craig Wright at the Hoover Presidential Library, and John Sherlock in UCD Special Collections for making exceptional efforts to answer my questions.

Many colleagues assisted me during this project. Lori Clune and Scott Pittman took time away from their research to photograph documents for me, and Scott's undergraduate honors thesis on General Ralph Van Deman inspired me to take my book in new directions. Dolores Janiewski and Simon Judkins shared their documents and pointed me to new leads. My agent, Lisa Adams, helped me focus my argument and explain its significance. My editor at The New Press, Marc Favreau, understood this project from the beginning and provided thoughtful editing. I would also like to thank Jed Gladstein for sharing memories of his mother, Caroline Decker Gladstein, and Daneet Steffens for allowing me to publish a snapshot of Ella Winter.

I refined the arguments of the book in several different forums. I would especially like to thank Rhodri Jeffreys-Jones and Robert Mason at the University of Edinburgh, and the group at the Conspiracy and Democracy Project at the University of Cambridge: Andrew McKenzie-McHarg, Alfred Moore, Hugo Drochon, Rachel Hoffman, Nayanika Mathur, David Runciman, Richard Evans, and John Naughton. Donald Critchlow and the anonymous reviewers at the *Journal of Policy History* gave me useful critiques for chapter 5, which appeared in revised form as "Bleeding Edge: New Deal Farm Labor Mediation in California and the Conservative Reaction" (Fall 2013):

48–72. Todd Edward Holmes helped me understand the politics of California agribusiness in a later era. My colleagues Casey Sullivan, Beth Slutsky, Jessica Mayhew, Ellen Hartigan-O'Connor, Joan Cadden, Matthew Stratton, Cecilia Tsu, and Louis Warren provided crucial insights. Ari Kelman read many drafts with humor, patience, and generosity.

I received financial support from the Committee on Research at the University of California, Davis. The humanities and social sciences faculty at UCD are fortunate to have such reliable support from the administration. In addition, the Herbert A. Young Society Deans' Fellowship furnished funds for me to travel to archives. Clare Hall and the Centre for Research in the Arts, Social Sciences and Humanities at the University of Cambridge provided fellowships that gave me time to write.

Julia Ainsworth located key documents for me, while Sarah Ainsworth was brave enough to make the trek to Imperial Valley on a 115-degree day in August to help me photograph the un-digitized, un-microfilmed *Brawley News*. Their sister Isabella never served as my research assistant, but she did make a lovely mug in ceramics class on the subject of my book. All three girls, along with Andrew and Jane Rauchway, regularly reminded me that there's more to life than work.

My husband and colleague, Eric Rauchway, shared his knowledge of the New Deal, read the manuscript many times, and supported me throughout the writing process. I dedicate this book to him.

NOTES

The following abbreviations are used for frequently cited archives and newspapers. Collections are listed alphabetically by abbreviation.

AHOH   Allan Hoover oral history, HHL
BN   *Brawley News*
CCT   Charles Collins Teague papers, Bancroft Library, University of California, Berkeley
CGOH-BAN   Caroline Decker Gladstein oral history, sound recording, no date, Bancroft Library, University of California, Berkeley
CGOH-WSU   Caroline Decker Gladstein oral history, 1976, Wayne State University, Detroit, MI
CMW   Carey McWilliams papers, University of California, Los Angeles
CRP   Chester Rowell papers, Bancroft Library, University of California, Berkeley
CSH   Center for Sacramento History, Sacramento, CA
DNC   Democratic National Committee files, FDRL
DOJ   RG 60, Records of the Department of Justice, National Archives and Records Administration, College Park, MD
ER   Eleanor Roosevelt collection, FDRL
EWOH   Ella Winter oral history, JBC
FDRL   Franklin D. Roosevelt Presidential Library, Hyde Park, NY
FPOH   Francis Perkins oral history, 1976, Columbia University Oral History Collection, New York, NY
FWOH   Francis Whitaker oral history, JBC
FWP   Federal Writers Project collection, Bancroft Library, University of California, Berkeley
GCP   George Clements papers, University of California, Los Angeles
GHP   George Hatfield papers, Bancroft Library, University of California, Berkeley
HHL   Herbert Hoover Presidential Library, West Branch, IA

IVP	*Imperial Valley Press*
JBC	Jackson Benson collection, Green Library, Stanford University, Stanford, CA
JKP	Joseph Knowland papers, Bancroft Library, University of California, Berkeley
JOCD	J.F.T. O'Connor diary, Bancroft Library, University of California, Berkeley
JWOH	Jack Warnick oral history, sound recording, Bancroft Library, University of California, Berkeley
LAHP	Lorena A. Hickok papers, FDRL
LARS	RG 233, L.A. Police Department Red Squad Files, Records of the House of Representatives Committee on Un-American Activities (Dies), Legislative Archives, National Archives and Records Administration, Washington, DC
LAT	*Los Angeles Times*
LGP	Leo Gallagher papers, Southern California Library for Social Studies and Research, Los Angeles, CA
LHP	Langston Hughes papers, Beinecke Library, Yale University, New Haven, CT
MKP	Margaret Ann Kerr papers, Hoover Institution Archives, Stanford, CA
NLB	RG 25, Records of the National Labor Relations Board, National Archives and Records Administration, College Park, MD
NLP	Norman Leonard papers, Labor Archives and Research Center, San Francisco State University, San Francisco, CA
NSP	Noel Sullivan papers, Bancroft Library, University of California, Berkeley
NYT	*The New York Times*
OF	Official Files, FDRL
PBOH	Philip Bancroft oral history, 1962, Bancroft Library, University of California, Berkeley
PBP	Philip Bancroft papers, Bancroft Library, University of California, Berkeley
PCOH	Pat Chambers oral history, sound recording, date unknown, Bancroft Library, University of California, Berkeley
PGP	Pelham Glassford papers, University of California, Los Angeles
PPF	President's personal file, FDRL
PPI	Post-Presidential individual file, HHL
PST	Paul S. Taylor papers, Bancroft Library, University of California, Berkeley, CA

PVC	*People v. Chambers* transcript, Crim1533, California State Archives, Sacramento
RTD	Rexford Tugwell diary, FDRL
SB	*The Sacramento Bee*
SBLC	*The Sacramento Bee* legal collection, Center for Sacramento History, Sacramento, CA
SDP	Samuel Darcy papers, Tamiment Library, New York University, New York, NY
SFC	*San Francisco Chronicle*
STP	Sam Tanenhaus papers, Hoover Institution, Stanford, CA
SU	*The Sacramento Union*
UCD	Special Collections, University of California, Davis
UCLA	Charles E. Young Library, University of California, Los Angeles
VDP	Ralph Van Deman papers, RG 46, Van Deman Collection, Records of the Senate Internal Security Subcommittee of the Senate Judiciary Committee, 1951–1975, Legislative Archives, National Archives and Records Administration, Washington, DC
VTD	*Visalia Times Delta*
W&B	Whitaker & Baxter Campaigns, Inc. Records, California State Archives, Sacramento
WCOH	Wofford B. Camp oral history, 1971, Bancroft Library, University of California, Berkeley
WMP	William Mullendore papers, HHL

Other works cited in the notes receive a full citation on their first appearance.

Introduction

1. Hoover to Henry Stoddard, July 8, 1933, "Stoddard, Henry L., 1933–44," PPI HHL; Hoover to Stoddard, June 6, 1933, in the same folder; Hoover to Fess, November 14, 1933, "Fess, Simeon D., 1933–36," PPI HHL.

2. Hoover to Mark Sullivan, August 9, 1933, "Sullivan, Mark, 1933–41," PPI HHL; Hoover to Irwin, November 18, 1933, "Irwin, Will, 1933–34," PPI HHL.

3. In January 1934, five hundred thousand cotton farmers had already agreed to participate in that year's program. U.S. Senate Committee on Agriculture and Forestry, *Operations of the Agricultural Adjustment Act*, 73rd Cong., 2nd sess., January 18, 1934, p. 18.

4. Hoover to Frank Knox, July 9, 1934, "Knox, Frank B., July–December, 1934," PPI HHL. Hoover's farm north of Bakersfield became controversial in 1928 when Democrats charged he hung a sign outside it saying only nonwhites could work there. Hoover denied this story for years afterward; see the letters in the "Hoover farm" folders in the

Misrepresentations subject file at the Hoover presidential library. He and his aides gave conflicting accounts of his ranch holdings, at times saying he had never owned a ranch, or that he had sold his interest in his ranch, or he had only helped other people buy ranches. However, his son Allan said in his oral history that he and his father owned four ranches in the 1930s, which Allan managed. See AHOH, part 3, 7–12, HHL. See also "Hoover Farm Interesting," *Fresno Republican*, December 16, 1923.

5. Bancroft to Henry Wallace, November 11, 1933, box 1, PBP.

6. Mark Arax and Rick Wartzman, *The King of California: J.G. Boswell and the Making of a Secret American Empire* (New York: PublicAffairs, 2003), 136.

7. See Barton C. Hacker, "The United States Army as a National Police Force: The Federal Policing of Labor Disputes, 1877–1898," *Military Affairs* 33, no. 1 (April 1969): 255–64; David Adams, "Internal Military Intervention in the United States," *Journal of Peace Research* 32, no. 2 (May 1995): 197–211.

8. Richard White, *"It's Your Misfortune and None of My Own": A History of the American West* (Norman: University of Oklahoma Press, 1991), 58.

9. On the Bolshevik Revolution's effect on politics, see John Gerring, *Party Ideologies in America, 1828–1996* (Cambridge: Cambridge University Press, 1998), 125–58.

10. See "Red Rehearsals to Pave Way for Revolt Are Told," *SB*, March 23, 1935.

11. By contrast, in 2010, the state had approximately 37 million residents, or more than 12 percent of the nation's total.

12. Richey to Koverman, July 18, 1933, in "Koverman, Ida, 1933–1954," PPI HHL.

13. On reapportionment and California, see Frances N. Ahl, "Reapportionment in California," *American Political Science Review* 22, no. 4 (November 1928): 977–80; Thomas Barclay, "Reapportionment in California," *Pacific Historical Review* 5, no. 2 (June 1936): 93–129; Zechariah Chafee Jr., "Congressional Reapportionment," *Harvard Law Review* 42, no. 8 (June 1929): 1015–47; "Eleven States Gain, 21 Lose House Seats," *NYT*, November 19, 1930; "Reapportionment Stirs Up California," *NYT*, April 26, 1931; "Prospectus for the National Democratic Farm Campaign," 1944, "Miscellaneous Papers, 1932–1948," box 583, DNC, FDRL.

14. Population figures from censuses of 1920, 1930, and 1940. On the phenomenal nature of the migration to California during the 1920s, see Carter Goodrich, *Migration and Economic Opportunity: The Report of the Study of Population Redistribution* (Philadelphia: University of Pennsylvania Press, 1936), 682–85. Goodrich says of the migration to California on p. 682: "Since the movement is abnormal in most respects, it is inconceivable that it will continue."

15. Howe to Harry Hopkins, March 5, 1934, "California H 1933–1945," box 11, OF 300, FDRL.

16. Carey McWilliams, *The Education of Carey McWilliams* (New York: Simon & Schuster, 1979), 66.

17. Wallace Stegner, "California: The Experimental Society," *Saturday Review*, September 23, 1967, 28.

18. For an overview of the scholarship on modern conservatism, see Kim Phillips-Fein, "Conservatism: The State of the Field," *Journal of American History* 98, no. 3 (December 2011): 723–43. The literature on conservatism is vast, but here are some of the books that have been most helpful to me (although I disagree with the emphasis in some): On conservatism and the West, Rick Perlstein, *Before the Storm: Barry Goldwater and the Unmaking of the American Consensus* (New York: Hill and Wang, 2001); Perlstein, *The Invisible Bridge: The Fall of Nixon and the Rise of Reagan* (New York: Simon & Schuster, 2014); Perlstein, *Nixonland: The Rise of a President and the Fracturing of America* (New York: Scribner, 2008); Lisa McGirr, *Suburban Warriors: The Origins of the New American Right* (Princeton, NJ: Princeton University Press, 2001); Darren Dochuk, *From Bible Belt to Sunbelt: Plain-Folk Religion, Grassroots Politics, and the Rise of Evangelical Conservatism* (New York: W.W. Norton, 2011); Donald T. Critchlow, *When Hollywood Was Right: How Movie Stars, Studio Moguls, and Big Business Remade American Politics* (Cambridge: Cambridge University Press, 2013); Matthew Dallek, *The Right Moment: Ronald Reagan's First Victory and the Decisive Turning Point in American Politics* (New York: Free Press, 2000). On conservatism and race, see Kevin Kruse, *White Flight: Atlanta and the Making of Modern Conservatism* (Princeton, NJ: Princeton University Press, 2005); Dan T. Carter, *The Politics of Rage: George Wallace, the Origins of the New Conservatism, and the Transformation of American Politics* (New York: Simon & Schuster, 1995); Matthew D. Lassiter, *Silent Majority: Suburban Politics in the Sunbelt South* (Princeton, NJ: Princeton University Press, 2006); Thomas J. Sugrue, *The Origins of the Urban Crisis: Race and Inequality in Postwar Detroit* (Princeton, NJ: Princeton University Press, 1996); Bruce J. Schulman, *From Cotton Belt to Sunbelt: Federal Policy, Economic Development, and the Transformation of the South, 1938–1980* (Durham, NC: Duke University Press, 1994); Robert O. Self, *American Babylon: Race and the Struggle for Postwar Oakland* (Princeton, NJ: Princeton University Press, 2003); Allan J. Lichtman, *White Protestant Nation: The Rise of the American Conservative Movement* (New York: Atlantic Monthly Press, 2008); and Thomas Byrne Edsall and Mary D. Edsall, *Chain Reaction: The Impact of Race, Rights, and Taxes on American Politics* (New York: W.W. Norton, 1992). For other scholars who find the origins of modern conservatism in the 1930s, see Joseph E. Lowndes, *From the New Deal to the New Right: Race and the Southern Origins of Modern Conservatism* (New Haven, CT: Yale University Press, 2008); Kim Phillips-Fein, *Invisible Hands: The Businessmen's Crusade Against the New Deal* (New York: W.W. Norton, 2010); Elliot A. Rosen, *The Republican Party in the Age of Roosevelt: Sources of Anti-Government Conservatism in the United States* (Charlottesville: University of Virginia Press, 2014); Clyde P. Weed, *The Nemesis of Reform: The Republican Party During the New Deal* (New York: Columbia University Press, 1994); Robert Mason, *The Republican Party and American Politics from Hoover to Reagan* (Cambridge: Cambridge University Press, 2012); and Jefferson Cowie and Nick Salvatore, "The Long Exception: Rethinking the Place of the New Deal in American History," *International Labor and Working-Class History* 74 (Fall 2008): 3–32.

19. "Rugged Individualism or Predatory Collectivism?," *San Francisco Examiner*, March 7, 1935.

20. See Kenneth Finegold and Theda Skocpol, *State and Party in America's New Deal* (Madison: University of Wisconsin Press, 1995), 38, 143.

1. Revolution and Reaction

1. "Terror Reign Threatened at Trial of Reds," *San Francisco Examiner*, March 28, 1935.

2. Steinbeck to George Albee, January 15, 1935, in *Steinbeck: A Life in Letters*, ed. Elaine Steinbeck and Robert Wallsten (New York: Viking, 1975), 98.

3. John Chamberlain, "Books of the Times," *NYT*, January 28, 1936.

4. Steinbeck to Mavis McIntosh, April 1935, in *Life in Letters*, 107.

5. Steinbeck to Elizabeth Otis, n.d., in *Life in Letters*, 162.

6. My account of the background of *In Dubious Battle* comes from oral histories in the Jackson Benson collection at Stanford University and the terrific research of Jackson Benson and Anne Loftis. See Benson and Loftis, "John Steinbeck and Farm Labor Unionization: The Background of 'In Dubious Battle,'" *American Literature* 52, no. 2 (May 1980): 200–201, 221; Benson, *The True Adventures of John Steinbeck, Writer: A Biography* (New York: Viking, 1984), 297–98; and Loftis, *Witnesses to the Struggle: Imaging the 1930s California Labor Movement* (Reno: University of Nevada Press, 1998), 55–56. Also see interviews with Ella Winter, Francis Whitaker, and James Harkins in the Jackson Benson collection in Special Collections at Stanford University.

7. Walton Bean and James J. Rawls, *California: An Interpretive History* (New York: McGraw-Hill, 1983), 396–99; Richard A. Walker, *The Conquest of Bread: 150 Years of Agribusiness in California* (New York: The New Press, 2004), 1–5.

8. U.S. Senate Subcommittee of the Committee on Education and Labor, *Violations of Free Speech and Rights of Labor*, 76th Cong., 3d sess. (Washington, DC: Government Printing Office, 1940) (hereafter La Follette hearings), part 54, 19884.

9. Carey McWilliams, *Factories in the Field: The Story of Migratory Farm Labor in California* (Berkeley: University of California Press, 1966). On California agribusiness, see also Walker, *Conquest of Bread*; Linda C. Majka and Theo J. Majka, *Farm Workers, Agribusiness, and the State* (Philadelphia: Temple University Press, 1982); Lawrence J. Jelinek, *Harvest Empire: A History of California Agriculture* (San Francisco: Boyd & Fraser, 1979); and Steven Stoll, *The Fruits of Natural Advantage: Making the Industrial Countryside in California* (Berkeley: University of California Press, 1998). David Vaught astutely points out that McWilliams's metaphor cannot explain all types of California agriculture, especially during the late nineteenth and early twentieth centuries. But this book concentrates on eras, areas, and environments in which McWilliams's phrase is apt. See Vaught, "Factories in the Field Revisited," *Pacific Historical Review* 66, no. 2 (May 1997): 149–84.

10. Federal Writers Project of the Works Progress Administration, *California in the 1930s: The WPA Guide to the Golden State* (Berkeley: University of California Press, 2013), 441.

11. On Boswell, see Mark Arax and Rick Wartzman, *The King of California: J.G. Boswell and the Making of a Secret American Empire* (New York: PublicAffairs, 2003).

12. "Who Are the Associated Farmers?," *Rural Observer*, September–October 1938. On Miller & Lux, see David Igler, *Industrial Cowboys: Miller & Lux and the Transformation of the Far West, 1850–1920* (Berkeley: University of California Press, 2001).

13. John Steinbeck, *The Harvest Gypsies: On the Road to the Grapes of Wrath* (Berkeley: Heyday, 1988), 49; "Sick and Needy Given Aid," *LAT*, January 20, 1932.

14. Paul Taylor, *On the Ground in the Thirties* (Salt Lake City: G.M. Smith, 1983), 14.

15. Ibid., 2.

16. La Follette hearings, part 54, 19859.

17. Quoted in Stoll, *Fruits of Natural Advantage*, 137.

18. Note cards, undated, box 80, GCP, UCLA.

19. For the ethnic and racial makeup of the farm labor force before the Okie migration, see "Racial Composition of Farm Labor Supply, California, 1930," in La Follette hearings, part 54, 19859.

20. Kevin Starr, *Endangered Dreams: The Great Depression in California* (New York: Oxford University Press, 1996), 67.

21. La Follette hearings, part 54, 19890.

22. Ibid., 19865.

23. Cletus Daniel, *Bitter Harvest: A History of California Farmworkers, 1870–1941* (Ithaca, NY: Cornell University Press, 1981), 101–102; Devra Weber, *Dark Sweat, White Gold: California Farm Workers, Cotton, and the New Deal* (Berkeley: University of California Press, 1994), 38–42; La Follette hearings, part 54, 19861.

24. "Communists Tried Under I.W.W. Law," *NYT*, January 29, 1935.

25. On the IWW, see Melvyn Dubofsky, *We Shall Be All: A History of the Industrial Workers of the World* (Urbana: University of Illinois Press, 1988).

26. On the IWW in California, see Daniel, *Bitter Harvest*, 81–91, and Starr, *Endangered Dreams*, 38–44.

27. Daniel, *Bitter Harvest*, 91; Starr, *Endangered Dreams*, 231–32.

28. Ahmed A. White, "The Crime of Economic Radicalism: Criminal Syndicalism Laws and the Industrial Workers of the World, 1917–1927," *Oregon Law Review* 85 (2006): 652. See also Woodrow C. Whitten, "Criminal Syndicalism and the Law in California, 1919–1927," *Transactions of the American Philosophical Society* 59, no. 2 (1969): 21.

29. Quoted in Stephen F. Rohde, "Criminal Syndicalism: The Repression of Radical Political Speech in California," *Western Legal History* 3 (1990): 316.

Notes to Pages 20–26

30. Throughout this book, I use small "c" communist to indicate those who agreed with the principles of the Communist Party but were not necessarily members, and big "C" Communist to indicate members of the Party or the Party itself. My sources do not always make this distinction.

31. Quoted in Harvey Klehr, *The Heyday of American Communism: The Depression Decade* (New York: Basic, 1984), 4.

32. See "Federal Sedition Bills: Speech Restriction in Theory and Practice," *Columbia Law Review* 35, no. 6 (June 1935): 917–27.

33. Michal R. Belknap, *Cold War Political Justice: The Smith Act, the Communist Party, and American Civil Liberties* (Westport, CT: Greenwood Press, 1977), 11; "Federal Sedition Bills," 918n5.

34. Klehr, *Heyday*, 5.

35. "Federal Sedition Bills," 921.

36. Lester V. Chandler, *America's Greatest Depression, 1929–1941* (New York: Harper & Row, 1970), 20.

37. Eric Rauchway, *The Great Depression and the New Deal: A Very Short Introduction* (New York: Oxford University Press, 2008), 40.

38. Chandler, *America's Greatest Depression*, 82.

39. Rauchway, *Great Depression and the New Deal*, 42–43; "500,000 in Chicago Facing Starvation," *Washington Post*, June 3, 1932.

40. On the Bonus Army, see Paul Dickson and Thomas B. Allen, *The Bonus Army: An American Epic* (New York: Walker and Company, 2006), and Donald J. Lisio, *The President and Protest: Hoover, Conspiracy, and the Bonus Riot* (Columbia: University of Missouri Press, 1974).

41. Klehr, *Heyday*, 38–39; Daniel, *Bitter Harvest*, 135.

42. Porter M. Chaffee, "A History of the Cannery and Agricultural Workers Industrial Union" (Oakland, CA: Federal Writers Project, 193?), 44.

43. See Daniel, *Bitter Harvest*, 130–35; Sam Darcy, "History of the Communist Party in California," folder 51, box 2, SDP, NYU.

44. Orrick Johns, *The Time of Our Lives* (New York: Octagon Books, 1973), 329–33.

45. See H.W. Brands, *Traitor to His Class: The Privileged Life and Radical Presidency of Franklin Delano Roosevelt* (New York: Doubleday, 2008); Frank Freidel, *Franklin D. Roosevelt: The Apprenticeship* (Boston: Little, Brown, 1952); Kenneth S. Davis, *FDR: The Beckoning of Destiny, 1882–1928, A History* (New York: G.P. Putnam's Sons, 1972); Geoffrey C. Ward, *Before the Trumpet: Young Franklin Roosevelt, 1882–1905* (New York: Harper & Row, 1985).

46. Quoted in Bernard Belush, *Franklin D. Roosevelt as Governor of New York* (New York: AMS Press, 1968), 140.

47. On Perkins, see Kirstin Downey, *The Woman Behind the New Deal: The Life of Frances Perkins, FDR's Secretary of Labor and His Moral Conscience* (New York: Nan A. Talese/Doubleday, 2009).

48. Elliott Roosevelt, ed., *The Roosevelt Letters: Being the Personal Correspondence of Franklin Delano Roosevelt*, vol. 3, *1928–1945* (London: George G. Harrap, 1952), 54.

49. "Roosevelt Hears 'Hunger Marchers,'" *NYT*, November 19, 1932.

50. John Spargo, "The Psychology of the Parlor Bolsheviki," *World's Work*, December 1919, 127.

51. "Fish Will Demand Deportation of Reds as Menace to Nation," *NYT*, January 10, 1931.

52. "Governor Starts His Tour," *NYT*, October 19, 1932.

53. Quoted in Ted Morgan, *Reds: McCarthyism in Twentieth-Century America* (New York: Random House, 2003), 121.

54. See Richard Breitman and Allan J. Lichtman, *FDR and the Jews* (Cambridge, MA: Belknap, 2013).

55. Frances Perkins, *The Roosevelt I Knew* (New York: Viking, 1946), 55. See also Molly Dewson, "Women and the New Deal," in *The Era of Franklin D. Roosevelt, 1933–1945: A Brief History with Documents*, ed. Richard Polenberg (Boston: Bedford/St. Martin's, 2000).

56. Ronald D. Rotunda, "The 'Liberal' Label: Roosevelt's Capture of a Symbol," in *Public Policy*, ed. John D. Montgomery and Albert O. Hirschman (Cambridge, MA: Harvard University Press, 1968), 17:377–408; and Samuel H. Beer, "In Search of a New Public Philosophy," in *The New American Political System*, ed. Anthony King (Washington, DC: American Enterprise Institute, 1978), 13–15.

57. Quoted in Arthur M. Schlesinger Jr., *The Age of Roosevelt*, vol. 3, *The Politics of Upheaval* (Boston: Houghton Mifflin, 1960), 620.

58. "Campaign Address on Progressive Government at the Commonwealth Club in San Francisco, California," September 23, 1932, http://www.presidency.ucsb.edu/ws/index.php?pid=88391.

59. First inaugural address, March 4, 1933, http://www.presidency.ucsb.edu/ws/?pid=14473.

60. See Theodore Saloutos, *The American Farmer and the New Deal* (Ames: Iowa State University Press, 1982), 269. On the subsidies in the San Joaquin Valley, see "Cotton Raisers Receive Checks," *LAT*, October 25, 1933.

61. For California examples, see the testimony of Enrique Bravo, La Follette hearings, part 54, 19927.

62. For discussions of the achievements and disappointments of the NIRA, see Ellis Hawley, *The New Deal and the Problem of Monopoly: A Study in Economic Ambivalence* (Princeton, NJ: Princeton University Press, 1966), 111–46, and Meg Jacobs, *Pocketbook Politics: Economic Citizenship in Twentieth-Century America* (Princeton, NJ: Princeton University Press, 2005), 104–35.

63. Eric Rauchway, "New Deal Denialism," *Dissent*, Winter 2010, 68–72, Romer quote at 68.

64. "A New Deal—Brings a New Deal In," *Touring Topics*, January 1934.

65. "Greet Prosperity Next Week," *SB*, October 7, 1933; "Parade of 10,000 Here Starts Buy Now Drive," *SB*, October 13, 1933; "Sacramento Exhibits Her Faith in NRA," *SB*, October 13, 1933.

66. William M. Leiserson, *Right and Wrong in Labor Relations* (Berkeley: University of California Press, 1938), 27.

67. Quoted in Irving Bernstein, *The New Deal Collective Bargaining Policy* (Berkeley: University of California Press, 1950), 23.

68. Quoted in J. Joseph Huthmacher, *Senator Robert F. Wagner and the Rise of Urban Liberalism* (New York: Atheneum, 1968), 147.

69. For the most complete discussion of the exclusion of farm workers from Section 7a, see Austin P. Morris, "Agricultural Labor and National Labor Legislation," *California Law Review* 54, no. 5 (December 1966): 1947–51. For the discriminatory nature of New Deal programs, see Ira Katznelson, *When Affirmative Action Was White: An Untold History of Racial Inequality in Twentieth-Century America* (New York: W.W. Norton, 2005).

70. Daniel, *Bitter Harvest*, 174; Morris, "Agricultural Labor," 1946.

71. Kyle Palmer, "Former President Finds Pleasure in Simple Life," *LAT*, July 30, 1933.

72. See Joan Hoff Wilson, *Herbert Hoover: Forgotten Progressive* (New York: HarperCollins, 1975), and David M. Kennedy, *Freedom from Fear: The American People in Depression and War, 1929–1945* (New York: Oxford University Press, 1999), 43–94.

73. Hoover to Henry Stoddard, June 6, 1933, "Stoddard, Henry L., 1933–1944," PPI HHL; Hoover to Will Irwin, November 18, 1933, "Irwin, Will, 1933–1934," PPI HHL; Hoover to Arthur Hyde, January 27, 1934, "Hyde, Arthur M., 1933–June 1934," PPI HHL.

74. Hoover to Lewis Strauss, April 4, 1933, "Strauss, Lewis L., Correspondence, 1933–June 1934," PPI HHL.

75. Hoover to Simeon Fess, December 18, 1933, "Fess, Simeon D., Correspondence, 1933–1936," PPI HHL.

76. Hoover to Mark Sullivan, October 26, 1934, "Sullivan, Mark, Correspondence, 1933–1941," PPI HHL. For Hoover's use of the phrase "march toward Moscow," see Hoover to Frank Knox, April 5, 1933, "Knox, Frank B., Correspondence, 1933–1934," PPI HHL.

77. Hoover to Frank Knox, March 10, 1934, "Knox, Frank B., Correspondence, 1933–1934," PPI HHL.

78. Hoover to Simeon Fess, December 27, 1933, "Fess, Simeon D., Correspondence, 1933–1936," PPI HHL.

79. Mullendore to C.C. Teague, April 4, 1934, WMP, HHL.

80. Teague to Henry Harriman, April 23, 1934, ibid.

81. "Los Angeles Is the World's White Spot," *LAT*, October 21, 1923. There are dozens of references to Los Angeles as a business "white spot" in *Los Angeles Times* stories in 1922 and 1923.

82. "Vigilance the Price of Liberty," *LAT*, June 3, 1922, quoted in Scott Allen Mc-Clellan, "Policing the Red Scare: The Los Angeles Police Department's Red Squad and the Repression of Labor Activism in Los Angeles, 1900–1940" (PhD diss., University of California, Irvine, 2011), 144.

83. Quoted in McClellan, "Policing the Red Scare," 192.

84. Rowell to George Cameron, August 8, 1934, "Rowell, Chester Harvey, 1932–1934," box 7, CRP.

85. David Halberstam, *The Powers That Be* (New York: Knopf, 1979), 116. See also "The Press: Half-Century," *Time*, December 7, 1931.

86. Ed Cray, *Chief Justice: A Biography of Earl Warren* (New York: Simon & Schuster, 1997), 79.

87. Telegram, E.D. Coblentz to Universal Service Bureaus and all Hearst editors, August 7, 1935, in "Hearst, William Randolph," PPF 62, FDRL.

88. For Republicans' views on Hearst, see the letters written to and by Hoover in September and October 1934 at the HHL, including Knox to Hoover, September 20, 1934.

89. On Giannini and the New Deal, see Felice A. Bonadio, *A.P. Giannini: Banker of America* (Berkeley: University of California Press, 1994).

90. Arax and Wartzman, *King of California*, 135.

91. "AAA Program Aids Farmer," *IVP*, March 1, 1934; Edwin G. Nourse, *Marketing Agreements Under the AAA* (Washington, DC: Brookings Institution, 1935), 15.

92. Mullendore to Teague, April 4, 1934, WMP, HHL; Address by C.C. Teague on the Agricultural Adjustment Act at the 10th Western Divisional Meeting of the Chamber of Commerce of the United States, Sacramento, California, December 4, 1933, in "Addresses and Papers, 1932–1934," box 2, CCT.

93. Bancroft to Justus Wardell, August 23, 1933, box 1, PBP.

94. Congressional Record, 73rd Cong., 1st sess., June 8, 1933, 5241, cited in Ira Katznelson, *Fear Itself: The New Deal and the Origins of Our Time* (New York: Liveright, 2013), 241.

2. The Great Strike

1. U.S. Senate Subcommittee of the Committee on Education and Labor, *Violations of Free Speech and Rights of Labor*, 76th Cong., 3d sess. (Washington, DC: Government Printing Office, 1940) (hereafter La Follette hearings), part 54, 19933.

2. La Follette hearings, part 54, 19932.

3. Federal Writers Project of the Works Progress Administration, *California in the 1930s: The WPA Guide to the Golden State* (Berkeley: University of California Press, 2013), 440.

4. Population figures from 1930 census.

5. Undated flyer, "National Labor Board, June–August 1934," OF 716, FDRL.

6. *Historical Statistics of the United States*, millennial edition online, series Ba4954-4964, 2-354; Austin P. Morris, "Agricultural Labor and National Labor Legislation,"

California Law Review 54, no. 5 (December 1966): 1947n38; Scott Allen McClellan, "Policing the Red Scare: The Los Angeles Police Department's Red Squad and the Repression of Labor Activism in Los Angeles, 1900–1940" (PhD diss., University of California, Irvine, 2011), 199. See also Irving Bernstein, *The Turbulent Years: A History of the American Worker, 1933–1941* (Boston: Houghton Mifflin, 1971), 37–91.

7. FPOH, book 4, 422. See also Robert Woodbury, *Introduction: Limits of Coverage of Labor in Industries Closely Allied to Agriculture under Codes of Fair Competition under NIRA* (Washington, DC: Office of National Recovery Administration, Division of Review, Labor Studies Section, 1936).

8. See Morris, "Agricultural Labor," 1947–51.

9. National Labor Board report, La Follette hearings, part 54, 20048.

10. W.N. Cunningham to J.H. Fallin, July 19, 1933, box 80, GCP.

11. On the Tagus strike, see Cletus Daniel, *Bitter Harvest: A History of California Farmworkers, 1870–1941* (Ithaca, NY: Cornell University Press, 1981), 156–58; Jackson Benson and Anne Loftis, "John Steinbeck and Farm Labor Unionization: The Background of 'In Dubious Battle,'" *American Literature* 52, no. 2 (May 1980): 204–6; and Marion R. Hardy, "The Political-Economic Implications of the Pat Chambers Criminal Syndicalism Trial" (master's thesis, Sacramento State College, 1964), 4–6.

12. See the Chambers entry in the Sacramento Police Department mug book, 15:280, CSH; and "Affidavit of Registration," April 24, 1934, box 46, LARS.

13. PCOH.

14. Benson and Loftis, "John Steinbeck and Farm Labor Unionization," 203.

15. PCOH.

16. Ibid.

17. Quoted in Benson and Loftis, "John Steinbeck," 204. See also PCOH.

18. Norman Thomas, *The Choice Before Us: Mankind at the Crossroads* (New York: AMS Press, 1970), 140.

19. Hardy, "Pat Chambers Criminal Syndicalism Trial," 7–10; Daniel, *Bitter Harvest,* 161–65; Stuart Jamieson, *Labor Unionism in American Agriculture* (Washington, DC: U.S. Bureau of Labor Statistics, 1945), 93–100.

20. Details of Decker's youth come from CGOH-WSU.

21. Ibid., 6, 17.

22. Ibid., 7, 15, 20.

23. Ibid., 32, 42.

24. Ibid., 40.

25. Ibid., 33.

26. On gender and sexuality in the CPUSA, see Rosalyn Baxandall, "The Question Seldom Asked: Women and the CPUSA," in Michael E. Brown, et al., *New Studies in the Politics and Culture of U.S. Communism* (New York: Monthly Review Press, 1993); Daniel Horowitz, *Betty Friedan and the Making of the Feminine Mystique* (Amherst: University of Massachusetts Press, 1998), 129–32; Van Gosse, "'To Organize in Every

Neighborhood, in Every Home': The Gender Politics of American Communists be-tween the Wars," *Radical History Review* 50 (Spring 1991): 109–41; Ellen Trimberger, "Women in the Old and New Left: The Evolution of a Politics of Personal Life," *Feminist Studies* 5 (Fall 1979): 432–61; Elsa Dixler, "The Woman Question: Women and the American Communist Party, 1929–1941" (PhD diss., Yale University, 1975); Kate Weigand, *Red Feminism: American Communism and the Making of Women's Liberation* (Baltimore: Johns Hopkins University Press, 2001), 15–27; and Beth Slutsky, "Three Generations of American Communist Women: Charlotte Anita Whitney, Dorothy Ray Healey, and Kendra Alexander, 1919–1992" (PhD diss., University of California, Davis, 2008).

27. Quoted in Harvey Klehr, *The Heyday of American Communism: The Depression Decade* (New York: Basic, 1984), 37.

28. CGOH-WSU, 38.

29. Paul F. Taylor, *Bloody Harlan: The United Mine Workers of America in Harlan County, Kentucky, 1931–1941* (Lanham, MD: University Press of America, 1990), 12.

30. Ibid., 14.

31. CGOH-WSU, 59; author's interview with Jed Gladstein, September 9, 2012.

32. "Miscellany," *Time*, April 29, 1929.

33. Helen Calista Wilson and Elsie Reed Mitchell, *Vagabonding at Fifty: From Siberia to Turkestan* (New York: Coward-McCann, 1929), 333.

34. CGOH-WSU, 30.

35. Ibid., 57.

36. Ibid., 55; author's interview with Jed Gladstein, September 9, 2012.

37. CGOH-WSU, 58.

38. Ella Winter, *And Not to Yield* (New York: Harcourt, Brace, and World, 1963), 188.

39. CGOH-WSU, 69.

40. CGOH-BAN.

41. Peggy Terry quoted in Studs Terkel, *Hard Times: An Oral History of the Great Depression* (New York: Pantheon, 1970), 49.

42. Sam Darcy, "Autobiography," 335, folder 20, box 3, SDP, NYU.

43. Darcy puts a positive spin on the union's efforts to get the workers to overcome their racism in ibid., 334–35. On the persistence of Anglo workers' racism, see Devra Weber, *Dark Sweat, White Gold: California Farm Workers, Cotton, and the New Deal* (Berkeley: University of California Press, 1994), 146–50, and James Gregory, *American Exodus: The Dust Bowl Migration and Okie Culture in California* (New York: Oxford University Press, 1989), passim, especially chap. 5.

44. WCOH, "Cotton, Irrigation, and the AAA," 21. On the importance of the Southern white migration to California, see Rodolfo F. Acuña, *Corridors of Migration: The Odyssey of Mexican Laborers, 1600–1933* (Tucson: University of Arizona Press, 2007), 271–72, and James N. Gregory, "Southernizing the American Working Class:

Post-War Episodes of Regional and Class Transformation," *Labor History* 39, no. 2 (1998): 135–54.

45. Guiberson interview, January 13, 1934, folder 50, carton 14, PST.

46. "People Getting Weary of Communist Agitators," *Fresno Bee*, October 6, 1933.

47. Quoted in Jamieson, *Labor Unionism in American Agriculture*, 103.

48. "Subia Rites Strip Camps of Families," *SFC*, October 17, 1933.

49. On McKiddy, see Jackson Benson, *The True Adventures of John Steinbeck, Writer: A Biography* (New York: Viking, 1984), 341. On Hammett, see ibid., 342; Anne Loftis, *Witnesses to the Struggle: Imaging the 1930s California Labor Movement* (Reno: University of Nevada Press, 1998), 33–36; and Daniel, *Bitter Harvest*, 321n45.

50. On Hammett and McKiddy as models for Casy and Joad, see Benson, *True Adventures*, 341–42.

51. CGOH-WSU, 81; "Cotton Strikers Vote War to Finish; Women Called into Picket Lines Today," *SFC*, October 15, 1933.

52. CGOH-WSU, 80.

53. "Food for Starving Strikers in Cotton Area Promised by Rolph; Arbitration Looms," *SU*, October 13, 1933.

54. "Starving Strikers to Be Fed," *SFC*, October 13, 1933.

55. "Communist Leader Granted Favor Denied Ranchers," *VTD*, November 20, 1933. See also, for example, "Strikers Go Back to Work," *Oakland Post-Enquirer*, October 27, 1933.

56. "Girl, 21, Laughs at Fear as She Directs Strike," *San Francisco News*, October 26, 1933.

57. *PVC*, 13:6346. All Communists were marginalized in this way, but Decker was erased from the history more often than the men.

58. "Burial Rites Mapped for Slain Picket," *SFC*, October 16, 1933; "San Francisco Girl Tells of Women's Hopeless View in War-Torn Strike Sector," *SFC*, October 13, 1933.

59. For descriptions of the Corcoran camp, see Winter, *And Not to Yield*, 196; Marie de L. Welch, "Camp Corcoran," in *This Is Our Own* (New York: Macmillan, 1940), 57–62; and Paul Taylor, *On the Ground in the Thirties* (Salt Lake City: G.M. Smith, 1983), 61–62.

60. Weber, *Dark Sweat, White Gold*, 90.

61. Quoted in Taylor, *On the Ground in the Thirties*, 33. The moment became legend among California Communists, one of whom, Dalton Trumbo, would write a similar scene in the 1960 movie *Spartacus*.

62. Interviews with Morgan and Kearney, folder 48, carton 14, PST.

63. Quoted in Porter M. Chaffee, "A History of the Cannery and Agricultural Workers Industrial Union" (Oakland, CA: Federal Writers Project, 193?), 2:7.

64. On Bravo's role in the strike, see Gilbert González, *Mexican Consuls and Labor Organizing: Imperial Politics in the American Southwest* (Austin: University of Texas Press, 1999), 134–58.

65. Chaffee, "History of the Cannery and Agricultural Workers Industrial Union," 2:28.

66. Ibid., 2:29.

67. Jamieson, *Labor Unionism*, 99.

68. "Cotton Men to Drive Out Agitators in San Joaquin," SB, October 9, 1933.

69. Carter interview, November 17, 1933, folder 48, carton 14, PST.

70. "State Labor War Spreading; Strike Affects 20,000," SFC, October 10, 1933.

71. Guiberson interview, folder 50, carton 14, PST.

72. "Growers Plan to Drive Out Agitators: Tri-County Mass Meeting Being Held in Corcoran," VTD, October 9, 1933.

73. Sam Darcy, "Autobiography," 336, 340, folder 20, box 3, SDP, NYU.

74. Perkins to Rolph, October 9, 1933, "Strikes, 1933," box 5, OF 407b, FDRL.

75. "Growers Plan to Drive Out Agitators," VTD, October 9, 1933.

76. La Follette hearings, part 54, 19935–36.

77. "State Labor War Spreading"; "Cotton Pickers Will Be Given Protection," *Bakersfield Californian*, October 9, 1933.

78. "News Writer Eye-witness to Shooting," *San Francisco News*, October 11, 1933.

79. See Weber, *Dark Sweat, White Gold*, 101; Daniel, *Bitter Harvest*, 196; and the accounts in the *San Francisco News*, *Visalia Times-Delta*, *Fresno Bee*, and other California newspapers on October 11.

80. "California Clash Called 'Civil War,'" NYT, October 22, 1933.

81. "U.S. Moves to Arbitrate California Labor Strikes," SU, October 13, 1933.

82. See Winter, *And Not to Yield*, 194; "Chambers Jury Still Out at Press Time," VTD, December 5, 1933; "Jury Indicts Eight Valley Ranchmen as Strike Slayers," SFC, October 19, 1933.

83. "Let This War Stop Now!," SFC, October 11, 1933. See also "Let Peace Be Restored in Harvesting State's Crops," SB, October 11, 1933.

84. Chaffee, "A History of the Cannery and Agricultural Workers Industrial Union," 2:53.

85. Quoted in James Worthen, *Governor James Rolph and the Great Depression in California* (Jefferson, NC: McFarland, 2006), 97.

86. Quoted in ibid., 36.

87. Ibid., 182.

3. A New Deal

1. John Dos Passos, Mr. *Wilson's War* (Garden City, NJ: Doubleday, 1962), 300.

2. Quoted in George Creel, *Rebel at Large: Recollections of Fifty Crowded Years* (New York: G.P. Putnam's Sons, 1947), 143.

3. Ibid., 275.

4. "Creel Out of NRA as Party Hesitates," NYT, October 8, 1933.

5. See the cables in "NRA Miscellaneous, Oct. 1–15, 1933," box 8, OF 466, FDRL.

6. Roosevelt to Creel, November 26, 1933, "NRA Miscellaneous, Oct. 1–15, 1933," box 8, OF 466, FDRL.

7. Creel to Stephen Early, October 14, 1933, "NRA Miscellaneous, Oct. 1–15, 1933," box 8, OF 466, FDRL.

8. "Strike Status in California Told in Brief," SFC, October 13, 1933.

9. See the numerous telegrams praising Creel in "NRA Miscellaneous, Oct. 1–15, 1933," box 8, OF 466, FDRL.

10. Creel to Parker Frisselle, November 7, 1933, box 1, case 3, NLB. Emphasis added.

11. "Plague Fear Stiffs Creel to End Strike," SFC, October 19, 1933.

12. Reichert to Rolph, October 9, 1933, Reichert letter file, carton 39, FWP. Creel was very supportive of Reichert. See letter, Creel to Louis S. Haas, October 6, 1933, in the same file.

13. Letter, Irving Reichert to H.C. Merritt, October 10, 1933, box 1, case 3, NLB.

14. "New Action Asked," SB, October 21, 1933.

15. Harry Hopkins, "Extension of Relief to Strikers," October 5, 1933, in "Strikes, 1933," box 5, OF 407b, FDRL.

16. Stuart Jamieson, Labor Unionism in American Agriculture (Washington, DC: U.S. Bureau of Labor Statistics, 1945), 104.

17. Paul Taylor, On the Ground in the Thirties (Salt Lake City: G.M. Smith, 1983), 95.

18. Porter M. Chaffee, "A History of the Cannery and Agricultural Workers Industrial Union" (Oakland, CA: Federal Writers Project, 193?), 2:39; Taylor, On the Ground in the Thirties, 95–96.

19. "Cotton Strike Comes to End," LAT, October 28, 1933.

20. "Strike Bands Flee to Camp in Open Air," SFC, October 11, 1933.

21. "Four Slain in State Strike Riots," SFC, October 11, 1933.

22. "Cotton Strike Comes to End," LAT, October 15, 1933.

23. "Cotton Pickers Parade 2000 Strong in Bakersfield," LAT, October 17, 1933.

24. "Plague Fear Stiffs Creel to End Strike," SFC, October 19, 1933.

25. Ibid.

26. Rodolfo F. Acuña, Corridors of Migration: The Odyssey of Mexican Laborers, 1600–1933 (Tucson: University of Arizona Press, 2007), 260.

27. Dietmar Rothermund, The Global Impact of the Great Depression, 1929–1939 (London: Routledge, 1996), 45.

28. "Jury Indicts Eight Valley Ranchmen as Strike Slayers," SFC, October 19, 1933; "Plague Fear Stiffs Creel to End Strike," SFC, October 19, 1933; "Creel Warns of Epidemics in Cotton Strikers' Camps," SFC, October 19, 1933; "Near-Riot Mars Creel's Visit to Strike Camp," VTD, October 19, 1933.

29. Interview with Buckner, December 20, 1933, field notes, folder 48, carton 14, PST.

30. Sam Darcy, "Autobiography," 346, folder 20, box 3, SDP.

31. See *A Century of Progress*, a 1934 film by Otto Hagel and Hansel Meith, at the San Francisco Labor Archives and Research Center.

32. Terry Ommen, "From the Unconventional to the Conventional," *VTD*, December 17, 2003. The auditorium was deemed structurally unsafe in 1963 and subsequently torn down.

33. "New Cotton Area Walkout Near as Growers Hit Rolph Group," *SFC*, October 20, 1933; "Martial Law Call Hinted in Cotton Strike," *SFC*, October 21, 1933.

34. Anne Loftis, *Witnesses to the Struggle: Imaging the 1930s California Labor Movement* (Reno: University of Nevada Press, 1998), 32.

35. Clark Kerr, *The Gold and the Blue: A Personal Memoir of the University of California, 1949–1967* (Berkeley: University of California Press, 2001), 1:4–5.

36. See Mary Ellen Leary, "California's Lonely Secret Agent," *LAT*, April 2, 1967.

37. Taylor, *On the Ground in the Thirties*, 103.

38. U.S. Senate Subcommittee of the Committee on Education and Labor, *Violations of Free Speech and Rights of Labor*, 76th Cong., 3d sess. (Washington, DC: Government Printing Office, 1940) (hereafter La Follette hearings), part 54, 19942.

39. "New Cotton Area Walkout Near as Growers Hit Rolph Group."

40. "Cotton Strike Comes to End," *LAT*, October 28, 1933.

41. Guiberson interview, folder 50, carton 14, PST.

42. La Follette hearings, part 54, 19926. The official transcript was recorded by the state Division of Labor reporter. See letter, George Techumy to George Creel, November 20, 1933, box 1, case 3, NLB.

43. La Follette hearings, part 54, 19932–33.

44. Ibid., part 54, 19934.

45. Ibid., part 54, 19940.

46. Ibid., part 54, 19936; "Martial Law Call Hinted in Cotton Strike," *SFC*, October 21, 1933.

47. La Follette hearings, part 54, 19939; Taylor, *On the Ground in the Thirties*, 103.

48. Taylor, *On the Ground in the Thirties*, 106. Some Americans referred to the NIRA as the "National Recovery Act" at the time.

49. La Follette hearings, part 54, 19941.

50. Letter, E.J. Hanna, Ira B. Cross, Tully Knoles, to George Creel and James Rolph, October 23, 1933, box 1, case 3, NLB.

51. Ibid.

52. "Farmers Foot the Bills and Stand the Losses," *VTD*, October 24, 1933.

53. Buckner interview, December 20, 1933, field notes, folder 48, carton 14, PST.

54. Cross to Edson Abel, January 6, 1934, folder 51, carton 14, PST.

55. Buckner interview, December 20, 1933, field notes, folder 48, carton 14, PST. See also "Berkeley Students Act as Cotton Strike Leaders," *LAT*, October 28, 1933.

56. See "Highway Police in Strike Area," October 24, 1933, *SB*, and "Troops Gather for Crisis of San Joaquin Strike," *LAT*, October 25, 1933.

57. Taylor, *On the Ground in the Thirties*, 112.

58. Chaffee, "History of the Cannery and Agricultural Workers Industrial Union," 2:60.

59. Ibid., no page number.

60. See Devra Weber, *Dark Sweat, White Gold: California Farm Workers, Cotton, and the New Deal* (Berkeley: University of California Press, 1994), 111.

61. Cletus Daniel, *Bitter Harvest: A History of California Farmworkers, 1870–1941* (Ithaca, NY: Cornell University Press, 1981), 219.

62. "Chronicle Reporter Has Another Pipe Dream," *VTD*, October 27, 1933.

63. "Sheriff Hits Creel Visit to Strikers," *SFC*, October 20, 1933.

64. Letter, John E. Pickett to Creel, January 16, 1934, box 1, case 3, NLB. See also Hill, Guiberson, Wilson, and Buckner interviews, folder 48, carton 14, PST.

65. Letter, Clark Kerr to Paul Taylor, February 8, 1934, in folder 50, carton 14, PST.

66. "Looks as Though Our Cotton Farmer Is the 'Forgotten Man,'" *VTD*, October 19, 1933.

67. "Creel Picks Body to Act in Strike in San Joaquin," *SB*, October 14, 1933.

68. Clarke Chambers, *California Farm Organizations: A Historical Study of the Grange, the Farm Bureau and the Associated Farmers 1929–41* (Berkeley: University of California Press, 1952), 39–41; La Follette hearings, part 55, 20075–91, 20235–41.

69. "Mob Breaks into Jail; Hart Killers Seized," *LAT*, November 27, 1933.

70. For the most complete account of the San Jose lynching, see Henry Farrell, *Swift Justice: Murder and Vengeance in a California Town* (New York: St. Martin's, 1992).

71. "Lynch Mob Trial Doubted and Pardons Promised," *LAT*, November 28, 1933.

72. "Woman to Give Chambers Bail," *LAT*, November 29, 1933.

73. "Chambers Jury Fails to Agree," *VTD*, December 6, 1933; "Chambers Case May Reach Jury This Afternoon," *VTD*, December 4, 1933; "Chambers Jury Still Out at Press Time," *VTD*, December 5, 1933.

4. Bohemians

1. Jackson Benson and Anne Loftis, "John Steinbeck and Farm Labor Unionization: The Background of 'In Dubious Battle,'" *American Literature* 52, no. 2 (May 1980): 200–201, 221; Benson, *The True Adventures of John Steinbeck, Writer: A Biography* (New York: Viking, 1984), 297–98; Loftis, *Witnesses to the Struggle: Imaging the 1930s California Labor Movement* (Reno: University of Nevada Press, 1998), 55–56. Also see interviews with Ella Winter, Francis Whitaker, and James Harkins in JBC.

2. Loftis, *Witnesses to the Struggle*, 55; Benson, *True Adventures*, 297.

3. Marc Grossman, "Chavez, Steinbeck: The Ties That Bind," *SB*, October 20, 2002.

4. Loftis, *Witnesses to the Struggle*, 55; Grossman, "Chavez, Steinbeck."

5. Benson and Loftis argue that Chambers must not have been Steinbeck's source. In *Witnesses to the Struggle*, Loftis notes on p. 56: "It is tempting to identify Chambers as Steinbeck's source, but there are logistical problems in doing so" because Chambers was in jail in Visalia in December 1933 and arrested in Imperial Valley, hundreds of miles away, in January 1934, while the interviews took place sometime in the winter of 1933–34. But there are two long stretches of time when Chambers was in hiding and could have met Steinbeck: from December 6, when he was released in Visalia, to a few days before January 18, when he was arrested in El Centro; and again from mid-February, when he was released in El Centro, to March 10, when he turned himself in again in El Centro. He could easily have gone from Visalia to a hiding place in Seaside, stayed there for a few weeks and met Steinbeck, and then traveled down to Imperial Valley in mid-January. Alternatively, it is possible (although less likely) that he could have met Steinbeck during the month he was missing from mid-February to mid-March. For the newspaper articles and court docket establishing his whereabouts, see "Chambers Jury Fails to Agree," *VTD*, December 6, 1933; Docket, folder P-4, carton 32, FWP; "Man and Woman Sought in Brawley Raid Last Week Captured; 'Pat' Chambers Apprehended at El Centro," *BN*, January 19, 1934; "Three Agitator Suspects Arrested," *LAT*, January 19, 1934. See also "Strike Gets Attention of Supervisors," *IVP*, February 17, 1934, and "Mrs. Johnson Arrested for Carrying Gun," *IVP*, March 28, 1934, to establish the February and March dates for his absence.

6. "East Swelters While Carmel Revels," *Carmel Sun*, August 2, 1934.

7. Federal Writers Project of the Works Progress Administration, *California in the 1930s: The WPA Guide to the Golden State* (Berkeley: University of California Press, 2013), 342. See also "Carmel," *Carmel Sun*, August 23, 1934, for a complete list of businesses and art galleries in the town.

8. Peter Hartshorn, *I Have Seen the Future: A Life of Lincoln Steffens* (Berkeley, CA: Counterpoint, 2011), 315. Steffens repeated many variations of this statement. Ella Winter, in the epigraph for *Red Virtue*, puts the quote as "I've seen The Future—and it works!"

9. Ella Winter, *And Not to Yield* (New York: Harcourt, Brace, and World, 1963), 53.

10. Ibid., 65.

11. Ibid., 53.

12. Ibid., 61.

13. Quoted in Hartshorn, *I Have Seen the Future*, 334.

14. Steffens, *The Autobiography of Lincoln Steffens* (New York: Harcourt, Brace, 1931), 820.

15. Winter, *And Not to Yield*, 136.

16. Ibid., 129.

17. Ibid., 136, 147. See also Nora Sayre, *On the Wing: A Young American Abroad* (Washington, DC: Counterpoint, 2001), 150–52.

18. Justin Kaplan, *Lincoln Steffens: A Biography* (New York: Simon & Schuster, 1974), 318.

19. Winter, *And Not to Yield*, 132, 134, 138.

20. Malcolm Cowley, *The Dream of the Golden Mountains: Remembering the 1930s* (New York: Viking, 1980), ix.

21. See Michael Denning, *The Cultural Front: The Laboring of American Culture in the Twentieth Century* (London: Verso, 1997), especially xix–xx.

22. Winter, *And Not to Yield*, 173.

23. Malcolm Muggeridge, *Chronicles of Wasted Time* (London: Collins, 1972), 1:245. On leftist tourists in the Soviet Union in the 1930s, see David Caute, *The Fellow-Travelers: Intellectual Friends of Communism* (New Haven, CT: Yale University Press, 1973), and Paul Hollander, *Political Pilgrims: Travels of Western Intellectuals to the Soviet Union, China, and Cuba, 1928–1978* (New York: Oxford University Press, 1981).

24. Quoted in Ros Pesman, "'Red Virtue': Ella Winter and the Soviet Union," in *Political Tourists: Travellers from Australia to the Soviet Union in the 1920s–1940s*, ed. Sheila Fitzpatrick and Carolyn Rasmussen (Carlton, VIC: Melbourne University Press, 2008), 110.

25. Winter, *And Not to Yield*, 149.

26. R.L. Duffus, "The Odyssey of a Reporter," *NYT*, April 12, 1931.

27. Winter, *And Not to Yield*, 154.

28. Ibid., 155.

29. Ella Winter, *Red Virtue: Human Relationships in the New Russia* (New York: Harcourt, Brace, 1933), 6.

30. Ibid., 95.

31. Winter, *And Not to Yield*, 175.

32. EWOH, April 25, 1977, JBC.

33. Winter, *And Not to Yield*, 186.

34. Sayre, *On the Wing*, 152.

35. Winter, *And Not to Yield*, 190.

36. Ibid., 173.

37. Steffens to Joe Freeman, July 5, 1934, in *The Letters of Lincoln Steffens*, ed. Ella Winter and Granville Hicks, vol. 2, *1920–1936* (New York: Harcourt, Brace and Company, 1938), 987.

38. Susan Duffy, ed., *The Political Plays of Langston Hughes* (Carbondale: Southern Illinois University Press, 2000), 6; Eric Homberger, *American Writers and Radical Politics, 1900–39* (London: Macmillan, 1986), 128–30.

39. To A. Winter, August 10, 1932, in *Letters of Lincoln Steffens*, 2:927.

40. "Fire Chief Orders John Reed Club Padlocked," *Carmel Pine Cone*, October 27, 1933.

41. "John Reed Club Told of Valley Cotton War," *Carmel Pine Cone*, November 10, 1933.

42. To Jo Davidson, June 3, 1932, in *Letters of Lincoln Steffens*, 2:923.

43. Winter, *And Not to Yield*, 203.

44. To Governor James Rolph, February 2, 1934, in *Letters of Lincoln Steffens*, 2:975.

45. Langston Hughes, "The Negro Artist and the Racial Mountain," *The Nation*, June 23, 1926.

46. Quoted in Arnold Rampersad, *The Life of Langston Hughes*, vol. 1, *1902–1941, I, Too, Sing America* (New York: Oxford University Press, 1986), 205.

47. Quoted in ibid., 239.

48. Langston Hughes, *I Wonder as I Wander: An Autobiographical Journey* (New York: Octagon, 1986), 285.

49. Hughes to Sullivan, undated, folder "Langston Hughes," box 40, NSP.

50. Hughes, *I Wonder as I Wander*, 284–85.

51. Quoted in Rampersad, *Life of Langston Hughes*, 288.

52. Winter, *And Not to Yield*, 195.

53. Hughes, "The Vigilantes Knock at My Door," folder 5902, box 266, LHP.

54. Winter, *And Not to Yield*, 197.

55. Ella Winter, "California's Little Hitlers," *New Republic*, December 27, 1933, 188–90. See also Winter, "Where Democracy Is a 'Red Plot,'" *New Republic*, June 6, 1934.

56. Quoted in Rampersad, *Life of Langston Hughes*, 291.

57. "Harvest," in Duffy, *Political Plays of Langston Hughes*, 93, 136.

58. Ibid., 81.

59. Federal Writers Project, *California in the 1930s*, 66. The best biography of Steinbeck is Benson, *True Adventures*.

60. FWOH, JBC.

61. John Steinbeck, "I Remember the Thirties," in *The Thirties: A Time to Remember*, ed. Don Congdon (New York: Simon & Schuster, 1962), 25; Benson, *True Adventures*, 256.

62. FWOH, JBC.

63. See Winter's profile of Steinbeck, "Sketching the Author of Tortilla Flat," *San Francisco Chronicle*, June 2, 1935, book page.

64. EWOH, JBC.

65. FWOH, JBC.

66. Ibid.

67. John Steinbeck, *In Dubious Battle* (New York: Penguin, 2006), 24.

68. Ibid., 26.

69. Ibid., 26–27.

70. Ibid., 48.

71. Ibid., 252.

72. To George Albee, January 15, 1935, in *Steinbeck: A Life in Letters*, ed. Elaine Steinbeck and Robert Wallsten (New York: Viking, 1975), 98.

73. See Mimi Gladstein's excellent analysis of the absence of women in much of Steinbeck's fiction: "Missing Women: The Inexplicable Disparity Between Women in Steinbeck's Life and Those in His Fiction," in *The Steinbeck Question: New Essays in*

Criticism, ed. Donald R. Noble (Troy, NY: Whitston Publishing Company, 1993), 84–98. See also the essays in Tetsumaro Hayashi, ed., *Steinbeck's Women: Essays in Criticism* (Muncie, IN: The Steinbeck Society of America, 1979).

74. Steinbeck to Elizabeth Otis, n.d., in *Life in Letters*, 162.

75. "Books of the Times," *NYT*, January 28, 1936.

76. Steinbeck to Elizabeth Otis, May 13, 1935, in *Life in Letters*, 109–10.

77. Steinbeck to Mavis McIntosh, April 1935, in *Life in Letters*, 107.

78. Benson, *True Adventures of John Steinbeck*, 317.

79. "'In Dubious Battle' and Other Recent Works of Fiction," *NYT*, February 2, 1936.

80. "Books of the Times," *NYT*, January 28, 1936; "No End of Books," *Washington Post*, January 29, 1936.

81. Paul Jordan-Smith, "Will Our Age Produce," *LAT*, February 16, 1936.

82. "'In Dubious Battle,'" *NYT*.

83. Mary McCarthy, "Minority Report," *The Nation*, March 11, 1936, 326–27.

84. Decker quoted in Loftis and Benson, "John Steinbeck and Farm Labor Unionization," 221.

5. Imperial

1. "Anti-Radical Mass Meeting Saturday at Fair Ground," *BN*, March 20, 1934; "'Anti-Red' Mass Meeting at Fair Grounds Friday," *BN*, March 22, 1934; "Anti-Radical Group Plans Big Meeting," *IVP*, March 20, 1934.

2. "Imperial Valley's Answer to 'Reds,'" *BN*, March 20, 1934.

3. "Attend This Americanism Mass Meeting," *BN*, March 22, 1934; "Nice Talks on 'Red' Menace Before Club," *BN*, March 22, 1934; "Wolford Raps Reds in Talk at Elks Club," *BN*, March 22, 1934; "Hugh Osborne May Talk at Elks Club in Brawley Tonight," *BN*, March 21, 1934.

4. Federal Writers Project of the Works Progress Administration, *California in the 1930s: The WPA Guide to the Golden State* (Berkeley: University of California Press, 2013), 458–62.

5. Donald Worster, *Rivers of Empire: Water, Aridity, and the Growth of the American West* (New York: Pantheon, 1985), 191–212; William deBuys, *Salt Dreams: Land and Water in Low-Down California* (Albuquerque: University of New Mexico Press, 1999), 71–163; Kevin Starr, *Material Dreams: Southern California Through the 1920s* (New York: Oxford University Press, 1991), 20–44.

6. Harold Bell Wright, *The Winning of Barbara Worth* (Chicago: The Book Supply Company, 1911), acknowledgment (unpaginated).

7. Postcard of lobby at the Hotel Barbara Worth, accessed January 15, 2015, http://gchudleigh.com/images/htl31.JPG.

8. Worster, *Rivers of Empire*, 208.

9. NLB report in U.S. Senate Subcommittee of the Committee on Education and Labor, *Violations of Free Speech and Rights of Labor*, 76th Cong., 3d sess. (Washington, DC:

Government Printing Office, 1940) (hereafter La Follette hearings), part 54, 20045, 20051; Exhibit 8903, La Follette hearings, part 55, 20288–89.

10. Richard Bransten, "Glassford in the Imperial Valley," *New Masses*, May 15, 1934.

11. Descriptions of Imperial County in the 1930s from Federal Writers Project, *California in the 1930s*, 460–62, 639–41.

12. La Follette hearings, part 54, 20039.

13. See "More Policemen Needed in Brawley," *BN*, January 10, 1934.

14. Carey McWilliams, "The Farmers Get Tough," *American Mercury*, October 1934, 241.

15. Cletus Daniel, *Bitter Harvest: A History of California Farmworkers, 1870–1941* (Ithaca, NY: Cornell University Press, 1981), 113.

16. Ibid., 113–26; Kevin Starr, *Endangered Dreams: The Great Depression in California* (New York: Oxford University Press, 1996), 66–68; Gilbert González, "Company Unions, the Mexican Consulate, and the Imperial Valley Agricultural Strikes, 1928–1934," *Western Historical Quarterly* 27, no. 1 (Spring 1996): 56–59.

17. MacCulloch Report, Exhibit 8765, La Follette hearings, part 54, 20040.

18. "Conditions Said Better," *BN*, December 30, 1933.

19. Daniel, *Bitter Harvest*, 225–27; Gilbert González, *Mexican Consuls and Labor Organizing: Imperial Politics in the American Southwest* (Austin: University of Texas Press, 1999), 173–77.

20. Stuart Jamieson, *Labor Unionism in American Agriculture* (Washington, DC: U.S. Bureau of Labor Statistics, 1945), 108.

21. Letter, Darcy to Decker, December 26, 1933, *PVC*, 864.

22. See Hancock's testimony in U.S. House, *Investigation of Communist Activities in the State of California*, part I, 83rd Cong., 2nd sess., February 24, 1954, 4517–63.

23. On Ray, see Dorothy Healey, *Dorothy Healey Remembers: A Life in the American Communist Party* (New York: Oxford University Press, 1990), and Beth Slutsky, "Three Generations of American Communist Women: Charlotte Anita Whitney, Dorothy Ray Healey, and Kendra Alexander, 1919–1992" (PhD dissertation, University of California, Davis, 2008), chap. 3.

24. Healey, *Dorothy Healey Remembers*, 46–47.

25. MacCulloch report, La Follette hearings, part 54, Exhibit 8765, 20039.

26. On the absence of media attention to the strike, see FPOH, book 4, 419; on grower control of the local media, see Pelham Glassford to Charles Wyzanski, April 28, 1934, folder 2, box 26, PGP.

27. Healey, *Dorothy Healey Remembers*, 45.

28. NLB report, La Follette hearings, part 54, 20050.

29. See the stories in the *Imperial Valley Press* and *Brawley News* for January 9–13. See also "Health Department Order to Evacuate Unsanitary Camps Carried Out at Calipatria," *IVP*, February 19, 1934.

30. PCOH.

31. Reporter's transcript of hearing before NLB committee, folder 3, box 25, PGP.

32. "Vigilantes Break Up Strikers," *BN*, January 12, 1934.

33. Telegram, strike committee to president, January 12, 1934, and note to Senator Wagner, January 13, 1934, in "Strikes 1934," box 5, OF 407b, FDRL.

34. Healey, *Dorothy Healey Remembers*, 49.

35. Docket, folder P-4, carton 32, FWP; "Man and Woman Sought in Brawley Raid Last Week Captured; 'Pat' Chambers Apprehended at El Centro," *BN*, January 19, 1934; "Three Agitator Suspects Arrested," *LAT*, January 20, 1934.

36. "Chapin Hall Discerns 'Old Gang's' Here," *BN*, January 15, 1934.

37. "New Agitators Arrive in Valley," *BN*, January 18, 1934.

38. NLB report, La Follette hearings, part 54, 20049.

39. "Sheriff Asks for State Militia," *BN*, January 11, 1934.

40. For more on the establishment of the National Labor Board and its regional boards, see James A. Gross, *The Making of the National Labor Relations Board* (Albany: State University of New York Press, 1974), 1:15–72.

41. MacCulloch to National Labor Board, January 25, 1934, Region 15, file 15-37, box 3, NLB.

42. Quoted in MacCulloch report, La Follette hearings, part 54, 20039.

43. MacCulloch to National Labor Board, January 25, 1934.

44. Judy Kutulas, *The American Civil Liberties Union and the Making of Modern Liberalism, 1930–1960* (Chapel Hill: University of North Carolina Press, 2006), 42, 49.

45. "Ernest Besig," *SFC*, November 21, 1998.

46. Peter Richardson, *American Prophet: The Life and Work of Carey McWilliams* (Ann Arbor: University of Michigan Press, 2005), 60.

47. McWilliams, "Farmers Get Tough," 241.

48. Jerry Voorhis, *Confessions of a Congressman* (Garden City, NY: Doubleday, 1947), 10.

49. "Chief Denies Wirin Permit for Meeting in Brawley," *BN*, January 22, 1934.

50. "A Serious Situation in Imperial Valley," *BN*, January 23, 1934.

51. "Board Hears Complaints on Attitude of J.R. Lester," *BN*, January 23, 1934.

52. Report of the special investigating committee, April 16, 1934, La Follette hearings, part 54 (hereafter Phillips report), 20059.

53. Porter M. Chaffee, "A History of the Cannery and Agricultural Workers Industrial Union," (Oakland, CA: Federal Writers Project, 193?), 2:9.

54. "Valley Quiet Today After Hectic Night During Which Brawley Stages Abduction," *IVP*, January 24, 1934; Chaffee, "A History of the Cannery and Agricultural Workers Industrial Union," 2:10.

55. Irving Bernstein, *The Turbulent Years: A History of the American Worker, 1933–1941* (Boston: Houghton Mifflin, 1971), 164.

56. "Not Mob Violence But Valley Spirit," *BN*, January 26, 1934. Quoted in National Labor Board report, La Follette hearings, part 54, 20050.

57. Joseph B. Keenan to Roger Baldwin, April 4, 1934, file 95-12-114, box 13987, DOJ.

58. MacCulloch to Federal Imperial Valley Commission, January 31, 1934, Region 15, file 15-37, box 3, NLB.

59. MacCulloch report, La Follette hearings, part 54, 20041.

60. Daniel, *Bitter Harvest*, 232–33.

61. NLB report, La Follette hearings, part 54, 20049, 20047.

62. Ibid, 20049.

63. Ibid., 20048.

64. Ibid., 20052.

65. Ibid.

66. "Time for Americanism to Assert Itself," *BN*, February 21, 1934.

67. "Trials Following Trouble in Imperial Valley, 1934," folder P-4, carton 32, FWP. See also "Lubin Slanders Imperial Valley Citizens," *BN*, March 24, 1934.

68. "Press and Personal Statements About Imperial Valley Terror," April 7, 1934, in folder X-157, carton 29, FWP.

69. Daniel, *Bitter Harvest*, 235; González, *Mexican Consuls and Labor Organizing*, 183–84.

70. "Press and Personal Statements About Imperial Valley Terror."

71. "General Glassford Reports," *LAT*, April 14, 1934.

72. "A Fair Deal for Imperial Valley," *BN*, February 27, 1934.

73. "Welcome Set for Glassford," *LAT*, April 1, 1934.

74. Telegram, National Labor Board to Lubin, Leonard, and French, February 24, 1934, "National Labor Relations Board, Jan.–May 1934," box 1, OF 716, FDRL. See also Charles Wyzanski to Pelham Glassford, March 27, 1934, folder 2, box 26, PGP; Lubin to MacCulloch, April 13, 1934, Region 15, file 15-37, box 3, NLB.

75. "Health Department Order to Evacuate Unsanitary Camps Carried Out at Calipatria," *IVP*, February 19, 1934.

76. Healey, *Dorothy Healey Remembers*, 52; PCOH; "Mrs. Johnson Arrested for Carrying Gun," *IVP*, March 28, 1934.

77. "Certain Phases of the Activities of Peace Officers Bearing Upon the Relations of Agricultural Employers and Employees in California, 1933–38," no date, folder 58, carton 14, 24, PST.

78. Clarke A. Chambers, *California Farm Organizations: A Historical Study of the Grange, the Farm Bureau and the Associated Farmers, 1929–1941* (Berkeley: University of California Press, 1952), 41.

79. George Clements quoted in La Follette hearings, part 54, 19865.

80. La Follette hearings, part 55, 20253; "American Institutions" reference, ibid., 20261.

81. See Nelson A. Pichardo, "The Power Elite and Elite-Driven Countermovements: The Associated Farmers of California during the 1930s," *Sociological Forum* 10, no. 1 (March 1995): 40.

82. For law enforcement's contribution to this effort, see "Activities of Various Peace Officers Groups, Citizens Groups, and Disaster Emergency Plans, in California, 1933–1938," 11–12, folder 58, carton 14, PST. See also folder labeled "Redbaiting," box 18, CMW; and "Communists Condemned by Speakers at Mass Meeting," *IVP*, March 24, 1934. On the Associated Farmers, see Pichardo, "The Power Elite and Elite-Driven Countermovements," and Nelson Pichardo Almanzar and Brian Kulik, *American Fascism and the New Deal: The Associated Farmers of California and the Pro-industrial Movement* (Lanham, MD: Lexington Books, 2013).

83. Letter from Guernsey Frazer to Frisselle, November 20, 1934, in La Follette hearings, part 55, 20256.

84. "Time for Americanism to Assert Itself."

85. "Activities of Various Peace Officers Groups, Citizens Groups, and Disaster Emergency Plans, in California, 1933–1938," folder 58, carton 14, 5, PST.

86. Memo from Arnoll to Clements, no date, "Milk Strike," in unnamed folder, box 64, GCP.

87. "Dr. Patmont Bares System of Communism as Observed During Journey in Russia," *BN*, May 16, 1934.

88. See, for example, Philip Bancroft, "The Farmer and the Communists," April 1935, in "Associated Farmers," carton 32, FWP, and "Is There a Red Menace in Los Angeles?," *LAT*, April 15, 1934. For discussions of the gendered nature of anticommunism, see Kim E. Nielsen, *Un-American Womanhood: Antiradicalism, Antifeminism, and the First Red Scare* (Columbus: Ohio State University Press, 2001); Kirsten Marie Delegard, *Battling Miss Bolsheviki: The Origins of Female Conservatism in the United States* (Philadelphia: University of Pennsylvania Press, 2012); Mary C. Brennan, *Wives, Mothers, and the Red Menace: Conservative Women and the Crusade Against Communism* (Boulder: University Press of Colorado, 2008); Michelle M. Nickerson, *Mothers of Conservatism: Women and the Postwar Right* (Princeton, NJ: Princeton University Press, 2012), 5–7.

89. "Is There a Red Menace in Los Angeles?"

90. "The Week-End Radical Meetings," *BN*, March 19, 1934.

91. "Nora Conklin Is Sentenced to 90 Days in Prison," *SB*, May 15, 1934.

92. "Week-End Radical Meetings."

93. "Wolford Raps Reds in Talk at Elks Club," *BN*, March 22, 1934.

94. "Pea Strike Collapses," *LAT*, February 20, 1934.

95. "Too Much Flirting with Radicals," *BN*, May 23, 1934.

96. Ibid.

97. CAWIU flyer reprinted in La Follette hearings, part 55, 20184. See also "Pat Chambers Will Have a Hot Time in Jail," *BN*, March 12, 1934.

98. "Reason for Imperial's Anti-Red Drive," *LAT*, March 18, 1934. See also "Two Reasons Why Valley Organizes Against 'Reds,'" *BN*, March 21, 1934.

99. PCOH.

100. "Reason for Imperial's Anti-Red Drive."

101. In his oral history, Chambers conceded it was a mistake.

102. Johnson to Pelham Glassford, June 22, 1934, folder P-91, carton 34, FWP, reprinted in La Follette hearings, part 55, 20143-45; Johnson testimony in La Follette hearings, part 55, 20158-62.

103. Johnson to Glassford, La Follette hearings, part 55, 20144.

104. FPOH, book 4, 422.

105. FPOH, book 4, 405–6.

6. Crooks or Tools

1. "Glassford and the Siege of Washington," *Harper's*, November 1932, 642.

2. Ibid., 642, 643.

3. Gardner Jackson, "Memories of a Chief," *Washington Post*, August 20, 1959.

4. Donald J. Lisio, *The President and Protest: Hoover, Conspiracy, and the Bonus Riot* (Columbia: University of Missouri Press, 1974), 73.

5. See ibid., chap. 12; and Paul Dickson and Thomas B. Allen, *The Bonus Army: An American Epic* (New York: Walker and Company, 2006).

6. "Heroes: Break Up?," *Time*, July 18, 1932.

7. FPOH, book 4, 409.

8. Ibid.

9. "Brig.-Gen. Glassford Named Federal Conciliator as Imperial Valley Demurs," *LAT*, March 28, 1934.

10. "The Glassford Appointment," *LAT*, March 29, 1934.

11. "State Sends New 'Kick' on Imperial Conciliator," *LAT*, March 30, 1934.

12. "Ending Communist Strikes," *LAT*, April 21, 1934.

13. U.S. Senate Subcommittee of the Committee on Education and Labor, *Violations of Free Speech and Rights of Labor*, 76th Cong., 3d sess. (Washington, DC: Government Printing Office, 1940) (hereafter La Follette hearings), part 54, 20061. The complete Phillips report is reprinted in the La Follette hearings, part 54, 20053–63.

14. FPOH, book 4, 432.

15. Charles Wyzanski to Glassford, March 27, 1934, folder 2, box 26, PGP.

16. FPOH, book 4, 418.

17. Bulletin, "To All Mexican Workers in Imperial Valley," April 30, 1934, folder 2, box 26, PGP; Richard Bransten, "Glassford in the Imperial Valley," *New Masses*, May 15, 1934.

18. Glassford to Wyzanski, April 28, 1934, folder 2, box 26, PGP.

19. Telegram, Glassford to Chester Williams, April 30, 1934, folder 2, box 26, and Glassford to Wyzanski, April 30, 1934, folder 2, box 26, PGP.

20. On the consul's role, see Gilbert González, *Mexican Consuls and Labor Organizing: Imperial Politics in the American Southwest* (Austin: University of Texas Press, 1999), 158–96.

21. See, for example, letter, anonymous to Glassford, June 16, 1934, folder P-91, carton 34, FWP.

22. Glassford to Wyzanski, June 13, 1934, folder 2, box 26, PGP; Glassford to Heald, June 12, 1934, folder P-91, carton 34, FWP; Statement by General P. D. Glassford, undated, folder P-91, carton 34, FWP.

23. "Glassford's Charges of Deliberate 'Red Scare' in Imperial Bring Hot Reply," *LAT*, June 27, 1934.

24. Roy Cantwell to Glassford, June 11, 1934, folder 7, box 26, PGP. See also the letters in folder 9, box 25.

25. Glassford to Wyzanski, April 28, 1934, folder 2, box 26; Glassford to Wyzanski, May 31, 1934, folder 2, box 26, PGP.

26. Glassford to Pierson Hall, May 23, 1934, folder 6, box 26, PGP.

27. "Federal Labor Moves Fought," *LAT*, May 6, 1934.

28. On Rolph's need for grower support in the election, see letter, O. C. Heitman to Glassford, April 9, 1934, folder 6, box 26, PGP.

29. Telegram, Glassford to Secretary of Labor, April 14, 1934, folder 2, box 26, PGP.

30. Wyzanski to Glassford, April 16, 1934, folder 2, box 26, PGP.

31. Ibid.

32. Telegram, Wyzanski to Glassford, May 10, 1934, folder 2, box 26, PGP. For the proposal, see Glassford to Wyzanski, May 6, 1934, in the same folder.

33. Glassford to Wyzanski, May 12, 1934, folder 2, box 26, PGP.

34. *Open Forum*, June 2, 1934, folder X-157, carton 29, FWP.

35. Glassford to Wirin, May 30, 1934, folder 2, box 26, PGP.

36. Bransten, "Glassford in the Imperial Valley," 12.

37. Robert Johansen to Glassford, July 28, 1934, folder 7, box 26, PGP.

38. Glassford to Wyzanski, June 20, 1934, folder 2, box 26, PGP.

39. Glassford to Wyzanski, May 31, 1934, folder 2, box 26, PGP.

40. Letter, Lucille Painter to "Uncle Ernie" (Besig), July 12, 1934, folder P-91, carton 34, FWP.

41. Porter M. Chaffee, "A History of the Cannery and Agricultural Workers Industrial Union" (Oakland, CA: Federal Writers Project, 193?), 2:22–23; "Assault on Attorney Ernest Besig of Los Angeles, Calif., Imperial Valley, June 8th, 1934," in folder 2, box 26, PGP.

42. Chaffee, 2:22–23; Glassford to Wyzanski, June 13, 1934, folder 2, box 26, PGP.

43. "General Glassford Charges Intimidation by Official," *IVP*, June 14, 1934.

44. "Gen. Glassford Changes Mind and Declares He Will Stay in Imperial Valley," *LAT*, June 15, 1934.

45. Ibid.; "Judge Hurls Denial at Glassford After Sensational Imperial Valley Clash," *LAT*, June 16, 1934.

46. News release, June 15, 1934, by Glassford, folder P-91, carton 34, FWP.

47. "Recommends Investigation by Grand Jury of Alleged Attacks on Wirin-Johnson," *IVP*, June 26, 1934. The Glassford report is reproduced in the La Follette hearings, part 55, 20302–5.

48. Wyzanski to Glassford, June 12, 1934, folder 2, box 26, PGP.

49. "The Strike Crumbling," *LAT*, July 19, 1934.

50. "The Red Menace," *LAT*, June 16, 1934.

51. "General Glassford Charges Intimidation by Official," *IVP*, June 14, 1934.

52. *Open Forum*, June 23, 1934, folder X-157, carton 29, FWP.

53. Chester Williams to Glassford, June 14, 1934, folder 6, box 26, PGP.

54. Telegram, Wirin to Wyzanski, June 14, 1934, folder P-85, carton 34, FWP.

55. "Government Lets Canal Contract," *IVP*, June 23, 1934.

56. "Additional Water Supply Arrives in Valley," *IVP*, July 12, 1934.

57. *Open Forum*, July 7, 1934, folder P-91, carton 34, FWP.

58. "Heald Condemns Statement Made by Taft," *IVP*, July 3, 1934.

59. Glassford to Wyzanski, June 14, 1934, folder 2, box 26, PGP.

60. Glassford to Besig, June 20, 1934, folder P-91, carton 34, FWP.

61. Besig to Glassford, June 21, 1934, folder 6, box 26, PGP.

62. Glassford to Wyzanski, June 13, 1934, folder 2, box 26, PGP.

63. Glassford to Wyzanski, June 14, 1934, folder 2, box 26, PGP.

64. FPOH, book 4, 411, 418.

65. Kevin Starr, *Material Dreams: Southern California Through the 1920s* (New York: Oxford University Press, 1991), 43.

7. Seeing Red

1. "Re: Special Communist Convention at Sacramento Cannery and Agricultural Workers Industrial Union," April 28, 1934, box 3, VDP.

2. On Van Deman, see Joan M. Jensen, *Army Surveillance in America, 1775–1980* (New Haven, CT: Yale University Press, 1991), 110–77, 205, 233, 264; Roy Talbert Jr., *Negative Intelligence: The Army and the American Left, 1917–1941* (Jackson: University Press of Mississippi, 1991), 6–28, 234–35; Marc B. Powe, "A Sketch of a Man and His Times," in *The Final Memoranda: Major General Ralph H. Van Deman, USA Ret., 1865–1952*, ed. Ralph E. Weber (Wilmington, DE: Scholarly Resources, 1988), ix–xxii; Robert W. Cherny, "Anticommunist Networks and Labor: The Pacific Coast in the 1930s," in *Labor's Cold War: Local Politics in a Global Context*, ed. Shelton Stromquist (Urbana: University of Illinois Press, 2008), 23–24; Alfred W. McCoy, *Policing America's Empire: The United States, the Philippines, and the Rise of the Surveillance State* (Madison: University of Wisconsin Press, 2009), 77–82, 298–300, 300–23; and Nathan Miller, *Spying for America: The Hidden History of U.S. Intelligence* (New York: Paragon House, 1989), 175–201.

3. Jensen, *Army Surveillance in America*, 133.

4. Ibid., 160–65, 171.

5. Talbert, *Negative Intelligence*, 113–14.

6. Roy Talbert says that Van Deman lost his job because Army Chief of Staff Peyton C. March disapproved of his involvement in staff politics; Joan Jensen argues that the Department of Justice was concerned about MID's size and scope and pressured Secretary of War Newton Baker to remove him. Talbert, *Negative Intelligence*, 27; Jensen, *Army Surveillance in America*, 171.

7. Van Deman to General Marlborough Churchill, November 13, 1918, in Weber, *Final Memoranda*, 173.

8. See the reports in VDP, especially box 2.

9. See, for example, the extensive correspondence between Van Deman and the California Un-American Activities Committee's chief counsel, Richard Combs, in VDP, especially in boxes 68 and 73. On the California Un-American Activities Committee, see M.J. Heale, "Red Scare Politics: California's Campaign against Un-American Activities, 1940–1970," *Journal of American Studies* 20, no. 1 (April 1986): 5–32.

10. On Roosevelt's expansion of the FBI, see Kenneth O'Reilly, "A New Deal for the FBI: The Roosevelt Administration, Crime Control, and National Security," *Journal of American History* 69, no. 3 (December 1982): 638–58.

11. Speech, James Davis, no date, box 49, LARS.

12. Robert Michael Smith, *From Blackjacks to Briefcases: A History of Commercialized Strikebreaking and Unionbusting in the United States* (Athens: Ohio University Press, 2003), 86.

13. See, for example, "Confidential Report No. 3," January 5, 1934, box 64, GCP. See also the reports in the SBLC, SHC.

14. "April 28th," memo, SBLC, SHC.

15. "Senate Panel Holds Vast 'Subversives' File Amassed by Ex-Chief of Army Intelligence," *NYT*, September 7, 1971.

16. Quoted in Jensen, *Army Surveillance in America*, 205.

17. McCoy, *Policing America's Empire*, 320.

18. "Confidential Memo," September 19, 1950, unmarked folder, box 1, MKP. For an overview of the BAF, see Edwin Layton, "The Better America Federation: A Case Study of Superpatriotism," *Pacific Historical Review* 30, no. 2 (May 1961): 137–47.

19. Report of Guernsey Frazer, June 25, 1934, reprinted in U.S. Senate Subcommittee of the Committee on Education and Labor, *Violations of Free Speech and Rights of Labor*, 76th Cong., 3d sess. (Washington, DC: Government Printing Office, 1940) (hereafter La Follette hearings), part 67, 24493–97; quotes at 24497 and 24494.

20. Stuart Jamieson, *Labor Unionism in American Agriculture* (Washington, DC: Government Printing Office, 1945), 111.

21. La Follette hearings, part 68, 25006, 24995–5009.

22. La Follette hearings, part 67, 24495.

23. "New Chief Ex-Iowan," *LAT*, June 3, 1934.

24. Franklin Hichborn, "California Politics, 1898–1939," 2746, available at UCLA Young Research Library and the Robbins Collection at UC Berkeley's Boalt School of Law.

25. "Governor Opposes Use of Vigilantes," *LAT*, June 8, 1934.

26. "Merriam Invokes Laws Against Red Agitators," *LAT*, June 13, 1934.

27. La Follette hearings, part 67, 24495.

28. See Raymond Haight's accusations in Upton Sinclair, *I, Candidate for Governor, and How I Got Licked* (Berkeley: University of California Press, 1994), 128.

29. "Merriam's Red Stand Lauded," *LAT*, June 15, 1934.

30. On Nixon's manufacturing of the appearance of public support for his policies, see Jonathan Schell, *The Time of Illusion* (New York: Knopf, 1976), 70.

31. On the San Francisco strike, see Kevin Starr, *Endangered Dreams: The Great Depression in California* (New York: Oxford University Press, 1996), chap. 4; Bruce Nelson, *Workers on the Waterfront: Seamen, Longshoremen, and Unionism in the 1930s* (Urbana: University of Illinois Press, 1988), chap. 4 and 5; Charles Larrowe, "The Great Maritime Strike of '34," *Labor History* 11 (Fall 1970): 403–51; Larrowe, *Harry Bridges: The Rise and Fall of Radical Labor in the United States* (New York: Lawrence Hill, 1972); John Kagel, "The Day the City Stopped," *California History* 63, no. 3 (Summer 1984): 212–23; David Selvin, *A Terrible Anger: The 1934 Waterfront and General Strikes in San Francisco* (Detroit: Wayne State University Press, 1996); Paul S. Taylor and Norman Leon Gold, "San Francisco and the General Strike," *Survey Graphic* 23 (September 1934): 405–11; Michael Johns, "Winning for Losing: A New Look at Harry Bridges and the 'Big Strike' of 1934," *American Communist History* 13, no. 1 (2014): 1–24.

32. Telegram, Creel to president, March 21, 1934, "National Labor Relations Board, Jan–May 1934," OF 716, FDRL.

33. "Port Strike Crisis Near," *SFC*, May 21, 1934.

34. "Blood Floods Gutters as Police, Strikers War," *SFC*, July 6, 1934.

35. Irving Bernstein, *The Turbulent Years: A History of the American Worker, 1933–1941* (Boston: Houghton Mifflin, 1971), 279.

36. "Armed Peace Descends on Water Front," *SFC*, July 7, 1934.

37. See pictures in the *SFC*, July 7, 1934.

38. Sinclair, *I, Candidate for Governor*, 128.

39. "Meat Men, Laundries, Taxi Drivers Among Those to Quit Jobs," *SFC*, July 13, 1934.

40. Parker Frisselle to Guernsey Frazer, July 6, 1934, in La Follette hearings, part 69, 25274.

41. Earl Burke, "Dailies Helped Break General Strike," *Editor & Publisher* 67, no. 11 (July 28, 1934): 5.

42. "Thousands of Union Men Called from Jobs; Reds Converging on City; Food Running Short" and "Reds March on S.F. to Preach Revolt in Strike," *SFC*, July 14, 1934.

43. "This Is Time for All to Keep Their Heads," *SFC*, July 14, 1934.

44. Rogers, "Will Rogers Finds Plenty of Common Sense Left," July 19, 1934, in *Will Rogers' Daily Telegrams, III-4*, ed. James Smallwood (Stillwater: Oklahoma State University Press, 1979), 198.

45. Ella Winter, *And Not to Yield* (New York: Harcourt, Brace, and World, 1963), 203–4.

46. Hiram Johnson to Harold Ickes, July 15, 1934, "Pacific Coast Longshoremen's Strike," box 11, OF 407b, FDRL.

47. Julius Meier to Roosevelt, July 16, 1934, "Pacific Coast Longshoremen's Strike," box 11, OF 407b, FDRL.

48. Perkins to president, July 15, 1934, "Pacific Coast Longshoremen's Strike," box 11, OF 407b, FDRL.

49. Perkins to Roosevelt, August 13, 1934, "Strikes, 1934," box 5, OF 407b, FDRL; Frances Perkins, *The Roosevelt I Knew* (New York: Viking, 1946), 312–15.

50. Howe to president, July 15, 1934, "Pacific Coast Longshoremen's Strike," box 11, OF 407b, FDRL.

51. September 5, 1934, in *The Complete Presidential Press Conferences of Franklin D. Roosevelt* (New York: Da Capo Press, 1972), 4:44–45.

52. "Coast Cities Join in Drive to Stamp Out Red Agitators," *SB*, July 21, 1934; "Police Jail More Reds as Vigilantes Beat Ten," *SFC*, July 20, 1934. See also David F. Selvin, "An Exercise in Hysteria: San Francisco's Red Raids of 1934," *Pacific Historical Review* 58, no. 3 (August 1989): 361–74.

53. "Reds Turn Black and Blue," *SFC*, July 18, 1934.

54. This account comes from Hughes's unpublished manuscript titled "The Vigilantes Knock at My Door," folder 5902, box 366, LHP. The editorials he quotes are "Story by Hughes in a Woman's Magazine," *Carmel Sun*, August 23, 1934, and "Edward Willett Burns Says Women to Blame," *Carmel Sun*, August 30, 1934.

55. Steffens to Perkins, July 19, 1934, in *The Letters of Lincoln Steffens*, ed. Ella Winter and Granville Hicks, vol. 2, *1920–1936* (New York: Harcourt, Brace and Company, 1938), 988–89.

56. George West, "California Sees Red," *Current History*, September 1934, 661.

57. Hickok to Aubrey Williams, August 15, 1934, "Reports to Harry Hopkins, May Through August, 1934," box 11, LAHP; partially reprinted in *One Third of a Nation: Lorena Hickok Reports on the Great Depression*, ed. Richard Lowitt and Maurine Beasley (Urbana: University of Illinois Press, 1981), 306.

58. "Address of Chief of Police Davis, LA, at St. Francis Hotel, 1934," folder 32:15, carton 32, JKP. See also "Attendance, July 26 Luncheon Meeting, St. Francis Hotel," folder 32:14 in the same carton.

59. "Americanism vs. Communism," *San Francisco Examiner*, July 23, 1934, quoted in David Nasaw, *The Chief: The Life of William Randolph Hearst* (Boston: Houghton Mifflin, 2000), 494.

8. Campaigns Inc.

1. On the campaign's financial trouble, see Baxter to Lois and Helene, July 21, 1934, folder "1934, Sacramento Headquarters Interoffice Correspondence," box 22, GHP.

2. Whitaker to Frances Vickers, July 22, 1934, "1934, Sacramento Headquarters Interoffice Correspondence," box 22, GHP.

3. Upton Sinclair, *The Brass Check: A Study of American Journalism* (Pasadena, CA: Published by the author, 1919), 147; *The Profits of Religion: An Essay in Economic Interpretation* (Pasadena, CA: Published by the author, 1918), 17; *The Goose-Step: A Study of American Education* (New York: Albert & Charles Boni, 1923), 384.

4. Upton Sinclair, *The Jungle* (Cambridge, MA: Robert Bentley Inc., 1946), 164, 36.

5. Upton Sinclair, "What Life Means to Me," *Cosmopolitan*, October 1906.

6. "Sinclair Held for Trial," *LAT*, May 17, 1923.

7. Upton Sinclair, *I, Candidate for Governor, and How I Got Licked* (Berkeley: University of California Press, 1994), 4.

8. Ibid., 5.

9. Ibid., 7.

10. See Mark Leff, *The Limits of Symbolic Reform: The New Deal and Taxation, 1933–1939* (Cambridge: Cambridge University Press, 2003).

11. Oswald G. Villard, "Los Angeles Kaleidoscope," *The Nation*, March 21, 1934, 321.

12. Carey McWilliams, *California: The Great Exception* (Berkeley: University of California, 1999), 192.

13. On California politics during this era, see J. Casey Sullivan, "Way Before the Storm: California, the Republican Party, and a New Conservatism, 1900–1930," *Journal of Policy History* 26, no. 4 (2014): 568–94.

14. Creel to "Mac" (Marvin McIntyre), June 3, 1934, PPF 2346, FDRL; Creel to Stephen Early, October 14, 1933, "Oct. 1–15, 1933," box 8, OF 466.

15. O'Connor to Louis Howe, October 29, 1934, "California C 1933–1937," box 10, OF 300, FDRL; Farley to Howe, July 2, 1934, "California O 1933–1937," box 12, OF 300, FDRL. See also Howe to Harry Hopkins, March 5, 1934, "California H 1933–1945," box 11, OF 300, FDRL.

16. Hickok to Hopkins, July 1, 1934, box 11, LAHP; partially reprinted in *One Third of a Nation: Lorena Hickok Reports on the Great Depression*, ed. Richard Lowitt and Maurine Beasley (Urbana: University of Illinois Press, 1981), 304.

17. Creel to Joseph Davies, May 26, 1934, "California C 1933–1937," box 10, OF 300, FDRL.

18. Eleanor Roosevelt to Upton Sinclair, January 26, 1934, "Sinclair, Upton," container 603, ER 100, FDRL.

19. Eleanor Roosevelt to Upton Sinclair, May 1, 1934, "Sinclair, Upton," container 603, ER 100, FDRL.

20. "Creel to Run for Governor," *LAT*, April 26, 1934.

21. George Creel, *Rebel at Large: Recollections of Fifty Crowded Years* (New York: G.P. Putnam's Sons, 1947), 287; Sinclair, *I, Candidate*, 57; Creel to Joseph Davies, May 26, 1934, "California C 1933–1937," box 10, OF 300, FDRL.

22. See Greg Mitchell's lively and informative account of the EPIC race, *The Campaign of the Century: Upton Sinclair's Race for Governor of California and the Birth of Media Politics* (New York: Random House, 1992).

23. Hoover to Merriam, August 29, 1934, "Merriam, Gov. Frank F., Correspondence, 1934–1944," PPI HHL.

24. "Is This Still America?," *LAT*, August 30, 1934.

25. Advertisement in *San Bernardino Sun*, October 21, 1934.

26. Teague to Knowland, September 20, 1934, "Campaigns: California, 1934," carton 32, JKP. Many scholars say the anti-Sinclair campaign spent at least $10 million to defeat him, but the source for this number is "one California official" cited in Charles Van Devander's 1944 book, *The Big Bosses* (New York: Howell, Soskin & Co.). As Van Devander notes, because so much of the money was spent directly by the business and financial interests opposed to Sinclair, the real cost of the opposition campaign is impossible to know. Van Devander, *Big Bosses*, 297.

27. Mitchell, *Campaign of the Century*, 200–202.

28. On Whitaker and Baxter, see Carey McWilliams, "Government by Whitaker and Baxter," *The Nation*, April 14, April 21, and May 5, 1951; Irwin Ross, "The Supersalesmen of California Politics: Whitaker and Baxter," *Harper's*, July 1959, 55–61; and Jill Lepore, "The Lie Factory," *New Yorker*, September 24, 2012.

29. For Hatfield campaign documents, see folders 5–8, box 1, W&B, and box 22, GHP.

30. Ross, "Supersalesmen of California Politics," 56, 57.

31. Sinclair, *I, Candidate*, 146.

32. Ross, "Supersalesmen of California Politics," 56–57.

33. Mitchell, *Campaign of the Century*, 225. Stanley Melvin Slome's master's thesis, "The Press Against Upton Sinclair: The 1934 California Gubernatorial Campaign" (University of California, Los Angeles, 1968), is an invaluable source for anti-Sinclair material in the press.

34. Sinclair, *I, Candidate*, 109.

35. Upton Sinclair, *The Lie Factory Starts* (Los Angeles: End Poverty League, 1934), pamphlet, UCD.

36. "Sinclair Says Nation Needs 'EPIC' Plan," *Washington Post*, September 6, 1934.

37. See Mitchell, *Campaign of the Century*, 369–72, 415–16, 499–501, and "Whitaker and Baxter—California Election News," at http://www.youtube.com/watch?v=-M9vfWjmONO.

38. Chester Rowell to George Cameron, August 8, 1934, "Rowell, Chester, 1932–1934," box 7, CRP. The Iowa attorney general's office told *Oakland Tribune* publisher

Joseph Knowland that the corruption charges were false and had been spread by a political rival. Walter F. Maley to Knowland, July 9, 1934, "Campaigns, California: 1934," box 32, JKP.

39. "The Corporation Purse Is Opened for Merriam," SB, July 20, 1934.

40. Sinclair, I, Candidate, 125.

41. Hoover to Frank Knox, October 2, 1934, "Knox, Frank P., correspondence July–December 1934," PPI HHL. The Hoover made similar comments to John Spargo (October 2), Lewis Strauss (October 1), Arch Shaw (October 8), Arthur Hyde (October 8), and Frank Kent (October 1).

42. J.J. Maguire to the president, October 30, 1934, "California M 1933–1937," box 12, OF 300, FDRL.

43. Martin Luther Thomas, Upton Sinclair's Open Insult! To the Stars and Stripes and Our Constitution (Los Angeles: Metropolitan Federated Church, 1934), UCD. For an analysis of Christian fundamentalist opposition to the New Deal, see Matthew Avery Sutton, "Was FDR the Antichrist? The Birth of Fundamentalist Antiliberalism in a Global Age," Journal of American History 98, no. 4 (March 2012): 1052–74.

44. Advertisement in LAT, October 20, 1934.

45. Press release, Sinclair state Democratic headquarters, September 1934, "Campaigns: California, 1934," JKP.

46. Alice Chase to Roosevelt, November 3, 1934, "California C 1933–37," box 10, OF 300, FDRL.

47. "We Have a Plan," Great Depression, Part 4, http://www.youtube.com/watch?v =6BcShxauDgk.

48. Robert Minor, "The 'EPIC' Mass Movement in California," The Communist 13 (December 1934): 1229, 1215.

49. Mitchell, Campaign of the Century, 265.

50. "Feminine body" quote in Redding Searchlight, October 21, 1934. See numerous other stories on female voters for Merriam in the Hatfield scrapbooks, box 44, GHP.

51. See, for example, "Women Warned of Menace in Sinclair Plan," Paso Robles Press, October 18, 1934; and "Shasta Women Organize to Elect Merriam and Hatfield, November 2," Redding Searchlight, October 21, 1934, in the Hatfield campaign scrapbooks, box 44, GHP.

52. "Great Body of Women Voters, Indifferent in Past, Support Merriam," San Jose Mercury-Herald, October 26, 1934, in scrapbooks, box 44, GHP.

53. "Merriam Clubs Formed by Women," San Francisco Call-Bulletin, October 4, 1934.

54. "Political Notes: ALL," Time, September 3, 1934. On the Liberty League, see Kim Phillips-Fein, Invisible Hands: The Businessmen's Crusade against the New Deal (New York: W.W. Norton, 2010), 10–13, 15, 19–25; and George Wolfskill, The Revolt of the Conservatives: A History of the American Liberty League, 1934–1940 (Boston: Houghton Mifflin, 1962).

55. President's note on enclosure in Marvin McIntyre to Frank Walker, January 25, 1936, "American Liberty League," PPF 3146, FDRL.

56. Telegram, Marvin McIntyre to Sinclair, August 29, 1934, "Sinclair, Upton–Jan.–Aug. 1934," box 1, OF 1165, FDRL.

57. "Sinclair Is Elated by Roosevelt Talk," NYT, September 5, 1934.

58. Sinclair, I, Candidate, 200–201.

59. Letter, O'Connor to Roosevelt, September 13, 1934, PPF 1135, FDRL.

60. Marvin McIntyre to George Inglish, October 29, 1934, "Sinclair, Upton, Oct. 29–31, 1934," box 2, OF 1165, FDRL. See the numerous similar letters in the same folder.

61. Letter, McAdoo to Roosevelt, September 24, 1934, "California M 1933–1937," box 12, OF 300, FDRL.

62. Frances Perkins, The Roosevelt I Knew (New York: Viking, 1946), 124. Roosevelt also told Jefty O'Connor that Sinclair made a "favorable impression" on him. October 3, 1934, JOCD.

63. Raymond Moley, After Seven Years (New York: Harper & Brothers, 1939), 298–99; letter, Sinclair to Roosevelt, October 5, 1934, "Sinclair, Upton, Oct. 1–20, 1934," box 1, OF 1165, FDRL.

64. There are many anti-Sinclair leaflets in box 1, OF 1165, FDRL.

65. In folder "Sinclair, Upton, Oct. 1–20, 1934," box 1, OF 1165, FDRL.

66. Letter, United for California League to Southern California employers, undated, "Sinclair, Upton, Oct. 1–20, 1934," box 1, OF 1165, FDRL.

67. "Roosevelt the Real Target," editorial, Los Angeles Daily News, no date, "Sinclair, Upton, Oct. 25–28, 1934," box 2, OF 1165, FDRL.

68. On the voter purge, see Mitchell, Campaign of the Century, 329–548, passim, quote at 476.

69. Sinclair, I, Candidate, 139.

70. "Poor Flock into State," LAT, October 24, 1934.

71. "Every Pauper Is Coming," SFC, October 16, 1934.

72. Letter, Creel to Sinclair, October 18, 1934, and memo, Stephen Early to Roosevelt, October 23, 1934, "California C 1933–1937," box 10, OF 300, FDRL; and memo, October 18, 1934, "Sinclair, Upton, Oct. 1–20, 1934," box 1, OF 1165, FDRL.

73. Memorandum for Mrs. Roosevelt from Stephen Early, October 23, 1934, "Sinclair, Upton, Oct. 21–24, 1934," box 2, OF 1165, FDRL.

74. George West, "Sinclair's Enemies Go 'Progressive,'" NYT, October 28, 1934.

75. Letter, O'Connor to Marvin McIntyre, November 2, 1934, "California O 1933–1937," box 12, OF 300, FDRL.

76. O'Connor diary entry for October 31, JOCD.

77. The state Senate remained solidly Republican, although ardent Sinclair supporter (and the state's next governor) Culbert Olson won a seat. Mitchell, Campaign of the Century, 546.

78. Sinclair, I, Candidate, 221.

79. Ibid., 108.

80. Ibid., 203.

81. Mullendore to E.F. Watkins, October 1, 1934, "State of the Nation, Correspondence, 1934," WMP.

82. Ibid.

9. Making History

1. "Reds Are Rounded Up Here in Raids by Flying Squads," SB, July 20, 1934; Mike Quin, *The C.S. Case Against Labor: The Story of the Sacramento Criminal Syndicalism Railroading* (San Francisco: International Labor Defense, 1935), 10–11, UCD. On the trial, see also Kevin Starr, *Endangered Dreams: The Great Depression in California* (New York: Oxford University Press, 1996), 166–73; Rick Wartzman, *Obscene in the Extreme: The Burning and Banning of John Steinbeck's The Grapes of Wrath* (New York: PublicAffairs, 2008), 121–34, 140–48; and Anne Loftis, *Witnesses to the Struggle: Imaging the 1930s California Labor Movement* (Reno: University of Nevada Press, 1998), 89–95.

2. "Webb Says Red Trial Here Is One of Great Importance," SB, March 20, 1935.

3. Herbert Solow, "Union-Smashing in Sacramento: The Truth About the Criminal Syndicalism Trial" (New York: National Sacramento Appeal Committee, August 1935), 28, UCD.

4. *PVC*, 13:6125.

5. "Defense Counsel Assails Webb," SB, March 27, 1935.

6. Travers Clement, "Red-Baiters' Holiday in Sacramento: The Criminal Syndicalism Trial," *The Nation*, March 13, 1935, 306.

7. Flyers in folder "Communists #4, Sacramento Workers School 1934," SBLC, CSH.

8. See Sacramento City Police Department Collection mug books, 15:269, CSH; Caroline Decker, "California's Terror Continues," *New Masses*, August 28, 1934; Quin, "C.S. Case Against Labor," 11.

9. "Nora Conklin Is Sentenced to 90 Days in Prison," SB, May 15, 1934.

10. "Re: Communist Investigation, Cannery & Agricultural Workers Industrial Union," May 6, 1934, box 3, VDP.

11. Charles K. McClatchy, *Private Thinks by C.K.* (New York: Scribner, 1936), 38.

12. Memos in SBLC, folder "Communists #2 Special Reports," CSH.

13. "Information," April 24, 1934, folder "Communists #2 Special Reports," SBLC, CSH.

14. "Reds Are Rounded Up Here in Raids in Drive-By Flying Squads," SB, July 20, 1934; Quin, "C.S. Case Against Labor," 10–11.

15. *Sacramento Bee* photographic morgue collection, 83/01/2421, CSH.

16. See Aubrey W. Grossman, "Who Is a Vagrant in California?," *California Law Review* 23, no. 5 (July 1935): 506–18.

17. The complete text of the act is in the appendix to Woodrow C. Whitten, "Criminal Syndicalism and the Law in California, 1919–1927," *Transactions of the American*

Philosophical Society 59, no. 2 (1969): 65. For background on the passage of state criminal syndicalism laws, see Ahmed A. White, "The Crime of Economic Radicalism: Criminal Syndicalism Laws and the Industrial Workers of the World, 1917–1927," *Oregon Law Review* 85 (2006): 650–770.

18. Whitten, "Criminal Syndicalism and the Law in California," 53; *Whitney v. California*, 274 U.S. 357 (1927).

19. F.A. Stewart to Edson Abel, August 1, 1934, in U.S. Senate Subcommittee of the Committee on Education and Labor, *Violations of Free Speech and Rights of Labor*, 76th Cong., 3d sess. (Washington, DC: Government Printing Office, 1940) (hereafter La Follette hearings), part 69, 25319.

20. "Sacramento Men Form Committee to Battle Reds," SB, July 20, 1934; "Anti-Red Group Meets for Lunch," SB, July 25, 1934.

21. "Witness Asserts Reds Held Here Urge Treason," SB, August 3, 1934.

22. Quin, "C.S. Case Against Labor," 11–12.

23. "Trials of Reds Are Set Here," SB, July 21, 1934.

24. "Sheriff Agrees Food in Jail Is Poor and Changes Menu," SB, February 8, 1935.

25. "Jurors Find Two Guilty of Vagrancy in Red Trial," SB, August 28, 1934.

26. "Eleven Radicals, Convicted Here, Face Sentences," SB, August 29, 1934.

27. "Injunction to Smother Communists Is Planned," SB, August 16, 1934.

28. The precise number of counts and indictments changed a few times in the course of the trial as the judge dismissed or consolidated the charges. In the end, fourteen defendants faced trial on two counts.

29. All stories in SB: "Witness in Red Trial Is Taken to Hiding Place," October 5, 1934; "Red Jury Threat Is Probed by Court Here," December 14, 1934; "Red Scheme to Enlist Pupils Is Bared Here," December 12, 1934; "Babcock Wants M'Allister to Stay in Red Case," December 31, 1934; "Red Plan for Drive on Capital Is Heard Here," January 12, 1935.

30. "Film Actor Named in Coast Red Plot," *NYT*, August 18, 1934.

31. "James Cagney, Film Star, Others Are Listed as Red Backers in Letters Here," SB, August 17, 1934.

32. Ibid.

33. "Movie Star Is Named as Red Backer," SB, August 17, 1934; "Names of Stars Are Linked in Red Probe," SB, August 18, 1934.

34. "Names of Stars Are Linked in Red Probe."

35. "Names of Velez, Del Rio and Novarro Sent to Los Angeles Police," *Washington Post*, August 20, 1934.

36. Babcock ad, *Sacramento Union*, November 4, 1934.

37. Marion R. Hardy, "The Political-Economic Implications of the Pat Chambers Criminal Syndicalism Trial" (master's thesis, Sacramento State College, 1964), 62–63.

38. Ibid., 63; "Group Demands Special Aid to Prosecute Reds," SB, January 8, 1935.

39. "Webb Names McAllister, Aide as Prosecutors in Radical Trial Here," *SB*, January 11, 1935; "Webb Says Trial Here Is of Great Importance," *SB*, March 20, 1935.

40. La Follette hearings, part 69, 25324. For the extensive correspondence regarding Hynes's charges, see "Accounts," box 45, LARS.

41. Scott Allen McClellan, "Policing the Red Scare: The Los Angeles Police Department's Red Squad and the Repression of Labor Activism in Los Angeles, 1900–1940" (PhD dissertation, University of California, Irvine, 2011), 206.

42. La Follette hearings, part 69, 25324.

43. Starr, *Endangered Dreams*, 170; Clement, "Red-Baiters' Holiday," 307.

44. Frazer to George Young, December 4, 1934, in La Follette hearings, part 69, 25321, and Frazer to Frisselle, January 15, 1934 [misprint in published hearings says 1923], part 69, 25324.

45. Frazer to Walter Garrison, February 2, 1935, 25324–25; Frazer to Garrison, August 30, 1934, 25328; and Frazer to Sowers, August 30, 1934, 25328, all in La Follette hearings, part 69.

46. Frazer to Clements, January 5, 1935, box 64, GCP.

47. Loftis, *Witnesses to the Struggle*, 206n27. Some of the AF's expenses for the trial are reproduced in the La Follette committee hearings, part 69, 25326–27.

48. See series of letters reprinted in La Follette hearings, part 69, 25322–23.

49. "Babcock Wants McAllister to Stay in Red Case," *SB*, December 31, 1934.

50. Caroline to Bert, December 18, 1934, folder "Criminal Syndicalism: Sacramento," box 6, CMW. Description of Decker's conditions in jail: CGOH-BAN and JWOH.

51. Clement, "Red Baiters' Holiday," 307.

52. PVC, 6:2852.

53. "Alleged Reds in Wild Riot at City Hall," *Los Angeles Evening Herald and Express*, February 15, 1933, folder 1, box 1, LGP. See also folder 28, box 1, "Cases: Sacramento Criminal Syndicalist Trial, Case Documents, 1934–36," and the biographical material in folder 1, box 1, LGP.

54. Carey McWilliams, "Leo Gallagher," *The Nation*, October 16, 1935.

55. "Red Counsel Is Scorned by Judge, Juror and Own Aide," *SB*, February 1, 1935.

56. PVC, 11:4896.

57. PVC, 13:6125. For an example of Gallagher's charges of conspiracy, see 13:6062.

58. "A Eulogy to Dal M. Lemmon," U.S. District Court for the Eastern District of California Historical Society, accessed October 18, 2013, http://courthistory.tripod.com/lemmonrotary.html.

59. "Radical Lawyer Is Excoriated as Publicity Seeker," *SB*, January 26, 1935.

60. See Lemmon's exchange with McAllister in PVC, 13:6044.

61. Quin, "C.S. Case Against Labor," 18.

62. "Radicals Linked to Revolt Plot," *SB*, February 7, 1935.

63. Quin, "C.S. Case Against Labor," 13.

64. *PVC*, 6:2635.

65. Ibid., 10:4308.

66. Ibid., 6:2678.

67. "Neil McAllister Faces Grill by Counsel of Reds," *SB*, February 18, 1935.

68. *PVC*, 10:4308, 4313.

69. Ibid., 10:3837–66.

70. "Defense Counsel Assails Webb in Radicals' Trial," *SB*, March 27, 1935.

71. Quin, "C.S. Case Against Labor," 24.

72. "C.S. Trial Nears Close; Swell Protests," *Western Worker*, March 25, 1935.

73. "Terror Reign Threatened at Trial of Reds," *San Francisco Examiner*, March 28, 1935.

74. *PVC*, 13:6042.

75. Ibid., 13:6034, 6044.

76. "City Prepares for Invasion of Reds, Jobless," *SB*, March 9, 1935. See also "Dean Prepares for Red March on Sacramento," *SB*, January 18, 1935.

77. "Red Rehearsals to Pave Way for Revolt Are Told," *SB*, March 23, 1935.

78. "Armed Troops as Guards in Red Peril Here Are Revealed," *SB*, February 19, 1935; "Exhibits at Reds' Trial Give Revolt Plot Plans," *LAT*, February 23, 1935.

79. Tugwell diary entry for December 28, 1934, 3, FDRL.

80. Tugwell diary, February 10, 1935, 44, FDRL.

81. Although according to Hiss, it was Telford Taylor, later the prosecutor in the Nuremberg trials after World War II, who actually drafted the provocative rule. See memorandum of conversation with Brigadier General Telford Taylor, October 29, 1948, Taylor file, STP.

82. Those fired were Jerome Frank, Gardner Jackson, Lee Pressman, Frank Shea, and Victor Rotnem. Pressman was a Communist; the rest were liberals. Hiss, who was working on a contract basis for the AAA at that time and was not a regular employee, escaped the purge.

83. For accounts of the purge, see Wartzman, *Obscene in the Extreme*, 134–38; Arthur M. Schlesinger Jr., *The Age of Roosevelt*, vol. 2, *The Coming of the New Deal* (Boston: Houghton Mifflin, 1959), 77–80; John C. Culver and John Hyde, *American Dreamer: The Life and Times of Henry A. Wallace* (New York: W.W. Norton, 2000), 152–57; Theodore Saloutos, *The American Farmer and the New Deal* (Ames: Iowa State University Press, 1982), 117–23; Donald H. Grubbs, *Cry from the Cotton: The Southern Tenant Farmers' Union and the New Deal* (Fayetteville: University of Arkansas Press, 2000), 53–61; Peter Irons, *The New Deal Lawyers* (Princeton, NJ: Princeton University Press, 1982), 173–80.

84. "Wallace Ousts Left Wingers 'for Harmony,'" *Chicago Tribune*, February 7, 1935.

85. Wartzman, *Obscene in the Extreme*, 140. I am indebted to Wartzman for discovering this connection.

86. RTD, February 10, 1935, 45, FDRL.

87. "Defense Counsel Assails Webb in Radicals' Trial," *SB*, March 27, 1935.

88. "Radicals' Fate Will Be Given to Jury To-day," *SB*, March 29, 1935; "Press and West Point Are Rapped by Reds' Counsel," *SB*, March 28, 1935.

89. "Criminal Syndicalism Trial Nears End," *Western Worker*, April 1, 1935.

90. Quoted in Loftis, *Witnesses to the Struggle*, 93.

91. "Radicals' Fate Will Be Given to Jury To-day."

92. *PVC*, 13:6125.

93. Quoted in Quin, "C.S. Case Against Labor," 26.

94. *PVC*, 13:6127–28.

95. Ibid., 13:6179.

96. "Friends of Reds Weep as Jury's Decision Is Read," *SB*, April 1, 1935.

97. "8 Guilty in Red Trial," *San Francisco Examiner*, April 2, 1935.

98. Ibid.

99. "Fight Begun to Free Frame-Up Trial Victims," *Western Worker*, April 4, 1935.

100. Quin, "C.S. Case Against Labor," 28.

101. Ibid.

102. *PVC*, 13:6341, 6346.

103. "State Has Farm Peace," *LAT*, September 29, 1935.

104. Herbert Klein and Carey McWilliams, "Cold Terror in California," *The Nation*, July 24, 1935, 97.

10. Harvest

1. "Patriotic Clubwomen Test Their Prowess at Range," *LAT*, August 25, 1935.

2. Creel to president, September 23, 1935, "Creel, George," PPF 2346, FDRL.

3. "Just as Radical as Russia," *LAT*, December 27, 1935.

4. Ira Katznelson, *Fear Itself: The New Deal and the Origins of Our Time* (New York: Liveright, 2013), 171, 260, 267–73.

5. Irving Bernstein, *The New Deal Collective Bargaining Policy* (Berkeley: University of California Press, 1950), 1.

6. Gary Dean Best, *The Life of Herbert Hoover: Keeper of the Torch, 1933–1964* (New York: Palgrave Macmillan, 2013), 55.

7. Larry Bartels argues that a state-by-state analysis of the 1936 vote shows that Roosevelt received the most support from states with the strongest income growth. Bartels, "The Irrational Electorate," *Wilson Quarterly* 32, no. 4 (Autumn 2008): 50.

8. John Steinbeck, *The Harvest Gypsies: On the Road to the Grapes of Wrath* (Berkeley: Heyday, 1988), 61.

9. On the migration of Southwesterners to California, see James Gregory, *American Exodus: The Dust Bowl Migration and Okie Culture in California* (New York: Oxford University Press, 1989), and James Gregory, *The Southern Diaspora: How the Great Migrations of Black and White Southerners Transformed America* (Chapel Hill: University of North Carolina Press, 2005).

Notes to Pages 222–224

10. Steinbeck, *Harvest Gypsies*, 23.

11. Ibid., 22–23.

12. Ibid., 60–61.

13. Steinbeck to Elizabeth Otis, July 28, 1938, in *Working Days: The Journals of The Grapes of Wrath, 1938–1941*, ed. Robert DeMott (New York: Viking, 1989), 154, quoted in Rick Wartzman, *Obscene in the Extreme: The Burning and Banning of John Steinbeck's The Grapes of Wrath* (New York: PublicAffairs, 2008), 246n40.

14. On Steinbeck's treatment of people of color in his narratives, see A. Saxton, "In Dubious Battle," *Pacific Historical Review* 73, no. 2 (May 2004): 259–60; and Devra Weber, *Dark Sweat, White Gold: California Farm Workers, Cotton, and the New Deal* (Berkeley: University of California Press, 1994), 146–47. On his exclusion of women strikers and his conservative views of gender roles, see Cyrus Ernesto Zirakzadeh, "John Steinbeck on the Political Capacities of Everyday Folk: Moms, Reds, and Ma Joad's Revolt," *Polity* 36, no. 4 (July 2004): 613–18; Mimi Gladstein, "Missing Women: The Inexplicable Disparity Between Women in Steinbeck's Life and Those in His Fiction," in *The Steinbeck Question: New Essays in Criticism*, ed. Donald R. Noble (Troy, NY: Whitston Publishing Company, 1993), 84–98; and Gladstein, "Deletions from the *Battle*; Gaps in the *Grapes*," *San Jose Studies* 18, no. 1 (Winter 1992): 43–51. On Hammett and McKiddy as models for Casy and Joad, see Jackson Benson, *The True Adventures of John Steinbeck, Writer: A Biography* (New York: Viking, 1984), 341–42.

15. Robert Brady in *Books* quoted in Kevin Starr, *Endangered Dreams: The Great Depression in California* (New York: Oxford University Press, 1996), 263.

16. On McWilliams, see Peter Richardson, *American Prophet: The Life and Work of Carey McWilliams* (Ann Arbor: University of Michigan Press, 2005); Daniel Geary, "Carey McWilliams and Antifascism, 1934–1943," *Journal of American History* 90, no. 3 (December 2003): 912–34; and Greg Critser, "The Making of a Cultural Rebel: Carey McWilliams, 1924–1930," *Pacific Historical Review* 55, no. 2 (May 1986): 226–55.

17. "Pro-Americans Hear 'Smear' Books Scored," *LAT*, August 22, 1939.

18. Wartzman, *Obscene in the Extreme*, 149–50.

19. *Congressional Record*, 76th Congress, 3rd sess., 1940, section 86, part 13, 140, quoted in Starr, *Endangered Dreams*, 257; Bancroft speech, "Does the Grapes of Wrath Present a Fair Picture of California Farm Labor Conditions?," 1940, p. 12, folder 8, carton 1, PBP.

20. "Aide to Gov. Olson Writes an Inflammatory Book and Tells Some Whoppers," *LA Daily News*, August 3, 1939; "Termites Steinbeck and McWilliams," July 29, 1939, *Pacific Rural Press*, both in folder 11, box 82, CMW.

21. J.W. Hawkins to Culbert Olson, August 2, 1939, folder 6, box 82, CMW.

22. On *American Exodus*, see Jan Goggans, *California on the Breadlines: Dorothea Lange, Paul Taylor, and the Making of a New Deal Narrative* (Berkeley: University of California Press, 2010), chapter 7.

23. Starr, *Endangered Dreams*, 266–67; Irving Bernstein, *The Turbulent Years: A History of the American Worker, 1933–1941* (Boston: Houghton-Mifflin, 1971), 451. On the La Follette committee, see Jerold S. Auerbach, *Labor and Liberty: The La Follette Committee and the New Deal* (Indianapolis: Bobbs-Merrill, 1966).

24. Testimony of Culbert Olson, U.S. Senate Subcommittee of the Committee on Education and Labor, *Violations of Free Speech and Rights of Labor*, 76th Cong., 3d sess. (Washington, DC: Government Printing Office, 1940) (hereafter La Follette hearings), part 47, 17243–66, quote at 17250. See also Carey McWilliams, *The Education of Carey McWilliams* (New York: Simon & Schuster, 1979), 79.

25. La Follette committee report, *Employers Associations and Collective Bargaining in California*, report 1150, part 1, 30, 61, 62, and part 4, 670–72.

26. Quoted in Nelson Pichardo, "The Power Elite and Elite-Driven Countermovements: The Associated Farmers in California during the 1930s," *Sociological Forum* 10, no. 1 (March 1995): 30.

27. "Farm Inquiry Held Red Aid," *LAT*, December 19, 1939.

28. La Follette committee report, *Employers Associations and Collective Bargaining in California*, report 1150, part 3, 394–99.

29. Walton Bean and James J. Rawls, *California: An Interpretive History* (New York: McGraw-Hill, 1983), 364.

30. Marilynn S. Johnson, *The Second Gold Rush: Oakland and the East Bay in World War II* (Berkeley: University of California Press, 1993), 8.

31. Gerald D. Nash, *The American West Transformed: The Impact of the Second World War* (Bloomington: Indiana University Press, 1985), 25–26.

32. On federal subsidy for California suburbanization, see Becky M. Nicolaides, *My Blue Heaven: Life and Politics in the Working-Class Suburbs of Los Angeles, 1920–1965* (Chicago: University of Chicago Press, 2002), 185–91.

33. U.S. Senate, Committee on Military Affairs, *Labor Shortages in the Pacific Coast and Rocky Mountain States*, 78th Cong., 1st sess., September 9–10, 1943, 59, cited in Johnson, *Second Gold Rush*, 37.

34. "Mexican Workers Sought by Olson," *NYT*, June 16, 1942, quoted in Richard B. Craig, *The Bracero Program: Interest Groups and Foreign Policy* (Austin: University of Texas Press, 1971), 39.

35. Roger Daniels, *Guarding the Golden Door: American Immigration Policy and Immigrants Since 1882* (New York: Hill and Wang, 2004), 90.

36. Ibid., 142–43.

37. Quoted in Ernesto Galarza, *Merchants of Labor: The Mexican Bracero Story* (Charlotte, NC: McNally and Loftin, 1964), 55.

38. Ernesto Galarza, *Strangers in Our Fields* (Washington, DC: Joint United States–Mexico Trade Union Committee, 1990), 22–58.

39. M.J. Heale, "Red Scare Politics: California's Campaign against Un-American Activities, 1940–1970," *Journal of American Studies* 20, no. 1 (April 1986): 14. See also

Ingrid Winther Scobie, "Jack B. Tenney and the 'Parasitic Menace': Anti-Communist Legislation in California, 1940–1949," *Pacific Historical Review* 43, no. 2 (May 1974): 188–211; and Edward R. Long, "Earl Warren and the Politics of Anti-Communism," *Pacific Historical Review* 51, no. 1 (February 1982): 53–56.

40. Mary Ellen Leary, "California's Lonely Secret Agent," *LAT*, April 2, 1967.

41. See Scobie, "Jack B. Tenney and the 'Parasitic Menace,'" 190.

42. Ella Winter, *And Not to Yield* (New York: Harcourt, Brace, and World, 1963), 258–93.

43. Arnold Rampersad, *The Life of Langston Hughes* (New York: Oxford University Press, 1986), 2:209–22, 260. Hughes says he occasionally "visited the migratory camps" and raised money for migrant workers but makes no mention of the play or his involvement with the CAWIU. Hughes, *I Wonder as I Wander: An Autobiographical Journey* (New York: Octagon, 1986), 283.

44. "Dates Are Interesting in the Bridges History," *LAT*, June 17, 1953; Dorothy Healey and Maurice Isserman, *Dorothy Healey Remembers: A Life in the American Communist Party* (New York: Oxford University Press, 1990), 46; testimony of Stanley B. Hancock in U.S. House, Committee on Un-American Activities, Hearings, *Investigation of Communist Activities in the State of California*, pt. 2, 83rd Cong., 2d sess. (Washington, DC: Government Printing Office, 1954), 4565–67.

45. Healey, *Dorothy Healey Remembers*, 86.

46. Alfred W. McCoy, *Policing America's Empire: The United States, the Philippines, and the Rise of the Surveillance State* (Madison: University of Wisconsin Press, 2009), 343–45; "Senate Panel Holds Vast 'Subversives' File Amassed by Ex-Chief of Army Intelligence," *NYT*, September 7, 1971.

47. Seth Rosenfeld, *Subversives: The FBI's War on Student Radicals and Reagan's Rise to Power* (New York: Farrar, Straus and Giroux, 2012), 51–54.

48. Clark Kerr, *The Gold and the Blue: A Personal Memoir of the University of California, 1949–1967* (Berkeley: University of California Press, 2001), 2:69.

49. Leary, "California's Lonely Secret Agent."

50. Senate of the State of California, *Thirteenth Report of the Senate Fact-Finding Subcommittee on Un-American Activities, 1965*, 68. For Kerr's account of the report, see Kerr, *Gold and the Blue*, 2:58–65.

51. *Thirteenth Report Supplement on Un-American Activities in California, 1966*, 134–35.

52. Quoted in Rosenfeld, *Subversives*, 322.

53. "Communistic Peril to America Told in Stirring Talks," *Riverside Daily Press*, September 29, 1936, in folder "Phillips, Senator John," box 17, CMW. See also Thomas's Christian American Crusade newsletter of November 28, 1938, in the same folder.

54. See "'Revolt Invading Church,'" January 8, 1935; "Crusading Pastor Escapes Shots; Pushes War on Reds," November 4, 1935; "Catholic Leader Assails Menace of Communism," March 10, 1934; "Reds Condemned by Jewish Meet," no date, all in folder

"Red baiting 2–20," box 18, CMW. No newspaper names on the clips. See also Chandler to Hoover, March 31, 1938, "Chandler, Harry, Correspondence, 1936–38," PPI HHL.

55. Eckard V. Toy, "*Faith and Freedom, 1949–1960*," in *The Conservative Press in Twentieth-Century America*, ed. Ronald Lora and William Henry Longton (Westport, CT: Greenwood Press, 1999), 153.

56. Irwin Ross, "The Supersalesmen of California Politics: Whitaker and Baxter," *Harper's*, July 1959, 59.

57. Ibid., 55.

58. Ibid., 61.

59. Greg Mitchell's *Campaign of the Century* is subtitled *Upton Sinclair's Race for Governor of California and the Birth of Media Politics* (New York: Random House, 1992). See also Mitchell's blog post "The Birth of Modern Politics—Beyond This Week's 'New Yorker' Probe," *The Nation*, September 21, 2012, http://www.thenation.com/blog/170083 /birth-modern-politics-beyond-weeks-new-yorker-probe.

60. See Hoover to Nixon, November 9, 1956, "Correspondence, Nixon, Richard M., 1950–1956," PPI HHL, and Nixon to Hoover, January 14, 1957, in the same folder, and the many fond notes the two men exchanged over the years. See also Richard Norton Smith, *An Uncommon Man: The Triumph of Herbert Hoover* (New York: Simon & Schuster, 1984), 360–61, on Hoover's role in Nixon's 1946 campaign. Irwin F. Gellman defends Nixon in his account of Nixon's early career. See Gellman, *The Contender: Richard Nixon, The Congress Years, 1946–1952* (New York: Free Press, 1999), 25–88.

61. Jerry Voorhis, *The Strange Case of Richard Milhous Nixon* (New York: Paul Eriksson, 1972), 8.

62. Paul Bullock, "'Rabbits and Radicals': Richard Nixon's 1946 Campaign against Jerry Voorhis," *Southern California Quarterly* 55, no. 3 (Fall 1973): 354. See also Bullock, *Jerry Voorhis: The Idealist as Politician* (New York: Vantage, 1978).

63. Roger Morris, *Richard Milhous Nixon: The Rise of an American Politician* (New York: Henry Holt, 1990), 572–74. The donors to Nixon's campaigns included oil magnate Henry Salvatori, tire executive Leonard Firestone, publisher Norman Chandler, broker Dean Witter, movie industry executive Louis B. Mayer, drugstore tycoon Justin Dart, and grower Robert Di Giorgio.

64. PBOH, 461–64.

65. David Halberstam, *The Powers That Be* (New York: Knopf, 1979), 122.

66. For a thorough discussion of the recent evidence of Hiss's guilt, see John Earl Haynes, Harvey Klehr, and Alexander Vassiliev, *Spies: The Rise and Fall of the KGB in America* (New Haven, CT: Yale University Press, 2009), chap. 1.

67. Quoted in Wartzman, *Obscene in the Extreme*, 140.

68. Hoover to Nixon, January 22, 1950, "Nixon, Richard M., Correspondence 1950–1956," PPI HHL.

69. David Greenberg, *Nixon's Shadow: The History of an Image* (New York: W.W. Norton, 2003), 29.

70. Greg Mitchell, *Tricky Dick and the Pink Lady: Richard Nixon vs. Helen Gahagan Douglas—Sexual Politics and the Red Scare, 1950* (New York: Random House, 1998), 171.

71. "Senate Panel Holds Vast 'Subversives' File Amassed by Ex-Chief of Army Intelligence"; McCoy, *Policing America's Empire*, 344–45. After the Watergate scandal, Voorhis noted with satisfaction that "Nixon turned out to be the subversive—not Voorhis." "Ex-Rep. Jerry Voorhis Dies; Lost to Nixon," *LAT*, September 12, 1984.

72. Hoover to Nixon, November 9, 1956, "Nixon, Richard M., Correspondence 1950–1956," PPI HHL.

73. "The Great Debate," undated, in folder "Nixon, Richard M., Correspondence, 1960–1965," PPI HHL.

74. Worthen, *Young Nixon and His Rivals: Four California Republicans Eye the White House, 1946–1958* (Jefferson, NC: McFarland, 2010), 13, quoting an article by Theodore White, "The Gentlemen from California," *Collier's*, February 3, 1956.

75. Greenberg, *Nixon's Shadow*, xvi, xii, xxxi, 7.

76. Anne Edwards, *Early Reagan* (New York: William Morrow, 1987), 489; Todd Holmes, "The Economic Roots of Reaganism: Corporate Conservatives, Political Economy, and the United Farm Workers Movement, 1965–1970," *Western Historical Quarterly* 41, no. 1 (Spring 2010): 59, 63; Bill Boyarsky, *Rise of Ronald Reagan* (New York: Random House, 1968), 105–6; Matthew Dallek, *The Right Moment: Ronald Reagan's First Victory and the Decisive Turning Point in American Politics* (New York: Free Press, 2000), 72–75; and Lou Cannon, *Governor Reagan: His Rise to Power* (New York: PublicAffairs, 2003), 134.

77. Holmes, "Economic Roots of Reaganism," 63.

78. Ronald Reagan with Richard G. Hubler, *Where's the Rest of Me?* (New York: Duell, Sloan and Pearce, 1965), 159. See also Garry Wills, *Reagan's America: Innocents at Home* (Garden City, NY: Doubleday, 1987), 247–50.

79. Rosenthal, *Subversives*, 8, 112–13, 120–26. For a discussion of Hollywood's role in creating modern Republicanism, see Donald T. Critchlow, *When Hollywood Was Right: How Movie Stars, Studio Moguls, and Big Business Remade American Politics* (Cambridge: Cambridge University Press, 2013).

80. The speech is available on many websites, including the Ronald Reagan Presidential Library and Museum's, accessed February 10, 2015, http://www.reagan.utexas.edu/archives/reference/timechoosing.html.

81. Quoted in Dallek, *Right Moment*, 194.

82. Rosenfeld, *Subversives*, 374–76.

83. The books on Chavez and the UFW include Matt Garcia, *From the Jaws of Victory: The Triumph and Tragedy of Cesar Chavez and the Farm Workers Movement* (Berkeley: University of California Press, 2012); Miriam Pawel, *Crusades of Cesar Chavez* (New York: Bloomsbury, 2014); Susan Ferriss and Ricardo Sandoval, *The Fight in the Fields: Cesar Chavez and the Farmworkers Movement* (New York: Harcourt Brace, 1997);

Ronald B. Taylor, *Chavez and the Farm Workers* (Boston: Beacon Press, 1975); Linda C. Majka and Theo J. Majka, *Farm Workers, Agribusiness, and the State* (Philadelphia: Temple University Press, 1982); and Dick Meister and Anne Loftis, *A Long Time Coming: The Struggle to Unionize America's Farm Workers* (New York: Macmillan, 1977).

84. Quoted in Holmes, "Economic Roots of Reaganism," 58.

85. Holmes, "Economic Roots of Reaganism," 72.

86. "Grape Boycott: Struggle Poses a Moral Issue," *NYT*, November 12, 1969; Holmes, "Economic Roots of Reaganism," 71; Majka and Majka, *Farm Workers, Agribusiness, and the State*, 193.

87. Holmes, "Economic Roots of Reaganism." On guest worker programs, see Cindy Hahamovitch, *No Man's Land: Jamaican Guestworkers in America and the Global History of Deportable Labor* (Princeton, NJ: Princeton University Press, 2011).

88. "Plaza Park Renamed for Chavez," *SB*, April 16, 1997.

89. Richard A. Walker, *The Conquest of Bread: 150 Years of Agribusiness in California* (New York: The New Press, 2004), 294; Jon Wiener, "Cesar Chavez and the Farmworkers: What Went Wrong?," January 5, 2012, *The Nation* online, http://www.thenation.com/blog/165479/cesar-chávez-and-farmworkers-what-went-wrong. In July 2014, the UFW had 4,443 members. Center for Union Facts, "United Farm Workers: Basic Information," accessed February 10, 2015, http://www.unionfacts.com/union/United_Farm_Workers.

90. Quoted in Best, *Life of Herbert Hoover*, 255.

91. Letter, Bancroft to Hoover, March 10, 1949, box 1, PBP.

92. See the mutually admiring correspondence between Goldwater and Hoover in "Goldwater, Barry, Correspondence: 1938–1960," and "1961–1964," PPI HHL.

93. Pichardo, "The Power Elite," 29; McWilliams, *Education*, 79.

94. On William Knowland, see Worthen, *Young Nixon and His Rivals*, passim.

95. Otis Graham, *An Encore for Reform: The Old Progressives and the New Deal* (New York: Oxford University Press, 1967), 16.

96. George Creel, *Rebel at Large: Recollections of Fifty Crowded Years* (New York: G.P. Putnam's Sons, 1947), 370.

97. "George Creel, Ex-Editor and FDR Aid, Dead," *Chicago Daily Tribune*, October 3, 1953.

98. Figures from USDA census of agriculture, accessed February 10, 2015, http://www.agcensus.usda.gov/Publications/2012/Full_Report/Volume_1,_Chapter_1_State_Level/California/st06_1_002_002.pdf (for California) and http://www.agcensus.usda.gov/Publications/2012/Full_Report/Volume_1,_Chapter_1_State_Level/Iowa/st19_1_002_002.pdf (for Iowa).

99. U.S. Bureau of Labor Statistics, "Agricultural Workers: Summary," *Occupational Outlook Handbook*, accessed February 10, 2015, http://www.bls.gov/ooh/farming-fishing-and-forestry/agricultural-workers.htm.

100. See Todd Edward Holmes, "Politics in the Fields: Democrats, Republicans, and the Political Economy During the United Farm Workers' Grape Strike and Boycott, 1965–1970" (master's thesis, California State University, Sacramento, 2007), 2–63.

101. Senator Sheridan Downey, *They Would Rule the Valley* (San Francisco: Sheridan Downey, 1947).

102. Upton Sinclair, *One Clear Call* (New York: Viking Press, 1948), 9.

103. Lauren Coodley, *Upton Sinclair: California Socialist, Celebrity Intellectual* (Lincoln: University of Nebraska Press, 2013), 149–69.

104. Benson, *True Adventures*, 748, 836.

105. "The Nobel Prize in Literature 1962: John Steinbeck," Nobelprize.org, accessed February 10, 2015, http://www.nobelprize.org/nobel_prizes/literature/laureates/1962/.

106. For the appeal documents, see 2.10.6, NLP. Much later, in 1969, the U.S. Supreme Court invalidated California's criminal syndicalism law when it struck down a similar law in Ohio as a violation of the First Amendment.

107. CGOH-BAN.

108. Anne Loftis, *Witnesses to the Struggle: Imaging the 1930s California Labor Movement* (Reno: University of Nevada Press, 1998), 95; Jackson Benson and Anne Loftis, "John Steinbeck and Farm Labor Unionization: The Background of 'In Dubious Battle,'" *American Literature* 52, no. 2 (May 1980): 221n72; author's interview with Jed Gladstein, September 9, 2012.

109. Jacques E. Levy, *Cesar Chavez: Autobiography of La Causa* (Minneapolis: University of Minnesota Press, 2007), 153.

110. Todd Holmes uses the term "corporate conservative" for Reagan in "The Economic Roots of Reaganism."

111. Bureau of Labor Statistics, "Union Members, 2014," press release, January 23, 2015, accessed February 10, 2015, http://www.bls.gov/news.release/union2.nr0.htm; Gerald Mayer, *Union Membership Trends in the United States* (Washington, DC: Congressional Research Service, 2004). On the political attacks on organized labor, see Elizabeth Tandy Shermer, "Origins of the Conservative Ascendancy: Barry Goldwater's Early Senate Career and the Delegitimization of Organized Labor," *Journal of American History* 95, no. 3 (December 2008): 678–709, and Nelson Lichtenstein and Elizabeth Tandy Shermer, eds., *The Right and Labor in America: Politics, Ideology, and Imagination* (Philadelphia: University of Pennsylvania Press, 2012).

112. On the relationship between the decline of unions and the rise in wealth and income inequality, see Jake Rosenfeld, *What Unions No Longer Do* (Cambridge, MA: Harvard University Press, 2014), and Rosenfeld and Bruce Western, "Unions, Norms, and the Rise in U.S. Wage Inequality," *American Sociological Review* 76, no. 4 (August 2011): 513–37.

113. Congressional Budget Office, "Trends in the Distribution of Household Income Between 1979 and 2007," October 25, 2011, accessed February 10, 2015, http://www.cbo.gov/publication/42729.

114. See "Koch-Backed Political Network, Built to Shield Donors, Raised $400 Million in 2012 Elections," *Washington Post*, January 5, 2014, accessed February 10, 2015, http://www.washingtonpost.com/politics/koch-backed-political-network-built-to-shield-donors-raised-400-million-in-2012-elections/2014/01/05/9e7cfd9a-719b-11e3-9389-09ef9944065e_story.html.

115. Franklin Roosevelt, address at Madison Square Garden, October 31, 1936, at the American Presidency Project, accessed February 10, 2015, http://www.presidency.ucsb.edu/ws/?pid=15219.

INDEX

Page numbers in italics refer to photographs.

ABOUT THE AUTHOR

Kathryn S. Olmsted is chair of the history department at the University of California, Davis. A historian of anticommunism, she is the author of *Challenging the Secret Government: The Post-Watergate Investigations of the CIA and FBI*; *Red Spy Queen: A Biography of Elizabeth Bentley*; and *Real Enemies: Conspiracy Theories and American Democracy, World War I to 9/11*. She lives in Davis, California.

PUBLISHING IN THE PUBLIC INTEREST

Thank you for reading this book published by The New Press. The New Press is a nonprofit, public interest publisher. New Press books and authors play a crucial role in sparking conversations about the key political and social issues of our day.

We hope you enjoyed this book and that you will stay in touch with The New Press. Here are a few ways to stay up to date with our books, events, and the issues we cover:

- Sign up at www.thenewpress.com/subscribe to receive updates on New Press authors and issues and to be notified about local events
- Like us on Facebook: www.facebook.com/newpressbooks
- Follow us on Twitter: www.twitter.com/thenewpress

Please consider buying New Press books for yourself; for friends and family; or to donate to schools, libraries, community centers, prison libraries, and other organizations involved with the issues our authors write about.

The New Press is a 501(c)(3) nonprofit organization. You can also support our work with a tax-deductible gift by visiting www.thenewpress.com/donate.